# FOUR
# THREATS

# FOUR THREATS

## THE RECURRING CRISES OF AMERICAN DEMOCRACY

SUZANNE METTLER

*and*

ROBERT C. LIEBERMAN

ST. MARTIN'S PRESS
NEW YORK

First published in the United States by St. Martin's Press, an imprint of
St. Martin's Publishing Group

FOUR THREATS. Copyright © 2020 by Suzanne Mettler and Robert C.
Lieberman. All rights reserved. Printed in the United States of America.
For information, address St. Martin's Publishing Group, 120 Broadway,
New York, NY 10271.

www.stmartins.com

Design by Meryl Sussman Levavi

Library of Congress Cataloging-in-Publication Data

Names: Mettler, Suzanne, author. | Lieberman, Robert C., 1964– author.
Title: Four threats : the recurring crises of American democracy / Suzanne
    Mettler and Robert C. Lieberman.
Description: First edition. | New York : St. Martin's Press, 2020. | Includes
    bibliographical references and index.
Identifiers: LCCN 2020012822 | ISBN 9781250244420 (hardcover) |
    ISBN 9781250244437 (ebook)
Subjects: LCSH: Democracy—United States—History. | Political culture—
    United States—History. | Polarization (Social sciences)—United States. |
    Racism—United States—History. | Income distribution—Political
    aspects—United States. | Executive power—United States—History. |
    United States—Politics and government. | United States—History.
Classification: LCC JK1726 .M48 2020 | DDC 320.973—dc23
LC record available at https://lccn.loc.gov/2020012822

Our books may be purchased in bulk for promotional, educational, or business
    use. Please contact your local bookseller or the Macmillan Corporate and
Premium Sales Department at 1-800-221-7945, extension 5442, or by email
    at MacmillanSpecialMarkets@macmillan.com.

First Edition: 2020

10   9   8   7   6   5   4   3   2   1

*To our children*

# Contents

# Introduction

## Democracy Under Siege

When the president used his power to target immigrants, the press, and his political opponents, the sheer overreach of his actions shocked many citizens.

Tensions among the nation's political leaders had been escalating for years. Embroiled in one intense conflict after another, both sides had grown increasingly distrustful of each other. Every action by one camp provoked a greater counterreaction from the other, sometimes straining the limits of the Constitution. Fights and mob violence followed.

Leaders of the dominant party grew convinced that their only hope for fixing the government was to do everything possible to weaken their opponents and silence dissent. The president signed into law provisions that made it more difficult for immigrants (who tended to support the opposition) to attain citizenship and mandated the deportation of those who were deemed dangerous or who came from "hostile" nations. He then put his pen to a law that would allow for the prosecution of those who openly criticized his administration, such as newspaper publishers.

The year just described was not 2017 or 2018. Rather, it was 1798, when President John Adams signed the Alien and Sedition Acts. His allies in Congress, the Federalists, argued that these measures were necessary, in anticipation of a possible war with France, to protect the country from internal spies, subversive elements, and dissent. The Federalists disapproved of immigrants, viewing them as a threat to the purity of national character. They particularly disliked the Irish—the largest group—because they largely favored their political opponents, the Republicans, and sympathized with the French. Or as one Federalist congressman put it, there was no need to "invite hordes of Wild Irishmen, nor the turbulent and disorderly of all the world, to come here with a basic view to distract our tranquility."[1]

Critics of the new laws raised their voices in protest. The Republicans charged that they amounted to barefaced efforts to weaken their faction, which happened to include most Americans not of English heritage. Two leading Republicans, Thomas Jefferson and James Madison, went so far as to advise state governments to refuse to abide by the Sedition Act, resolving that it was unconstitutional.

Political conflicts boiled over into everyday life. Federalists and Republicans often resided in different neighborhoods and attended different churches. Federalists, centered particularly in New England, prized their Anglo-American identity, and even after the Revolution they retained their affinity with the mother country. Republicans saw themselves as cosmopolitan, cherishing Enlightenment ideals of liberty and equality, and they championed the French Revolution and held disdain for Britain. By 1794, partisans in urban communities were holding separate Fourth of July ceremonies. Republicans read aloud the Declaration of Independence—penned by the founder of their party, Thomas Jefferson—as evidence that independence had been their own achievement, while the Federalists offered toasts to their leader, President George Washington. The Republicans viewed themselves as the party of the people; one prominent politician among them chided the Federalists for celebrating not "we the people" but "we the noble, chosen, privileged few."[2]

To many people at the time, the Alien and Sedition Acts bore an unsettling resemblance to the kinds of government overreach that had spurred them to fight a war for independence just a few decades earlier. The acts comprised four laws, three of which placed restrictions on immigrants and appeared to be a strategic attempt to shape the electorate by excluding potential voters for the opposition in order to tip the scales of power. The fourth, the Sedition Act, made it illegal to publish "any false, scandalous, and malicious writing or writings against the

Government of the United States, or either House of the Congress of the United States, with intent to defame ... or to bring them ... into contempt or dispute." By denying freedom of speech and freedom of the press, it outlawed criticism of the government and deprived citizens of the opportunity to become more fully informed by hearing alternative points of view. The measures gave the president power to exert control over Americans' lives in ways removed from congressional authority, and therefore less accountable to popular control. Some state governments outright refused to abide by the new federal law, intensifying divisions. And on the streets, mock violence—the burning of effigies—was swiftly transforming into the genuine article, as politically motivated beatings and open brawls proliferated. In one case, on July 27, 1798, Federalists in New York marched up Broadway singing "God Save the King" just to antagonize the Republicans; the latter responded by singing French revolutionary songs. Soon the "singing contest" gave way to violence as fighting ensued.[3]

Watching the growing chaos and division, Americans of all stripes worried that their experiment in self-government might not survive the decade. They feared that monarchy would reassert itself, aristocracy would replace representative government, or some states might secede from the Union, causing its demise. The early beginnings of democracy in the United States were fragile—even at a time when some of the Constitution's framers themselves, along with other luminaries of the era, held public office.

❖

Should we contemporary Americans worry about the future of our democracy? Is it in danger? While we do not share our predecessors' fears that the British crown might rule us once again or that the nation might lapse into civil war, subtler signs of danger abound. We face the weakening of the checks and balances that prevent democracy from sliding into tyranny. The rule of law, long taken for granted by Americans, has been eroded by a president who sees the government as an instrument to advance his own personal and political interests. Elections, the foundation of democracy, are becoming less free and fair due to the distorting influence of money, misinformation, and foreign meddling. While the United States has long distinguished itself by its relative absence of outright corruption, public office now increasingly appears to be—for some—a platform for private gain rather than an opportunity for public service. Hard-won civil rights, civil liberties, and voting rights face challenges; even journalists engaged in routine investigative reporting have been subjected to intimidation. And above all, American politics is becoming a matter of "us" against "them" among political leaders and ordinary Americans alike, dividing families and communities, fostering hostility, and impeding our collective capacity to solve problems and govern ourselves productively.

Many remain confident that democracy will endure, and certainly reasonable arguments can be made to support that assumption. After all, the United States boasts the world's longest-functioning constitution and a long-standing reputation as a beacon of democracy for the world. We typically regard our political institutions as bulwarks against the emergence of tyranny or authoritarianism.[4] And although American democracy developed slowly and haltingly—thwarted at the outset by the enslavement of African Americans, the subordinate status of women of all races, and the suppression of Native Americans—still the nation's history is often depicted as a story of progress toward the fulfillment of a democratic ideal.

The trouble is, however, that a closer look at American history reveals a far more tumultuous past than this familiar narrative suggests. This book delves into our history in order to try to understand whether democracy today is in danger or not. We turn to several periods in which many Americans were worried about whether rule by "we the people" could endure. We investigate them to uncover the elements that presaged each crisis, how our institutions withstood serious threats, and what ensued. What we have learned from this history is that American democracy has been far from invincible. To the contrary, it has been under threat time and again, and has often proven to be fragile in the face of danger. In many instances, moreover, real harm occurred, sometimes with long-lasting consequences.

From the beginning of the republic to the present, the United States has endured repeated crises when the nation's promise of popular government was in peril. At each of these junctures, political combat escalated to a point where Americans feared that the government might collapse, that the Union might dissolve, or that unrest, violence, or even civil war might break out. In the 1790s, people worried that political conflict over the Alien and Sedition Acts would plunge the nation into armed conflict or dissolve it through secession. In the 1850s, divisions over slavery *did* tear the country apart, leading to a destructive civil war in the next decade. In the 1890s, amid the convulsive changes in the industrial era and the upsurge in labor conflict and farmers' political organizing, nearly four million African Americans were stripped of their voting rights. During the Great Depression of the 1930s, many Americans welcomed a president who was willing to use greater executive power than his predecessors, but some worried that it paved the way for a strongman leader like those on the rise in several European countries. During the Watergate scandal of the 1970s, the president tried to use the tools of executive power that were developed in the 1930s as political weapons to punish his own enemies.

At each of these five moments we saw clear signs of damage to the pillars of democracy. Ambitious politicians frequently trampled the principle of free and fair elections, using intimidation, stuffing of ballot boxes, and other techniques to win office. They often dispensed with the rule of law and resorted to power and force instead, from the time when President George Washington led fifteen thousand troops into western Pennsylvania to suppress the Whiskey Rebellion to when President Franklin D. Roosevelt, during World War II, signed an executive order that sanctioned the imprisonment of more than a hundred thousand Americans of Japanese descent in detention camps. Parties openly undermined the legitimacy of the opposition, from the conflict over slavery in Kansas, when pro- and antislavery citizens adopted separate constitutions, held separate elections, and chose separate legislatures, to President Richard Nixon's underhanded and illegal efforts to destroy those he regarded as his political enemies. The integrity of hard-won rights suffered, from the damage to freedom of the press and freedom of speech caused by the Sedition Act to the loss of voting rights by African Americans in the 1890s.

These crises of democracy did not occur randomly; rather, they developed in the presence of four specific threats: political polarization, conflict over who belongs in the political community, high and growing economic inequality, and excessive executive power. We know from the study of the rise and fall of democratic regimes elsewhere in the world that these conditions are harmful to the sustainability of democracy. When they are absent, democracy tends to flourish; when one or more of them are present, democracy is prone to decay.

Each of these threats by itself can damage democracy. Polarization tends to divide citizens into opposing "teams" that are geared more toward defeating one another than governing effectively. Disputes over who belongs in the political community and the status of members—categorized along lines of race, gender, national origin, or religion—can engender deep divisions that result in political exclusion, the widespread denial of rights, and violent reprisals. Economic inequality can pit society's haves against its have-nots and induce the wealthy to use their resources to protect their privileged place in the social order. And the growth of executive power enables the concentration of authority in the hands of a single person, which is precisely what the framers of the Constitution hoped to avoid.

In none of these periods of democratic fragility in American history were all four threats present simultaneously. Each of the threats has waxed and waned at different times, and on only some occasions have a few joined forces. And it is these combinations that have proven particularly dangerous. In the 1850s, for example, the paired emergence of extreme political polarization and the intensification of conflict over the status of African Americans pushed the country into a calamitous civil war. In the 1890s, polarization and ardent white supremacy resurged, and in combination with the soaring economic inequality of the Gilded Age they led to the wholesale exclusion of African Americans from rights of citizenship. Democracy has not fared well in these periods when the threats coalesced.

Now, for the first time in American history, we face all four threats at the same time. As in the 1790s, or during the conflict that led to the Civil War, we confront deep political polarization. Political leaders exaggerate their differences in order to win elections, and they have grown more willing to circumvent long-established norms in order to gain, wield, and keep power. And ordinary Americans are increasingly sorting themselves into separate camps based on where they live, where they go to school, where they work, what they read, listen to, and watch—and how they vote. In the process, they have grown more polarized and antagonistic toward the opposing party. Increasingly, partisans view one another not as honorable competitors but as an existential threat to everything they stand for.

What's more, partisan divisions today overlap with other conditions that are also familiar from the history of American politics—rising racial antagonism, pitched battles over gender, and soaring economic inequality. The combination of intense political combat, social tribalism, and plutocracy now threatens to undermine our government's legitimacy and its capacity to seek common solutions to collective problems. No corner of contemporary politics has been spared from this dysfunction: not Congress, the bureaucracy, the courts, the media, or the presidency. Making matters worse, today's merger of threats, unlike that of earlier periods, coexists with extreme and growing executive power. This creates the opportunity for excessively partisan presidents to use the government to serve their own personal and political ends.

It is this unprecedented confluence of all four threats—more than the rise to power of any particular leader or party—that lies behind the contemporary crisis of American democracy. The threats have grown deeply entrenched, and they will likely persist and wreak havoc for some time to come. These circumstances are troubling indeed, and we make light of them at our peril. In order to understand what the combination of threats might portend for American democracy, in this book we will consider how the nation navigated them in the past—or, in some instances, failed to do so—and then apply what we have learned to the present.

# 1

## Threats to Democracy

Many Americans think of the United States as synonymous with democracy. After all, the nation was born through a revolution against tyranny and monarchy. Emboldened colonists insisted on the creation of a government in which authority flows from the people themselves. The nation's founding documents herald democratic ideals, from the Declaration of Independence's claim that "all men are created equal" to the Constitution's preamble identifying "We the People" as its source. The ancient Greeks, in city-states such as Athens, had practiced direct democracy, in which citizens made decisions by deliberating face-to-face in assemblies. It was Americans who brought the concept to scale for a larger society, particularly through the Constitution, which established national institutions of government with representatives selected by the people themselves, through a combination of direct and indirect means. By the early nineteenth century, states extended the vote to nearly all white men, regardless of whether they owned property. These measures made the United States more inclusive than its European counterparts in that era, and the nation became renowned for its boisterous, highly participatory politics that included newly enfranchised men of modest means.[1]

Yet the young nation simultaneously repudiated democracy in crucial ways that would shape its development down to the present. It did this by embedding social hierarchies into the Constitution and cementing them with the power of law. When the Constitution was ratified, nearly one in five Americans—all of them of African descent—were enslaved, and the document itself sanctioned the practice. In the case of women's status, which was among the topics relegated to the states under the Tenth Amendment, once women married—as was expected of them—they relinquished their legal and economic rights to their husbands. As the country moved toward universal voting rights for white men, inclusion occurred on the basis of race and gender, establishing the United States in its early years as a "white man's republic."[2] Full membership in the political community—entailing the right to vote and to participate fully in public affairs—expressly excluded women and African Americans.

Over two centuries of struggle and contention, the United States democratized. The nation's conception of "the people" slowly grew more inclusive and more Americans gained the rights of citizenship. But it was not until the 1960s and 1970s that the United States formally extended civil and political rights to all Americans regardless of race or gender.[3] The road toward full democracy was neither straight nor smooth. Generations of Americans organized, signed petitions, and marched in the quest for equal rights of citizenship, and they often faced violence, defeats, and reversals of progress.

But even though the United States has not been a full democracy from the beginning, the American Revolution established the modern *idea* of democracy—a system of government in which those who govern are held accountable to the people through competitive elections. However imperfectly the principles of American democracy may be realized, inherent in them are standards by which we can measure the state of American politics. At any given time, a regime can be more or less democratic, depending on how close it comes to meeting these standards of democracy. Think of democracy as a continuum rather than an on-off switch. A country can be somewhere between being a full democracy and not being a democracy at all. As we look at democracy through American history, we can assess where on the continuum it is.

Democratic regimes can also move along the continuum in either direction. A regime might be moving toward more complete democracy, as the United States did during Reconstruction after the Civil War and in the 1960s. But regimes might also move in the other direction, toward less democracy, a process known as "backsliding."[4] There is no guarantee, even in the United States, that we will move in the right direction, and it is a grave mistake to assume either that the United States is automatically democratic because of what our Constitution says or that we have moved steadily and inexorably toward greater democracy.

History reveals that neither assumption is correct.

## THINKING ABOUT DEMOCRACY . . . AND BACKSLIDING

The United States has not always been democratic. Moreover, American democracy has not developed through steady progress over time; sometimes it has been subject to decay or derailment, and the question is whether that is occurring again now. Before we can assess the prospects of democratic deterioration, what do we mean by democracy?

We tend to think of democracy as a political system in which authority flows from the people, rather than from an individual leader or a small group of powerful elites. But of course many autocrats around the world also claim to be the people's true representative. How then can we distinguish democracies from authoritarian governments—or, more to the point, identify whether a single nation exhibits signs of becoming more or less democratic?

Democracy is a system of government in which citizens are able to hold those in power accountable, primarily through regular competitive elections, and in which representatives engage in collective decision-making, seeking to be responsive to the electorate. Modern democracies that conform to this definition are systems of representative government, not direct democracies or systems of mob rule. Successful democracies also tend to be *liberal* democracies, regimes that effectively protect their citizens' rights to express their views, participate in the political process, and have their voices heard. Effectively functioning democratic systems tend to share four key attributes.[5]

*Free and fair elections* constitute the most fundamental feature of any representative democracy. Elections permit societies to resolve conflict without bloodshed, by using the ballot box rather than bullets. They also provide a means for citizens to choose their rulers and to hold them accountable, "throwing the bums out" if they disapprove of how they govern.[6]

Inherent in representative democracy is also the idea that all members of society, including those in government, must adhere to the *rule of law*.[7] This means that society is not run by individuals who exercise sheer personal power, by vigilantes who take the law into their own hands, or by hereditary or religious leaders. Rather, it is run according to rules that apply to everyone and to the operations of government itself. No individual can be considered to be above the law, no matter how powerful; the legal code is to be applied to all citizens evenly, by impartial courts. The rule of law also mandates procedures for elections and representation and establishes checks and balances between branches of government, limiting the power of any one branch. It prevents tyranny, arbitrary and cruel dominance by an autocrat, rule by sheer force and violence, and corruption.

Democracy necessitates the *legitimacy of the opposition*: those on different sides of a policy debate or with different political parties must recognize each other not as enemies or as an existential threat who must be stopped at any cost, but as fellow citizens with equal stakes in the contest and an equal right to participate. The ongoing struggle for power between those with different points of view is intrinsic to democratic politics. This competition for influence, carried out according to previously agreed-upon rules of the game, is a good and necessary thing. Being part of a democracy requires participating over and over again in the quest to promote one's values, interests, or ideas—and actually being permitted to do so. Democracy ceases if one party makes it impossible for another party to compete effectively or to govern when it wins elections. Democracy means that the loser of a contest must still be able to look to the future, to aim to win the next election or prevail in the next policy battle.[8]

While these three features came to be regarded as pillars of American democracy by the nineteenth century, only in the twentieth century did the United States embrace the idea that the government must also protect the *integrity of rights*, including civil liberties, such as freedom of speech, freedom of religion, and freedom of the press; civil rights, for example, ensuring that people cannot be turned away from jobs, schools, restaurants, or housing on the basis of their race or sex; and voting rights.

Democracy means little for those who do not enjoy these protections, which foster equal civic standing among citizens and their meaningful inclusion in the democratic process.[9] When the US Constitution was ratified in 1788, and even with the Bill of Rights added to it in 1791, states retained jurisdiction over rights and denied them to most people; the development of robust rights, guaranteed to citizens broadly by national government, involved a slow and uneven process of democratization, punctuated by instances of egregious backsliding.

These four attributes of democracy—free and fair elections, the rule of law, the legitimacy of the opposition, and the integrity of rights—provide us with clear indicators that we can use as standards to assess whether democracy is advancing or retreating in any given period of history. Nations that call themselves democracies may have some of these attributes but not others; variation abounds. Many nations, for example, hold democratic elections but do not respect their citizens' freedom of expression or dissent, and they have leaders who rule arbitrarily with little heed to the rule of law. Scholars describe such regimes as "competitive authoritarianism," a hybrid form of governance that combines democratic and nondemocratic elements.[10] Just because a nation has attained a robust combination of all four attributes of democracy, moreover, is no guarantee that it will continue to maintain them: lapsing toward weakened or hybrid forms is common.

In recent years, some critics have begun to wonder whether the United States itself is undergoing democratic backsliding. Freedom House, an independent watchdog organization that is highly regarded for its rankings of democratic fitness based on political rights and civil liberties, downgraded the United States from a score of 94 (out of 100 points) in 2010 to 86 in 2019. While the nation still ranks among the eighty-seven countries regarded as "free," its rank fell from thirty-first to fifty-first in less than a decade. In a democracy index prepared annually by *The Economist*, the United States slipped from the classification of "full democracy" to that of "flawed democracy" in 2017. In doing so, it departed the ranks that included most western European countries and Canada, and joined Argentina, Greece, and several eastern European countries, among others.[11]

Some scholars who study democratic deterioration worldwide seek to evaluate the United States today by comparing and contrasting it to

Germany under Hitler and Italy under Mussolini and, more recently, to Hungary under Viktor Orbán, Russia under Vladimir Putin, and Peru under Alberto Fujimori.[12] But none of those cases involves a country with such a long constitutional tradition and established political institutions, not to mention the United States' wealth—all features assumed to ensure the continuation of democracy.[13] For these reasons, we are better off turning to American history in order to understand the threats that have confronted the nation in the past and how well the attributes of democracy survived them.

## THE FOUR THREATS

The history of American democracy has hardly been serene; to the contrary, it has involved extreme conflict and frequent violence and bloodshed. While developments in the past sixty years went far to deepen and expand democracy, earlier periods often witnessed it in peril and even being rolled back. In order to make sense of the conditions that most put democracy at risk, we have learned a great deal from scholars who study its rise and fall in countries around the world. In particular, we discern four major threats that can endanger it: political polarization, conflict over who belongs in the political community, high and rising levels of economic inequality, and executive aggrandizement.

### POLITICAL POLARIZATION

Americans have heard plenty in recent years about the dangers of rising political polarization. Not many years ago, lawmakers in Washington frequently cooperated across party lines, forging both policy alliances and personal friendships. Now, hostility more often prevails, and it has been accompanied by brinksmanship and dysfunction that imperil lawmaking on major issues.

The public is no different. In the 1950s, when pollsters asked Americans whether they would prefer that their child "marry a Democrat or a Republican, all other things being equal," the vast majority—72 percent of Americans—either didn't answer or said they didn't care. By contrast, in 2016 the majority—55 percent—did express a partisan preference for their future son-or daughter-in-law.[14] For many Americans, partisanship has become a central part of their identity.

But could rising polarization actually harm democracy? At first blush, this might seem unlikely; in fact, many political scientists have long argued that vibrant political parties are actually essential to the functioning of democracy. They bring elected officials together around a common set of priorities and foster cooperation so that they can accomplish goals on behalf of the public. They help citizens, who lack the time and expertise to study every issue, to make sense of politics and decide which candidates to support; this enables them to participate in elections and hold elected officials accountable. Distinctions between parties help make democracy work by presenting citizens with meaningful choices. Yet when parties divide both lawmakers and society into two unalterably opposed camps that view each other as enemies, they can undermine social cohesion and political stability. Democracy is put at risk.

The framers of the US Constitution, attuned to such threats from England's previous century of experience with violent parties and factions, hoped the new nation could avoid them altogether. They worried that if groups organized around different priorities, they might exacerbate social and political divisions and pursue their own goals at the expense of the public good. They aimed to design government in ways that would manage and mitigate those differences. Yet no sooner was the new government up and running than political leaders—including some of the founders themselves—began to choose sides on the critical issues of the day, leading to the formation of the Federalist and Republican factions, which were really "proto-parties" or precursors to formal political parties, which were firmly in place not long afterward.

In fact, throughout much of the United States' history, contrary to the framers' fears, political parties have actually mitigated political and social conflict. The two-party system often compelled both parties to compete for middle-of-the-road voters rather than those at either extreme and thus it had a moderating influence. In addition, American society tended to generate "cross-cutting cleavages," meaning multiple, overlapping ties that reinforce connections among citizens instead of a single overarching divide between them, as was the case in European countries, which were more often riven by overriding conflicts of class, religion, or language.

In the United States of the mid-twentieth century, from the 1930s to the early 1970s, for example, two moderate parties prevailed. The Republicans embraced not only fiscal conservatives but also some supporters of civil rights and proponents of the Equal Rights Amendment, while the Democrats' big tent took in both urban ethnic liberals and white southerners—who liked the federal government's largesse but resisted its intervention in how they ran their affairs, particularly with respect to race. In some other periods of American history, however, parties exacerbated divisions.

Polarization grows when citizens sort themselves so that, instead of having multiple, cross-cutting ties to others, their social and political memberships and identities increasingly overlap, reinforcing their affinity to some groups while setting them apart from others. In the mid-twentieth century, this process commenced as white southerners, beginning as early as the 1940s and accelerating by the 1970s, distanced themselves from the Democratic Party and shifted gradually toward the Republicans while the Democrats increasingly embraced the cause of racial equality. These new groupings diverged more from each other on ideology (conservative versus liberal) and views of particular issues (such as civil rights, abortion, and more recently gun rights).[15]

Polarization intensifies as ambitious political entrepreneurs take advantage of growing divisions to expand their power. They may do this by adopting opposing positions on issues, highlighting and promoting underlying social differences, and using polarizing rhetoric and tactics in order to consolidate their supporters while weakening their opponents.[16]

Contemporary polarization in Congress advanced in this way starting in 1978. A young Republican congressman named Newt Gingrich, lamenting his party's decades of minority status, launched a long-term scorched-earth strategy, attacking the institution of Congress itself in order to undermine public trust and convince voters that it was time for a change. He told Republicans, "Raise hell all the time. . . . This party does not need another generation of cautious, prudent, careful, bland, irrelevant, quasi-leaders. . . . What we really need are people who are . . . willing to stand up in a . . . slug fest and match it out with their opponent." He rallied the base, found ways to embarrass the Democratic majority, and proved masterly at attracting media attention.[17]

As a political strategy, polarization delivered effectively: congressional elections became more competitive than they had been for the previous half century. Every election from 1980 to the present presented an opportunity for either party to take control of each chamber of Congress. In 1994, Republicans finally took the House majority (after being in the minority for fifty-eight of the preceding sixty-two years), electing Gingrich to be the Speaker.[18] Partisan control of Congress has seesawed back and forth ever since.

Party leaders from Gingrich onward encouraged their fellow partisans to act as loyal members of a team, prioritizing party unity. They shifted staff and resources away from policy committees and toward public relations, allowing them to communicate constantly to voters about the differences between their party and the opposition. This messaging to the party "base" helps parties to be competitive in elections.

But this approach hinders democratic governance by making it more difficult for Congress to work across party lines and address the major issues that most concern Americans today.[19] This occurs in part because polarization makes many of the attributes of a well-functioning polity— such as cooperation, negotiation, and compromise—more costly for public officials, who fear being punished at the polls if they engage in these ways with opponents. After the conservative political movement known as the Tea Party emerged in 2009, rallying against taxes, government programs, and immigration, its activists lambasted moderates and threatened them with primary challenges from the right. This strategy bore fruit in 2010, when the newly elected Republican majority contained several fewer moderates and many more hard-core conservatives.[20]

As division escalates, the normal functioning of democracy can break down if partisans cease to be able to resolve political differences by finding middle ground, through mutual accommodation. Politics then instead becomes a game of mortal combat in which winning is the singular imperative and opponents are seen as enemies to be vanquished. Furthermore, polarization is not a static state but a process that feeds on itself and creates a cascade of worsening outcomes.[21] Over time, those who created it may find it difficult to control what they have wrought, as members of the base become less and less trustful of elites and believe that none are sufficiently devoted to their core values. These dynamics give rise to less-principled actors, as epitomized by Donald Trump's ascendance. During the 2016 campaign, numerous established Republican politicians—such as Senators Lindsey Graham and Marco Rubio—expressed their strong disdain for him, only to eat their words once he was elected and to support him faithfully once he was in the White House.

Deep, almost tribal partisanship divides not only elected officials but also ordinary Americans today. People who identify with one party have become more distinct in terms of race, religiosity, and ideology from those identifying with the other. They are also more socially distant and more likely to hold stereotypes and negative views of one another. Partisans are animated even more by their shared dislike for the other party than by their own shared perspectives, and this "negative partisanship" spurs them to react emotionally and to harbor anger toward members of the other party.[22] Such polarization can affect social life, making gatherings between partisans of different stripes—including family occasions—fraught with tension.

As such dynamics intensify, people come to view society and politics as divided between "us" and "them." This occurred in recent years in Hungary, for example, where a traditional left-right political divide was replaced by one between cultural nationalists and cosmopolitans, and in Venezuela, where Hugo Chávez rallied the poor and middle class against the elite.[23] In these nations and in others that have experienced similar developments, partisans begin to see those in the opposition as a threat to the nation itself. Polarization fosters tribalism, resentment, and disdain for members of the opposing party, and that in turn weakens democratic norms.

The culmination of polarization can indeed endanger democracy itself. If members of one political group come to view their opponents as an existential threat to their core values, they may seek to defeat them at all costs, even if it undermines normal democratic procedures in the process. They may cease to view the opposition as legitimate and seek permanent ways to prevent it from gaining power, such as by stacking the deck in their own favor. They may become convinced that it is justifiable to circumvent the rule of law and defy checks and balances or to scale back voting rights, civil liberties, or civil rights for the sake of preserving or protecting the nation as they see fit. Political polarization presents these very threats today, and they show no sign of abating.

## WHO BELONGS?

Democracy has been built most successfully in places where citizens share broad agreement about the boundaries of national community: who should be included as a member, and on what terms, meaning whether all should have equal status or if rights should be parceled out in different ways to different groups. Conversely, when a nation features deep social divisions along lines of race, gender, religion, or ethnic group, some citizens may favor excluding certain groups or granting them subordinate status. When these divisions emanate from "formative rifts" that either predated or emerged with the nation's founding, they can prove particularly pernicious, and persist as formidable undercurrents in politics.[24] Unless such rifts are purposely eliminated, conflict over them can habitually resurface and spur deep divisions, making democracy vulnerable.

Formative rifts may come to a head as the result of political change that prompts the two parties to take divergent stands over the status of implicated groups. Politicians may deliberately seek to inflame divisions as a political strategy that can unite and mobilize groups who would not otherwise share a common goal.[25] Or social movements might mobilize people on one side of a rift, leading to a countermobilization by those on the other side. For example, the civil rights movement sought to include more Americans within the boundaries of full citizenship, and that prompted racial conservatives to mobilize themselves to resist such changes; similarly, the feminist and LGBTQ movements each led to backlash movements by evangelical Christians. In either case, when such divisions are triggered, those who favor a return to earlier boundaries of civic membership and status may be convinced that they must pursue their goals at all costs, even if democracy is curtailed in the process. They may support political leaders who flout the rule of law and trample on voting rights, civil liberties, and civil rights, justifying it as necessary to preserve or restore the nation.

The United States at its inception divided the political community by race, creating a formative rift that has organized our politics ever since. A commitment to white supremacy has often prevailed, impelling many Americans to build coalitions around appeals to racism and segregation in order to further their political interests. After the Constitution itself sanctioned slavery, the quest to preserve it drove politics for decades. Even after slavery ended, white supremacy often reigned in American politics, through decades of voting restrictions, denial of rights, discrimination, and segregation. This tradition has been one of the most important antidemocratic forces in American history.

Yet a countervailing commitment to equality and inclusion also emerged in American politics, fueled by the ideals of the Declaration of Independence. This tradition repeatedly and powerfully challenged slavery and white supremacy and brought about critical reforms that expanded rights and advanced American democracy. It continues to do so today.

The American gender divide, also codified in law, made men's dominance in politics and society appear to be natural and it rendered gender hierarchy resistant to change. A countervailing commitment to equality emerged, however, in the nineteenth-century women's movement, articulated in the 1848 Declaration of Sentiments at Seneca Falls: "We hold these truths to be self-evident: that all men and women are created equal." Yet not until 1916 would the two major political parties embrace the cause of women's suffrage at the national level, ushering in the Nineteenth Amendment's ratification in 1920. Numerous other aspects of women's status remained defined at the state level for decades.[26]

Despite sweeping reforms in the twentieth century, legacies of formative rifts around both race and gender linger. Liberal democratic ideals championing equality and freedom have evolved over time and promoted broader inclusion within the rights and responsibilities of democratic citizenship. Yet they continuously contend with persistent traditions that sanction race or gender hierarchies.[27]

Certainly some tendencies of human nature help explain why formative rifts can prove potent. Many people trust communities that seem familiar to them and that they associate with virtue and safety, while they feel distrustful of other groups, whose customs strike them as strange and even dangerous. When political figures or events ignite voters' anger, particularly around matters pertaining to gender or race, it elevates political participation particularly among those who favor traditional hierarchies.[28]

Yet these views about who belongs in the political community do not always consistently foster political conflict and threaten democracy;

it all depends on how they map onto the political party system. In some periods, for example, neither party strongly challenged white supremacy, in which case the status quo prevailed. In other periods, the conflict between racially inclusive and white supremacist visions of American society and democracy has overlapped with partisan divisions and fueled intense political conflict. At such moments, democracy stood on the brink. When egalitarian forces gained the upper hand, democracy became more robust, as occurred during Reconstruction after the Civil War and in the mid-twentieth-century civil rights movement.[29] But when politicians defending old hierarchies effectively aroused their supporters, democracy was put at risk.

In the historical episodes we will explore, battles over race will take center stage, particularly as they relate to the inclusion and status of African Americans. To be sure, other power dynamics, including those related to gender, the status of Native Americans, and other ethnic groups, also shaped civic membership and status during these and other periods of American history. Racism, however, plays a particularly overt and prominent role in these crises, and in our analyses. As we will see, over and over again, it is corrosive to democracy.

In the contemporary period, once again, conflict between white supremacist and egalitarian visions of American society overlaps with the party system, and it coincides with intense polarization. Over the past several decades, while the US population has become more racially and ethnically diverse, the composition of the Republican Party has grown to be far whiter than the population at large, while the Democratic Party has embraced a more diverse coalition. Attitudes among party members have diverged as well: since the 1980s, Republicans have become far more likely to express racist views and Democrats far less so.[30]

For decades, Republican candidates and public officials mostly refrained from overtly invoking those views in their campaigns and public rhetoric, but Trump seized the opportunity to do so, and it helped him win the 2016 election. Contemporary American politics, more than ever before, features a party system sharply divided between proponents of racial egalitarianism and defenders of a system that has privileged whites. This political chasm is further exacerbated by rising hostility to immigration and simmering disagreement about the status of immigrants in American society. The resulting divergence makes for extremely volatile politics, and the potential expansion of democracy—or its rollback—is at stake.

## ECONOMIC INEQUALITY

High rates of economic inequality can undermine the institutions and practices of existing democracies. Countries in which inequality is on the rise are more likely to see democracy distorted, limited, and potentially destabilized. By contrast, countries in which inequality is low or declining are less likely to suffer democratic deterioration.[31]

People typically assume that inequality could make democracy vulnerable by increasing the chances that the less well-off will rise up against the wealthy, but that is rarely the case. Rather, as inequality grows, it is the affluent themselves who are more likely to mobilize effectively. They realize that working- and middle-class people, who greatly outnumber them, tend to favor redistributive policies—and the higher taxes necessary to fund them, which would fall disproportionately on the rich. Fearful of such policy changes, the rich take action to protect their interests and preserve their wealth and advantages. For a time, this may skew the democratic process by giving the rich an outsized voice, but it can eventually cause more fundamental problems, endangering democratic stability itself. This can occur when the wealthiest citizens seek to solidify their power even if it entails harm to democracy. They may be willing to abide a polarizing politics of "us versus them" and the adoption of repressive measures if that is what it takes for leaders to protect their interests.[32]

Among wealthy democracies in the world today, the United States is the most economically unequal nation. After a period during the mid-twentieth century when low- and middle-income Americans experienced quickly rising incomes, they have seen slow or stagnant wage growth and shrinking opportunities since the late 1970s. The affluent, meanwhile, continued to experience soaring incomes and wealth, particularly among the top 1 percent. CEO pay skyrocketed from 30 times the annual pay of the average worker in 1978 to 312 times as much by 2017.

Early on, the United States did not feature such economic inequality. Of course, in the late eighteenth century and the nineteenth century up through the Civil War, the widespread existence of slavery made for extreme inequality in the American South. Other regions of the nation during that same period, however, featured greater egalitarianism than Europe, being unencumbered by feudalism and the inherited structure of rigid social classes. But as the nineteenth century proceeded, economic inequality grew, and by the late nineteenth century—the Gilded Age, as Mark Twain called it—the United States had nearly caught up with Great Britain. These disparities would endure until the stock market crashed in 1929. The wealthy lost much through the Great Depression, and then, after World War II, the strong economy and government policies fostered upward mobility and the growth of a large middle class, otherwise known as "the great compression." By later in the twentieth century, however, economic inequality grew once again, owing not only to deindustrialization and globalization but also to changes (and failure to update policies amid transformed circumstances) in tax policy, labor policy, and other areas that favored the affluent. The fortunes of the wealthy soared higher than ever, outpacing those of their European counterparts.[33]

Greater political inequality generally accompanies rising economic inequality, and the United States has been no exception in this regard. In the age of the robber barons in the late nineteenth and early twentieth centuries, the industrial revolution generated vastly unequal wealth paired with unequal political power, as we will see. Decades of bloody repression of workers ensued as an ascendant class of capitalists enjoyed protection by the courts and the prevailing interpretation of the Constitution. Progressives and populists made some policy advances that restricted business power, and the New Deal and the postwar era brought a contraction between the rich and poor. As a middle class grew in the United States, a wider swath of Americans took part in public life, and democracy advanced.

As economic inequality has soared since the 1970s, however, the affluent and big business in the United States have become more politically organized than ever, in ways that present major obstacles to democracy. The amount of money spent on politics—both in campaign contributions and lobbying—has escalated sharply since the 1990s, owing to the deep pockets and motivation of wealthy Americans and corporations. Even more striking is the degree to which the rich have organized themselves politically, through highly effective groups such as Americans for

Prosperity, American Crossroads, and Heritage Action, which pursue their policy agenda on the state and national levels. The wealthy have reaped windfalls in the signature achievements of the Trump presidency: the immense 2017 tax cuts, which primarily benefited the top 1 percent and big companies, and the extensive scaling back of regulations. When government responds primarily to the rich, it transforms itself into oligarchy, and they gladly help usher in the new regime, which better protects their interests. Keeping watch over democracy is not their concern.[34]

## EXECUTIVE AGGRANDIZEMENT

The final threat to democracy is "executive aggrandizement," the enlargement of the powers wielded by a nation's top leader.[35] Democratic backsliding is often associated with the demise of checks on executive power, which typically results when powerful leaders expand their power and autonomy relative to more broadly representative legislatures and courts that are expected to protect rights. These executive actions might be perfectly legal, such as filling the courts and government agencies with political allies. But executives might also be tempted to stack the deck against their political opponents, making it hard to challenge their dominance; circumvent the rule of law; or roll back civil liberties and civil rights. Such actions can diminish democracy.

The American founders sought to thwart executive tyranny and to prevent a single group of leaders from seizing control of all the levers of government power at once. One of the ways they aimed to do this was to distribute power among different institutions, as James Madison explained in *Federalist* 51. Madison did not expect politicians to act with restraint in wielding power. He assumed, rather, that they would tend to be ambitious people bent on acquiring power and that the separation of powers would help prevent the concentration of power in a single individual or group.

The framers of the Constitution clearly gave the legislature pride of place. Article I establishes Congress as the first branch among three and lays out its powers in detail. The tersely worded Article II, by contrast, offers few specifics about presidential power, and makes constraints on the office—including the power of Congress to decide whether or not to enact measures the president recommends, and also to impeach and convict him—more evident than its powers.

But separation-of-powers systems such as that of the United States are notoriously prone to intractable political conflict between the executive and legislative branches, each of which can claim democratic legitimacy because it is independently elected. Moreover, a president engaged in such a conflict might be tempted to assume a populist mantle—to equate his supporters with "the people" as a whole and present his preferred policies as reflective of a single popular will as opposed to the multiplicity of voices and interests represented in the legislature.[36]

Across most of the first 125 years of the nation's history, with a few exceptions that we will examine in the early republic and the Civil War period, the very idea of a president achieving autocratic powers would have seemed inconceivable because the office was limited and Congress prevailed as the dominant branch. In the early twentieth century, however, presidential power began to grow.

By the time of Trump's election, the presidency had become a much more capacious and dominant office than the framers ever envisioned. Certainly the president cannot singlehandedly create or repeal laws, as those powers are vested in Congress. But in other respects an aspiring autocrat who occupies the White House would find considerable authority awaiting him. Presidents throughout the twentieth century have expanded the powers of the office, whether through the use of executive orders and proclamations, the administrative state, an enlarged White House staff and creation of the Executive Office of the Presidency, or the presidency's control over foreign policy and national security. Meanwhile, Congress—typically in moments of crisis, whether related to foreign policy crises or domestic travails—has ceded considerable authority to the executive branch and enabled presidents to act unilaterally and often without oversight. As a result, the ordinary checks and balances that the framers intended to ensure democratic accountability have grown weaker.

This process of executive aggrandizement, which has been supported by both parties, fueled the development of what has been called the "imperial presidency."[37] It has afforded presidents near-complete autonomy in foreign policy decisions and allowed them to commit the nation to expensive and risky interventions abroad, only later seeking congressional

Table 1.1  Major threats to democracy by historic period

|  | Polarization | Conflict over Who Belongs | Rising Economic Inequality | Executive Aggrandize-ment |
|---|---|---|---|---|
| 1790s | X | | | |
| 1850s | X | X | X | |
| 1890s | X | X | X | |
| 1930s | | | | X |
| 1970s | | | | X |
| 2010s | X | X | X | X |

approval. A vast national security apparatus has grown in tandem. It has secretly conducted domestic surveillance and political repression, often targeted at immigrants, minorities, and the politically vulnerable.

In the hands of a leader who envisions himself above the law, these tools provide ample means to further the leader's own agenda, at great cost to accountable democratic government.

## THE DANGER AND PROMISE OF DEMOCRACY

The four threats have waxed and waned over the course of American history, each according to its own pattern. Table 1.1 above shows which threats were present in each of the periods we investigate, including the present. When even one threat existed, the course of democracy was put at risk. In the 1790s, the emergence of intense polarization single-handedly led to escalating crises and ultimately threatened to launch the country into civil war. In two twentieth-century cases, executive aggrandizement loomed, as presidents wielded far more power than those in earlier periods. These circumstances worried Americans during the 1930s, when they witnessed totalitarianism on the rise in Europe and saw President Franklin D. Roosevelt embracing new powers to respond to the Great Depression. Such concerns reemerged when the abuses of Watergate came to light in the 1970s. In each instance, however, in the absence of the other threats, little backsliding occurred.

When several threats coalesced at one time, however, democratic progress grew deeply endangered. In the 1850s, polarized conflict over slavery created an intractable conflict that could not be healed by democratic means, leading to civil war. In the 1890s, the combination of polarization, economic inequality, and racial conflict produced a dramatic episode of democratic backsliding.

Today, for the first time ever, we face the confluence of all four threats at once. We would be foolhardy to ignore these circumstances, which undeniably make democracy more vulnerable. Polarization has become extreme, prompting members of Congress to act more like members of a team than as representatives or policymakers; their unwillingness to cooperate and compromise makes it impossible to address many major issues. Among ordinary citizens, polarization is prompting a sense of politics as "us versus them," in which people's political choices are highly motivated by their hostility toward the opposition. Polarization coincides with a sharp divide between an increasingly strident vision of white dominance in American society, on one side, and an increasingly diverse and inclusive coalition, on the other.[38] Economic inequality has skyrocketed, and wealthy Americans and business leaders are highly motivated and organized to protect their interests and expand their riches, whatever the costs to democracy. If the embrace of racist, nativist politics is required to achieve their goals, they are undeterred. And in the face of growing governmental dysfunction and stalemate, a massively powerful presidency has enabled President Trump to pursue much of his agenda by circumventing Congress. In this context of four threats, all the ingredients for democratic backsliding are in place.

Yet democratic decay is not inevitable. Although this combination of conditions makes democracy more precarious, it does not determine what will unfold, nor does it make the demise of government by the people unavoidable. Rather, it is politics that determines what will ensue. Politics does not adhere to mechanical principles, in which given circumstances foreordain a particular outcome. Rather, politics is driven by human beings who exercise agency and choice, and who can set their sights—if they so choose—on preserving and restoring democracy.

Democracy contains within it many seeds, including some that would hasten its own demise, but they must be selected and nurtured to produce such devastating outcomes. Ambitious political leaders engaged in intense competition can choose to pursue a strategy of political polarization if they wish. Up to a point, polarization can foster positive developments, such as boosting political participation, strengthening political parties, and simplifying voters' choices. But it must not be permitted to grow out of control.[39] Leaders can decide whether to promote and amplify racism and nativism as a polarizing strategy. They can also decide whether to do the bidding of the most affluent, who will willingly support them, or whether to cast their lot with ordinary Americans instead. Finally, they can decide whether to unleash the executive powers of the presidency, or whether to counter an increasingly powerful president by reasserting the representative power of Congress.

Conversely, democracy also contains the seeds of its own regrowth and renewal. Political leaders and citizens can—through politics—rescue democracy, but they must act before it is too late. Responsible public officials need to tend the garden of democracy in such a way that seeds of destruction do not take root, and if those seeds do sprout, leaders must make it their first priority to curtail their growth and to find ways to guard against their proliferation. In addition, they must bolster the laws and procedures that ensure free and fair elections, the rule of law, the legitimacy of the opposition, and integrity of rights. For their part, citizens must demand the preservation of democracy itself over any particular policy issues and seek to foster its revitalization.

Yet nurturing democracy has not come easily or automatically to Americans. To the contrary, no sooner was the US Constitution ratified and the new government established than the troubles began. Within just a few years, political leaders and ordinary citizens divided into camps that viewed each other as a fundamental threat to the nation's future.

# 2

## Polarization Wreaks Havoc in the 1790s

As the 1800 presidential election neared, Americans braced themselves. The Federalists, who dominated the presidency and both chambers of Congress, had become convinced that the Republicans, who functioned as the emerging opposition party, wanted to bring down the government itself and undermine the Constitution. A Connecticut Federalist predicted that if the Republicans won, "there is scarcely a possibility that we will escape a Civil War. Murder, robbery, rape, adultery and incest will all be openly taught and practiced, the air will be rent with the cries of distress, the soil will be soaked with blood, and the nation black with crimes."[1]

To Republicans, on the other hand, it seemed that the Federalists were using their power repeatedly to stifle any political opposition. Since the nation began, the Federalists had been pretty much in control: both presidents had been Federalists, and their faction had held the majority in the Senate continually and in the House in all but four years during the mid-1790s. Moreover, they viewed opposition as tantamount to insurrection, and had launched one action after another to repress it. By 1798, the Republicans found themselves shut out of power completely while the Federalists stacked the deck against them and prosecuted journalists who dared to criticize the government. The election of 1800, therefore, seemed to represent Republicans' last chance to gain a foothold—and for the fledgling government to demonstrate that it was not beholden to a particular faction. They believed that if they failed, neither the Constitution nor the Union could survive.[2]

Once the voting got under way, however, and then the states' electors made their choices, the election yielded an unbelievable result: deadlock. Republicans Thomas Jefferson and Aaron Burr tied for first place with seventy-three electoral votes each, while President John Adams netted sixty-five and two other Federalists, Charles Pinkney and John Jay, earned sixty-four and one, respectively.[3] Though Republicans had intended for Jefferson to be the presidential candidate and Burr the vice presidential candidate, the ballots used at the time did not make that distinction. Burr, moreover, whether because of opportunism or other motives, did not stand down but instead let the ambiguity linger. Without a clear winner, the decision—as dictated by the original language of Article II, Section I—was thrown into the House of Representatives, where each state would have a single vote in its presidential choice, and the victorious candidate had to attain a majority.

The Federalist majority in the House entertained three possible ways forward. The most obvious would be to honor the intent of the Republicans for Jefferson to be the presidential candidate and to declare him the winner. Alternatively, northern Federalists, many of whom abhorred Jefferson, could throw their support to Burr, whom they preferred; this option was also appealing because it would likely divide the Republicans and weaken them. A third option, a particularly controversial one, gained support among Federalists as well, and that was to usurp the presidency altogether. A law enacted in 1792, the Presidential Succession Act, mandated that if the office of the presidency lay vacant and no vice president stood by ready to step into the position, then the Senate's president pro tempore would become the new president. The Federalists cleverly observed that if they delayed making a decision until after inauguration day, this rule would take effect, meaning that one of their own would succeed Adams.

The nation lurched with anxiety for three long months, from December 1800 to February 1801, as it awaited a decision by the House. Rumors spread of plots and intrigue. Some reported hearing of threats to assassinate Jefferson. Mysterious fires broke out in Washington, damaging both the War and Treasury Departments, and each faction blamed the other for setting them. Republicans charged that Federalists sought to destroy evidence of corruption that had occurred while they dominated government.[4]

The framers had hoped the nation could avoid parties and designed the Constitution in ways intended to check their power if they did emerge. Already during President George Washington's first term in office, however, political polarization became apparent, and it intensified steadily throughout the 1790s. Federalist and Republican political leaders spent the decade locked in a series of battles, strategizing and plotting against each other through every constitutional, legal, and political means they could think of. Ordinary citizens also became highly involved in politics, the vast majority through peaceful civic engagement, though a few turned to violence. Even civic organizing outraged the Federalists, who saw it as a threat to their authority and responded forcefully.

Politics took on the proportions of mortal combat because both sides believed that the other presented an existential challenge to the nation's survival. Each was convinced that the circumstances justified taking extreme actions. The Federalists, who held political power, ran roughshod over several principles that were fundamental to the new American experiment: they violated the rule of law, trampled on the legitimacy of the opposition, and harmed rights of freedom of the press, freedom of speech, and freedom of assembly.

As Americans awaited the result of the 1800 election, the potential for violence loomed, and both parties expected bloodshed if a candidate preferred by the opposition was declared victorious. Republicans saw the nation's project of self-government being overrun by ascendant tyranny and believed that all would be lost unless they won. Yet if they did, Federalists would believe that a faction bent on undermining the nation had taken the reins. Both braced themselves for civil war and the possible destruction of the Union. Just fourteen years after the Constitution was drafted in Philadelphia, and only eleven years after the final states ratified it, the government it established stood poised to meet its demise.

## DEMOCRACY ON THE RISE AND RESTRICTED IN THE 1790S

In the 1790s, the groups that today we would call political parties got their start, though those who instigated them avoided that term: they preferred to view themselves as a "band of patriots" who were temporarily joined together to save the country from the treachery of a few. Within just a couple of years of trying to govern, political leaders found themselves at odds over policies; they also sought practical ways to achieve tasks for which the Constitution provided no mechanisms, such as coordinating elected officials to support specific policy goals. Madison and Jefferson took the initiative to create a nascent party structure to make it easier to gather politicians from far-flung parts of the country around shared principles and policy positions, to recruit candidates who would support those same views, and to indicate to voters what they stood for. The Republicans thus took shape and defined themselves against the Federalists, who mostly controlled the government.[5]

But political leaders in the 1790s, particularly the Federalists, had not yet developed the idea of a legitimate political opposition: they did not think that healthy self-government could thrive when groups with different approaches to governing competed with each other routinely through a political process. Rather, they thought that opposing views and competition could prove fatal to the government, and so they took a no-holds-barred approach to help their side prevail. As rancor and division spread, many Americans came to fear that the new nation was in dire peril.[6] Polarization could wreak plenty of havoc all on its own, as we will see.

All of this occurred in a context in which democracy was flourishing in some respects and nonexistent in others. The Revolution had toppled monarchy, and the Constitution had demolished titles of nobility and established freedom of religion. Several subsequent developments proved to be conducive to democratization. The framers' assumption that elites would rule a deferential citizenry was soon upended, not least because ordinary people themselves became politically active. States quickly expanded suffrage to include nearly all white men, regardless of whether they owned property. In economic terms, American society in the late eighteenth century was relatively egalitarian, outside of the South.[7]

Congress, elected through procedures that made it closer to the people than the president, figured prominently in the national government, and although the early presidents surprised many with the degree of power they asserted, their office lacked the institutional capacity that would enable twentieth-century presidents to go far beyond them. Each of these factors was conducive to democracy.

Yet despite these democratizing tendencies, the civic realm simultaneously remained circumscribed by rigid boundaries of membership and definitions of status that defied democracy entirely. Among the national population of 5.3 million Americans in 1800, close to one in five were African American, and nearly all of them—approximately 900,000 people—were enslaved.[8] Free women, under the principle of coverture, held no legal status once they were married. While Federalists and Republicans disagreed on many issues, race and gender were not among them, and so they did not contest the complete denial of freedom and equality to most people.

## THE PARTISAN MEDIA IS BORN

In September 1792, the anonymous author of an essay published in the *National Gazette* issued a thinly veiled attack on Treasury Secretary Alexander Hamilton and others associated with the Federalists. When the Constitution had been proposed, among those who embraced it, the writer recalled, "the great body were unquestionably friends to republican liberty," and yet "there were, no doubt, some who were openly or secretly attached to monarchy and aristocracy." Now this divide had given rise to public officials who were "more partial to the opulent than to the other classes of society; and having debauched themselves into a persuasion that mankind are incapable of governing themselves, it follows with them, of course, that government can be carried on only by the pageantry of rank, the influence of money and emoluments and the terror of military force." In a bound volume of the *National Gazette* now stored at the Library of Congress, the handwritten initials "JM" reveal the author of this essay— and many others that are similarly critical—to have been James Madison.[9]

Hamilton responded just one week later, also writing anonymously, in the rival *Gazette of the United States*. He castigated the Republicans as "the never to be satiated lovers of innovation and change—the tribe of pretended philosophers, but real fabricators of chimeras and paradoxes." He called them "seducing and treacherous leaders" who are known for "leading the dance to the tune of liberty without law" and who "endeavor to intoxicate the people with delicious but poisonous draughts to render them the easier victims of their rapacious ambition."[10] This was but one skirmish in what became an ongoing war that featured prominent political leaders fighting over their differences through the written word, published in the nation's first partisan news outlets.

Political polarization was fueled at the outset by political leaders themselves, ironically dividing some who had worked together just a few years earlier. During the Constitutional Convention in 1787, Madison, representing Virginia, had served as the document's chief architect, while Hamilton was a delegate from New York. The two worked in unity over the next two years, writing the Federalist Papers to make the case for ratification. After President George Washington was inaugurated in April 1789, the first order of business for the new government was to raise money to pay off the Revolutionary War debt; it was not clear how this could be done, since direct taxation seemed out of the question politically. In 1789 Congress enacted a tariff on goods imported by ship, but more revenues were needed. After public officials struggled unsuccessfully to come up with alternatives, the ambitious and brilliant treasury secretary stepped forth in January 1790 with the first of four bold financial plans. That is when the trouble began.

Over the course of the next two years, Hamilton would propose to employ and expand the federal government's power in ways that startled public officials and citizens alike. He firmly believed that the merchant class provided the key to the nation's economic growth, as it stood poised to use its resources to provide goods, engage in trade, and develop markets. He called for restructuring the national debt by shifting state debts to the federal government, and for creating a national bank, tariffs to promote manufacturing, and an excise tax on whiskey and other distilled spirits. These ideas won the support of wealthy individuals, speculators, and states with large debts, each of whom stood to gain from them, but they spurred distrust among others, particularly those from rural parts of the country that were reliant on agriculture. Some of Hamilton's peers thought that the plans, by imposing strong federal power, were "repugnant to the Constitution" and "dangerous to the rights and subversive of the interests of the people," as Patrick Henry put it.[11]

Chief among Hamilton's critics was Secretary of State Thomas Jefferson, who hated the idea of a republic centered around business and finance. He extolled the virtue of the "yeoman farmer," "those who labor in the earth," whom he described as "the chosen people of God."[12] Jefferson feared that if Hamilton had his way, the innate civic-mindedness of ordinary Americans would be overrun by the greed and self-interest of a small elite. And he found an ally against Hamilton in James Madison, who would later become the country's fourth president, and who was then serving as a congressman from Virginia. Madison made his opposition to Hamilton's plans known in Congress, but he and Jefferson believed that in order to protect the well-being of the nation, mere speeches would not be enough. The United States now needed a political opposition, and they would have to organize it.

Madison and Jefferson hoped to carry out their nascent partisan warfare through the media, but first they would need to create their own outlet. Their opponents already had one: a newspaper called the *Gazette of the United States*. In the words of its creator, John Fenno, the paper had been established for "the purpose of disseminating favorable sentiments of the federal Constitution and the Administration," and it offered unequivocal support for Hamilton's plans. Jefferson was appalled not just by the newspaper's "servile" posture toward Hamilton but also by the fact that its major advertisers were brokerage houses that handled government securities—which is to say they had a lot to gain financially by backing Hamilton.[13]

The pair set out to establish a competing newspaper that would offer opposing viewpoints. Seeking a skilled writer who was up to the task, Jefferson settled on Philip Freneau, a poet and journalist who had written vitriolic satire against the British and Tories during the Revolution and had later become a newspaper columnist at the *New York Daily Advertiser*. In order to support Freneau financially, Jefferson went so far as to offer him a "clerkship for foreign languages" in the State Department (a move that Hamilton later lambasted as corrupt).[14] Freneau agreed to Jefferson's request and established the *National Gazette*, which published its first issue on October 31, 1791. Thus the partisan media was born, with some of the founding fathers themselves serving as midwives.

Immediately the two rival newspapers brimmed over with anonymous op-eds engaging in a vociferous war of words. Many of those in the *National Gazette*, written by Jefferson and Madison under pseudonyms, blasted Hamilton's proposals, condemning the dangerous "consolidation" of national power at the expense of the states.[15]

Meanwhile, an all-out public feud erupted between Hamilton and Jefferson, with President Washington—the seeming embodiment of nonpartisan politics—caught in the middle. In a letter to the president, Jefferson offered a scathing indictment of Hamilton's plans, which he thought risked nothing less than the corruption of Congress, and the destruction of the Union and the underpinnings of republican government.

Hamilton, already incensed by the messages conveyed in the *National Gazette*, responded in kind, writing critical essays himself—also under various aliases—in the *Gazette of the United States*. He excoriated Jefferson for using "public money" to pay the editor to produce a newspaper that would be "an exact copy of the politics of his employer." He noted Jefferson's failure to support administration policies and charged that, in light of his opposition, he had the responsibility to resign. Washington, concerned that his administration would be destroyed from within, implored both men to make peace. "My earnest wish, and my fondest hope," he wrote to Jefferson, "is, that instead of wounding suspicions and irritable charges, there may be liberal allowances, mutual forbearances, and . . . yieldings on all sides." He conveyed the same request to Hamilton.[16] The president would not get his wish; the newspaper wars were just the beginning, and they would be but the first events in a decade of intensifying political conflict.

Congress, just three years old at this point, began to develop partisan divisions. In 1792, Jefferson and Madison recruited congressional candidates to promote a "Republican" agenda on policy issues, one that resisted the federal encroachment on liberty they associated with the Washington administration. Many of these individuals succeeded in getting elected. Soon the majority of roll-call votes were decided along what were for practical purposes party lines.[17]

Political opposition from public officials, evident in the newspaper wars, enraged the Federalists, but they also had to confront the unthinkable: resistance from rank-and-file citizens. Ordinary Americans themselves began to take sides on issues, whether simply as engaged citizens or as militant rebels. Some who used each of those approaches took part in the Whiskey Rebellion.

## WASHINGTON SUPPRESSES SUBVERSION IN THE WHISKEY REBELLION

Hamilton's financial plan included a federal excise tax on distilled spirits, such as whiskey, and once it was implemented in 1791, it generated opposition from citizens in several states. Reactions were swift—and not always peaceful. In Washington County, Pennsylvania, which bordered what was then the nation's western frontier, sixteen men disguised in women's dress accosted a federal tax collector named Robert Johnson who had been sent to collect the excise. They cut off his hair and then tarred and feathered him, meaning that they subjected him to a form of torture in which he was stripped naked, covered with hot tar, and rolled in feathers. Then they stole his horse and left him in the forest. By law, the offenders would have to be punished, but someone would have to arrest them first. The federal marshal responsible for serving their arrest warrants was fearful of receiving the same treatment as Johnson, so he hired an unsuspecting cattle drover named John Connor to go in his place. Connor was not only tarred and feathered but also whipped, robbed, and left tied to a tree. Other federal officials in the area soon began to fear for their lives. A belligerent crowd set out to attack another tax collector, an army officer named William Faulkner. Not finding him at home, the marauders broke in, rampaged through the house, and then shot holes through the ceiling in every room.[18] Figure 2.1 below depicts a tax collector who was not only tarred and feathered but also required to ride a rail, another form of vigilante justice common during the period.

Violence was an extreme way of protesting the excise tax, to be sure; most opponents of the tax objected through peaceful means such as petitions. At a public meeting in western Pennsylvania in late summer of 1792, those gathered considered the tax "oppressive upon the poor" and a threat to rural people's liberty. People declared themselves obligated

2.1  Famous Whiskey Insurrection in Pennsylvania

to "obstruct the operation of the law until we are able to obtain its total repeal."[19]

The Whiskey Rebellion would simmer for a few more years, as discontent swelled its forces while the US government struggled to maintain order. In the summer of 1794, US marshal David Lenox arrived with writs ordering sixty distillers to appear in court, announcing them in the presence of local federal excise inspector General John Neville. Soon after, an armed mob of five hundred men, members of local militia groups, attacked Neville's house. In defending themselves, Neville and his family killed two of the rebels, including the commander, and injured six before escaping. The mob then ransacked the house and burned it to the ground. Later they took Lenox captive to prevent him from collecting any more excise taxes. Some weeks later, six thousand rebels converged in a field just outside Pittsburgh, where Neville's headquarters were located, offering a powerful show of force. Some wanted to disrupt the federal mail service, others to attack Pittsburgh to seize ammunition from the garrison. At this point a delegation of more moderate leaders intervened and talked the rebels down from these more extreme actions.[20]

President Washington learned of these developments from two competing sources. One was a local congressman named William Findley, who viewed the rebels sympathetically. The other was Hamilton, who saw the Whiskey Rebellion as far more than mere hostility to a particular policy. He portrayed the rebels' disagreement with the excise tax as subversion, as opposition to the legitimacy of the federal government itself, which they were aiming to "render ... unpopular and odious." Hamilton therefore believed the uprising demanded quick and unequivocal suppression by the power and authority of the federal government.[21] The president found Hamilton more persuasive, and he became fearful that civil war might be imminent. He began to think that he should meet the insurrection with force.

Pennsylvania's governor, Thomas Mifflin, who was hostile to the Washington administration, let it be known that he did not support sending troops to put down the insurrection. As a last-ditch effort, Washington sent a commission to talk with the rebels, offering amnesty in exchange for submission, but the Pennsylvanians were not willing to back down. As the prospect of military force grew more likely, an editorial in the Philadelphia *General Advertiser* implored, "Shall Pennsylvania be converted into a slaughter house because the dignity of the United States will not admit of conciliatory measures? Shall torrents of blood be spilled to support an odious excise system?"[22] Criticism of Washington's plans to summon troops was mounting, but he did not relent.

In late September, Washington ordered a fifteen-thousand-man militia, gathered from four states—Virginia, New Jersey, Maryland, and Pennsylvania—to march to the region. Raising the army proved challenging: through some patriotic gentlemen soldiers volunteered, most troops had to be drafted, and draft evasion and desertion ran high. Those who stayed in were mostly poor and immigrant men who relied on the pittance they would earn. The troops were racked by disease, including dysentery with its fevers and diarrhea.[23]

Washington and Hamilton met the troops in Carlisle. Acting as commander in chief, the president led the mission himself, riding serenely on horseback at the front, accompanied by the governors and dignitaries of the states represented. Hamilton, thrilled with the federal show of force, stayed with the militia for the duration. Yet when the troops arrived near Pittsburgh in late October, there was no rebel army gathered to meet it, and the insurrection appeared to have already subsided.

Determined to complete the mission, mounted soldiers stormed the homes of suspected rebels on November 13, dragged 150 from their beds, and marched them to Pittsburgh, where some were housed in muddy pens or wet stables for days. Then Hamilton and several judges began interrogating the suspects, seeking "examples" whose trials would help deter other citizens from plotting rebellion themselves. But as they did, it became clear that the most notorious rebels—as many as two thousand— had already fled into the frontier, leaving behind only those who had played minor roles. The federal authorities lacked compelling evidence against the vast majority of those they questioned, and most were in dire straits that would evoke sympathy, having lost much of their land in recent years or been victims of hardship. Ultimately they arrested only ten men and brought them back to Philadelphia to stand trial. All were eventually acquitted except two, both of whom eyewitnesses had seen at Neville's house. The pair were sentenced to hang, but Washington issued stays of execution on two occasions and finally pardoned them.[24]

Despite this final act of mercy by the president, the incident would sully the reputation of a man who had been held in great reverence by Americans when he took office. More importantly for the state of democracy, the events also tarnished the principle of the rule of law. Before Washington sent in troops, Pennsylvania's secretary of state, Alexander Dallas, had implored, "The military power of the government ought not to be employed until its judicial authority . . . has proved incompetent to enforce obedience or to punish infractions of the law."[25] The administration had stalled a bit, but ultimately proceeded undeterred. This would also be the first and only time in the nation's history when the president himself led troops to put down a domestic rebellion. The debacle showed that the Federalists would regard any opposition to federal policies as treasonous and respond with force. To Americans who believed the Revolution had brought triumph over tyranny, this approach by the nation's first presidential administration smacked of overreach and the abuse of power.

## WASHINGTON CONDEMNS CIVIC ORGANIZING

Meanwhile, the Washington administration faced popular opposition from yet another quarter: the so-called Democratic-Republican societies.[26] These civic groups were forged by men who felt that the new government failed to live up to the ideals of the American Revolution: they believed that it catered to the few and was unresponsive to the many, threatened excessive power over the lives of citizens, and was undermining civic virtue among Americans. They openly criticized the Washington administration, which they viewed as having monarchical and aristocratic tendencies. They were not formally partisan groups, however, but rather saw their primary goal as nurturing civic engagement. By their very existence, the groups repudiated the vision of society held by the Federalists, who considered citizens to have a role only in electing their representatives, and aside from that thought that public officials—presumably elites—should be left alone to govern, and treated with deference.[27] Members of the Democratic-Republican societies, by contrast, felt adamantly that citizens needed to be informed and active.

Defenders of the administration assumed that these societies had their origins abroad and associated them with the revolutionary Jacobin societies in France, but historians find greater evidence of domestic sources. Several of the groups took inspiration from the *National Gazette,* whose editor, Freneau, wrote that citizens had both the right and the duty to criticize actions taken by government. He advocated the establishment of societies "for the purpose of watching over the rights of the people, and giving an early alarm in case of governmental encroachments thereupon." The groups also seem to have been the successors to Revolutionary-era groups such as the Sons of Liberty.[28]

Forty-two such societies were established, mostly in 1793 and 1794, in localities ranging from Maine to South Carolina. They drew together men from different classes of society; among the members were numerous craftsmen, printers, small farmers, and mechanics, as well as some professionals, merchants, and planters. The few wealthy and famous members included, for example, Peter Muhlenberg, who represented Pennsylvania in the US House and later in the Senate, and David Rittenhouse, an inventor and mathematician who became the first director of the US Mint. But in the main, society members were not affluent, and they criticized the administration for catering to "the rich and well born," particularly the merchants and bankers.[29]

The Democratic-Republican societies aimed to make government more responsive to the people. They promoted the "equal rights of man," which included freedom of speech, press, and assembly, and the right to criticize government officials. They sought to develop a democratic political culture, enabling Americans to transition from the role of monarchical subjects to republican citizens, and in the process to hold government officials accountable. The more hierarchical views of the Federalists threatened, in the words of a Massachusetts society, to "undermine the foundation of freedom, and to erect on her ruins the fabric of despotism." The members of the societies contended that it was "the duty of the people, to watch the conduct" of elected officials, and if those officials failed to live up to their responsibilities, "the people ought to be assiduous in exercising their constitutional authority to remove them from office."[30]

The societies educated citizens on issues, serving as "schools of political knowledge," as one minister referred to them. In their gatherings and deliberations, their members eschewed the use of traditional terms of address such as "sir" and "esquire," instead calling one another "citizen" in the spirit of the French Revolution. The groups fostered public discussion by hosting speakers and discussion meetings, and they aimed to influence public opinion through "dissemination of political information," in newspapers and by issuing pamphlets and resolutions. They took stands on numerous issues, promoting the development of universal public education, the end of debtors' prison and the adoption of legal reforms that favored debtors, and the eradication of capital punishment. In some associations, members promoted the abolition of slavery, though elsewhere slaveholders belonged to the groups.[31]

The societies' antagonism toward the Federalists worsened as foreign policy took center stage following the French Revolution's intensifying radicalism. Initially Americans had applauded France's battle against tyranny, honoring the allegiance between the two nations that had developed when France supported the colonies during the American Revolution. France's struggle appeared to signal that Americans had been in the vanguard of a new historical trend toward rule by the people. Yet once the French Revolution took a more violent turn—Louis XVI and Marie Antoinette were both executed on the guillotine, and then France declared war on Great Britain, Spain, and Holland—Americans grew sharply divided. Hamilton and other Federalists worried that the nation, still establishing itself and having only a small military, would be put at risk if it were drawn into the conflict. They were also concerned that Americans who remained loyal to France would soon promote radical egalitarianism, anarchy, and instability in the United States. They recommended that President Washington issue a proclamation of neutrality in the conflict between France and Great Britain, forbidding any aid to France from the United States. This development enraged Jefferson and many others, who perceived it not only as a betrayal of an ally but more fundamentally as a repudiation of republicanism and a threat to the Constitution. As Madison put it, the proclamation reflected "seeming indifference to the cause of liberty."[32]

As Americans confronted the choice between allegiance to Britain and allegiance to France, polarization spiraled. Hamilton, writing under the pseudonym "Pacificus," defended neutrality as being in the self-interest of the United States. Jefferson quickly urged Madison, the most persuasive writer among the Republicans, to respond: "For god's sake, my dear Sir, take up your pen, select the most striking heresies and cut him to pieces in the face of the public."[33] Madison proceeded to write essays charging the administration with the aggrandizement of executive power.

Then a popular and flamboyant French minister, Edmond-Charles Genêt (called "Citizen Genêt"), traveled throughout the country, courting Americans—including members of the Democratic-Republican societies—who enthusiastically supported France. He arrived in Charleston, South Carolina, on April 8, 1793, and took over a month to travel to Philadelphia, where he belatedly presented his credentials to Washington. Along the way he fanned the popular flames of support for America's entry into war with England. He went so far as to recruit and outfit privateers to sail from American ports on missions to attack British naval vessels. Washington and his advisors were irate; even Jefferson had to agree that Genêt had overplayed his hand in failing to respect the neutrality proclamation. They delicately requested that the French government recall Genêt, but many Americans sympathized with the minister. The swirling politics of the neutrality proclamation and the Genêt affair further polarized Americans over the appropriate posture the nation should take toward France. It also once again dented Washington's reputation: he was called a "tyrant" by critics, and one poster, titled "The Funeral of George Washington," depicted him placed on a guillotine.[34]

Several Federalists, who thought that such opposition to government by citizens threatened to break the nation apart, turned their ire to the Democratic-Republican societies. The Federalists considered the organizations inherently "unlawful" because they aimed to influence government by getting citizens involved in politics—something to which common people had no right, they thought. To discredit the groups, they attempted to malign the term "democracy," distinguishing it from "republicanism" and associating it instead with the anarchy, lawlessness, and sedition they observed in the French revolutionaries. As one Federalist said, "The clubs consist of hot-headed, ignorant or wicked men devoted entirely to their views of France."[35] To be clear, many of the members of the societies did tend to sympathize with the French, but their motivation emanated from the same homegrown spirit as the American Revolution.

President Washington, who generally tried to remain above the fray, became incensed by the Democratic-Republican societies because they violated the norm that between elections citizens should be deferential to government. To him, it was inappropriate for such groups to organize politically because they were what he called "self-created": they were formed voluntarily by citizens themselves, rather than being established by government or through elections. He was appalled by their ambition to influence government, writing, "Can any thing be more absurd, more arrogant, or more pernicious to the peace of Society than for self created bodies, forming themselves into permanent Censors, and under the shade of Night in a conclave." Washington was sure, moreover, that the societies had instigated the Whiskey Rebellion, though evidence pointed to the contrary. Washington saw the groups as an existential threat: "My mind is so perfectly convinced that, if these self-created societies cannot be discountenanced, they will destroy the government of this country."[36]

Washington appealed to Congress to stand behind him on the matter, and his Federalist allies who controlled the Senate quickly passed a resolution blaming "certain self-created societies" for misleading citizens and fomenting insurrection. In the House, by contrast, where Republicans were effectively in control, three days of debate ensued. Madison, though cautious about disagreeing with the president, said that it was not appropriate for Congress to take such a stand, for "the censorial power is in the people over the Government, and not in the Government over the people." He affirmed the "good sense and patriotism of the people" and downplayed the harm that could come from groups that only wanted to express their opinions. The House voted down the first resolution, which would have condemned the societies, and passed a second, more moderate version that defended the public order and expressed concern about "any misrepresentations . . . of the Government and its proceedings," whether made by individuals or by groups.[37]

In Jefferson and Madison's view, Washington had essentially asked members of Congress both to declare their loyalty to him and to denounce political opposition among ordinary citizens. Jefferson saw it as a partisan response unbefitting the head of the nation, while Madison termed it "the greatest error" of the president's political life. Writing to James Monroe, he said, "The game was to connect the Democratic societies with the odium of insurrection, to connect the Republicans in Congress with those Societies," and for the president to put his own prestige "in opposition to both."[38]

While the societies' presence would fade after just a few years, they had shown Americans how citizens could organize and hold government accountable even between elections. That their efforts were so openly despised by public officials demonstrates yet again that political opposition was not yet seen as a normal part of the functioning of a democracy. Civic engagement and civic groups would later become a hallmark of American public life, but in that polarized era they were seen, at least by some, as an existential threat to government requiring an adamant response.

## WASHINGTON CIRCUMVENTS CONGRESS

Soon another foreign policy crisis threatened to launch the United States into war with Great Britain, and the Washington administration's response to it—to negotiate a treaty with the nation's former mother country—further heightened the acrimony between Federalists and Republicans. As events unfolded, Republicans viewed the Washington administration as seizing an inappropriate amount of executive power, in ways that sidelined Congress and denied its authority. In essence, the president made light of the rule of law by violating the strictures of checks and balances. Some saw in this further evidence that the Federalists were taking the nation down a slippery slope toward monarchy.

The controversy began over trade policy. As the United States sought to settle its debts and improve its economy, it needed to forge more equitable trading relationships with other countries, not least with Britain. The Federalists, at Hamilton's urging, favored free trade, believing that a lack of restrictions would best promote American wealth and power. Republicans, by contrast, preferred to take a harder line, not least because southern planters still owed debts to Britain that they had incurred prior to the Revolution and they wanted those debts forgiven before they would agree to any conciliatory behavior toward the nation.[39]

The Republican-dominated House of Representatives wanted, therefore, to impose trade sanctions against Britain. But President Washington in effect circumvented the body by sending Chief Justice John Jay to Britain to negotiate a treaty ensuring open trade between the two countries and dealing with other grievances, such as the continued presence of British troops in the Northwest Territory. Jay succeeded and signed a treaty on November 19, 1794, at which Republicans grew livid. They claimed it was evidence that Federalists intended to reestablish ties with the very nation from which the United States had declared its independence. Ordinary citizens became embroiled in the polarizing debate, holding protests against the treaty in several northeastern cities and burning an effigy of Jay—and copies of the treaty—in Charleston, South Carolina. The most outspoken opponents even began to call for Washington's impeachment, and to criticize the House for being slow to pursue it.[40]

Unmoved by the furor, Washington signed the treaty, and the Federalist-dominated Senate ratified it. An outraged Jefferson charged: "A bolder party-stroke was never struck, for it certainly is an attempt of a party, which finds they have lost their majority in one branch of the Legislature, to make a law by the aid of the other branch and of the executive, under the color of a treaty." House members retaliated first by snubbing the president: they rejected, 50 to 38, a motion for a half-hour adjournment to commemorate his birthday; one year earlier, only 13 had voted against the same motion.[41]

Next, radical members of the opposition, led by Congressman Edward Livingston of New York, attempted to engage in oversight: they promoted a resolution demanding that the Washington administration share with it all correspondence and other documents related to the Jay Treaty. Washington flatly refused, arguing that the president and Senate retained the power to make treaties, and that to comply with the request for documents would "establish a dangerous precedent." Madison termed Washington's intransigence "improper and indelicate," as it undermined Congress's legitimate authority to gather information on the activities of the executive.[42] Both sides rallied their supporters, and petitions both for and against the treaty poured into the House. Finally, the House voted in favor of implementing it.

Washington, who had never envisioned the emergence of such polarization nor the abandonment of deference to political leaders, chose to retire rather than run again. The 1796 election would be the first contested by two parties. Of the several candidates who ran, Federalist John Adams won the most votes, followed by Republican Thomas Jefferson. This meant—according to procedures described in Article II, Section 1 (later modified by the Twelfth Amendment, ratified in 1804)—that they would serve as president and vice president, respectively. Initially, some observers thought that this bipartisan team would mend the partisan divisions in the country, but such hopes proved to be short-lived.

## POLITICAL OPPOSITION AND DISSENT UNDER ATTACK

As divisions over foreign policy grew, polarization continued to intensify among Federalist and Republican leaders and ordinary Americans alike. Citizens in each group expressed patriotism, but in different ways. It was at this stage that partisans held their own separate Fourth of July celebrations, with Republicans venerating the Declaration of Independence and Federalists the Constitution. One night in May 1798, a riot broke out in Philadelphia between young men who were wearing hats adorned with a cockade, or knot of ribbons, in black to demonstrate solidarity with England and those who were wearing red and blue ones, seemingly in support of France. The latter group later explained they intended for their cockades to honor the colors of the American Revolution. Whether or not that was the case, violence erupted. As Jefferson put it: "A fray ensued. The light horse were called in, and the city was so filled with confusion . . . that it was dangerous to go out."[43]

Hamilton, identifying in such events what he called a surging "spirit of patriotism"—in this case, a euphemism for partisanship—saw opportunity in the crisis. He proposed that Federalists take steps that would ensure "national unanimity," by which he actually meant to destroy the political opposition.[44] Politically, the time was ripe to go on the offensive. The previous year, in 1797, Republicans had lost the majority in the House, so now Federalists dominated both chambers. Hamilton took advantage of the situation to encourage his party in Congress to enact several new laws. Each of them aimed to weaken Republicans and, in so doing, consolidate Federalists' power.

Federalists' dislike of immigrants, who they believed supported the Republicans, led them to enact three "anti-alien" policies. The Naturalization Act increased the period of residency required in the United States before an individual could gain citizenship from five years to fourteen years. The Alien Enemies Act and the Aliens Act, in combination, made it easier for presidents to deport or imprison those who were deemed dangerous or were from a nation that was considered a threat to national security. They also established a registration and surveillance system for foreign nationals. Jefferson denounced the enacted provisions as "worthy of the 8th or 9th century" and reported that their passage had prompted French immigrants to depart immediately.[45]

In addition, to squelch political dissent, Congress enacted the Sedition Act that same year. It promised punishment for those who would "unlawfully combine or conspire together, with intent to oppose any measure . . . of the government of the United States." It also permitted the prosecution of anyone who published or wrote anything "false, scandalous or malicious" about government officials "with intent to defame . . . or to bring them . . . into contempt or disrepute; or to excite against them . . . the hatred of the good people of the United States."[46]

Proponents of the Sedition Act saw the activities of the Republican opposition as synonymous with treason. In the House of Representatives, Federalist Robert Goodloe Harper of South Carolina said that the opposition's goal was "to completely stop the wheels of Government, and to lay it prostrate at the feet of its external and internal foes." Congressman "Long John" Allen of Connecticut—so named because he was six feet five inches tall—accused Republican newspapers of seeking to "overturn and ruin the Government" by publishing "shameless falsehoods" and encouraging citizens to mount "an insurrection" at the polls.

In response, Republican congressman Albert Gallatin, from Pennsylvania, depicted the Sedition Act as a power grab by the Federalists, and noted that it equated any disapproval of "men now in power" with being an enemy of the Constitution itself. He distinguished between opposition to a presidential administration or a group of partisans, on the one hand, and opposition to the nation's system of government, on the other. But Gallatin was quite alone in articulating the legitimacy of political opposition; most of his contemporaries viewed opposition as intolerable and as a threat to the future of the republic.[47] That conviction drove the entire decade of spiraling conflict between the parties.

What the Alien and Sedition Acts clearly epitomized, to many Republicans, was the authoritarian tendencies of the Federalists. Both exerted real harm on crucial features of the nation's embryonic democracy. The immigration measures aimed to tilt the playing field in ways that would undermine Republicans' capacity to operate as an opposition party. The Sedition Act curtailed freedom of the press and freedom of speech. As a result, the Republicans felt compelled to resist the new laws in ways that further escalated the mounting conflict and presented a challenge to the federal government itself.

## FIGHTING FEDERALISTS WITH FEDERALISM

Thomas Jefferson believed that in enacting the Alien and Sedition Acts, the Federalists had endangered the basic right of dissent and engaged in an illegal usurpation of power. Further, though vice president, he determined that Republicans needed to abandon the moderate approaches of working through Congress and the electoral process and contest Federalist power grabs more strategically. The key to fighting the Federalists would be through federalism—that is, the American system of government, in which individual states were not wholly subservient to the national government but rather retained considerable authority in their own right. Jefferson advocated turning to the state governments, many of which were dominated by Republicans, and using their authority as independent sovereigns to resist. In 1798 and 1799, the states of Kentucky and Virginia issued resolutions declaring that the Alien and Sedition Acts represented an unconstitutional use of power by the national government to restrict Americans' liberties, and that on that basis those two states would declare them null and void.[48]

Jefferson himself, acting anonymously, had drafted the Kentucky resolutions. He argued that the states themselves had formed the federal government through a "compact," granting it "certain definite powers," but that they had reserved to themselves "the residuary mass of rights to their own self-government." As a result, in instances in which the federal government claimed "undelegated powers," meaning those not explicitly granted to it by the Constitution, "its acts are unauthoritative, void, and of no force." The resolutions argued that the Alien and Sedition Laws represented just such an unconstitutional usurpation of power, and urged other states to resist as well. Jefferson went so far as to call for a special committee to communicate between the states on the matter. State nullification of federal law represented an extreme measure, but one that Jefferson considered to be necessary. When it came to protecting liberty, he wrote, state governments had proven themselves as the "very best in the world," whereas the federal government "has, in the rapid course of 9 or 10 years, become more arbitrary, and has swallowed more of the public liberty than even that of England."[49]

In Kentucky, where the Alien and Sedition Acts had already been condemned at numerous public meetings, state legislator John Breckinridge took the lead on promoting the resolutions. He moderated Jefferson's language, dropping the insistence that states had the right to nullify laws, and requested instead that Congress repeal the offensive acts. The state legislature then passed the resolutions unanimously.[50] Soon thereafter, similar resolutions, drafted anonymously by Madison but edited by Jefferson to reinsert the stronger nullification language, were adopted in Virginia.

To Federalists, these resolutions were nothing less than a direct threat to the authority of the federal government. To Republicans, they were a last-ditch effort to resist federal repression of political dissent and to save the Union, using the leverage provided by the Constitution.

Behind the scenes, Virginia, fearing retaliation from the federal government, began to stockpile arms for possible military conflict.

## THE FEDERALISTS STRIKE BACK

Since the height of the newspaper wars and the Democratic-Republican societies, many Federalists had been concerned that their political opponents ultimately aimed to discredit the legitimacy of government itself and cause political instability. Now, in the wake of the Virginia and Kentucky resolutions and after getting wind of Virginia's military preparations, they saw their worst fears being realized. More troubling still, the opposition was spreading, as the two southern states were now joined by an unlikely corner of the North.

German Americans—who lived mostly in the southeastern counties of Pennsylvania—were second in number among the nation's ethnic populations after Irish Americans. In the early 1790s, Irish Americans became more visibly engaged in national politics, but those of German descent had remained neutral. By decade's end, however, several factors coalesced to enrage them: the Alien and Sedition Acts, a new federal property tax, and talk of an enlarged federal military, which Hamilton had promoted. In 1798, they united under the leadership of John Fries, a Revolutionary War veteran and auctioneer who was fluent in both English and German, and began to intimidate the assessors who were charged with carrying out the new federal property tax. They mobilized a local militia of 140 men who pressured the local US marshal to release eighteen people imprisoned in Bethlehem for refusing to pay the tax.[51]

Facing this new and unexpected threat, the Federalists felt besieged. They viewed the Fries Rebellion as part of a larger conspiracy to bring down the federal government. Although President Adams himself was somewhat reluctant, Hamilton—as he had during the Whiskey Rebellion—pushed for a powerful show of military force, lest the government risk "magnifying a riot into an insurrection." He declared that when "government appears in arms, it ought to appear like a Hercules, and inspire respect by the display of strength."[52] In fact, once the army marched into the region—a full four weeks later—it seemed more like an inept bully. In another echo of the Whiskey Rebellion, the troops met with no resistance and found that all signs of the rebellion had dissipated. They swarmed the area, tracking down suspects and making arrests, sometimes on the basis of little more than rumors. Fries himself saw the cavalry coming and took to the woods, but his dog barked and gave him away, prompting his arrest.

Several of the soldiers themselves later expressed revulsion at what they had been asked to do. One wrote, "The scenes of distress that I witnessed I cannot describe. . . . Conceive your home entered at the dead of night by a body of armed men, and yourself dragged from your wife and screaming children." Another worried that "these poor, well-meaning but ignorant Germans" were "treated in no respect like citizens of the same country." Still another called the entire expedition "not only unnecessary, but violently absurd," and said that one officer and a handful of assistants could have accomplished the task as well as the massed federal troops.[53]

The soldiers brought sixty prisoners to Philadelphia, where the Federalist newspapers urged harsh treatment of them by the courts, for "the principle of insurrection must be eradicated, or anarchy will ensue." Ultimately, however, only Fries and two others were tried for treason and found guilty. All three were eventually pardoned by Adams, against the wishes of his fellow Federalists. Meanwhile, the Federalists' overreach succeeded in bringing all the counties in the region—full of people who had been previously unengaged in politics—firmly into the Republican camp.[54]

Undeterred by this failure, the Federalists turned to another weapon: the Sedition Act. They used it to prosecute editors of numerous Republican newspapers that had published material critical of government leaders. After the law had been enacted, James Thomson Callender, one of the most outspoken Republican journalists, fled from Philadelphia to Virginia, where he continued to write scathing critiques of the Federalists. In one essay, he referred to President Adams as a "hoary headed incendiary." In May 1800, after Callender published his pamphlet *The Prospect Before Us*, he was arrested on the grounds that he had maliciously defamed President Adams in a manner aimed to turn Americans against him. The next month, he was tried and convicted by the ardent Federalist judge Samuel Chase—whom Republicans despised almost as much as Hamilton—and was fined and sentenced to nine months in jail.[55]

The Federalists also went after William Duane, editor of the Republican newspaper *Aurora* in Philadelphia. Duane had used his platform to denounce the Alien Acts, and later published the text of a bill promoted by the Federalists that would have changed the method of counting electoral votes in order to stack the deck permanently in their favor. The Senate charged him with a "high breach of privileges" for publishing a bill that was not yet enacted, ordered him to appear before the chamber to be tried, and informed him that while he could be accompanied by lawyers, they could not defend him. Duane went into hiding to avoid a likely conviction.[56]

These highly publicized events only intensified the political divide. To Federalists, they showcased the necessity for a law to silence those who were critical of the government. To Republicans, they clearly manifested the Federalists' strengthening grip on power and their willingness to repress any who dissented from it. Amid such fractious polarization, the possibility of secession or civil war seemed ever closer.

## PRESSING THE LIMITS OF REPUBLICANISM

As 1800 got under way, Americans looked to the fall election to help move the country forward. New York was one of several states in which electors for the presidential election were chosen by state legislators. And so when in the spring of 1800 Republicans won control of the New York state legislature, previously dominated by Federalists, it seemed to mark a decided shift in favor of the Republican cause. Republican ascendancy in the state also fueled the political fortunes of New Yorker Aaron Burr, who had distinguished himself as a party operative during the spring elections. Soon state Republican leaders met and declared their support for Burr as vice president.[57]

Meanwhile, the Federalists were racked by internecine conflicts. Adams despised Hamilton, whom he described as "a man devoid of every moral principle," and came to believe that Hamilton's hubris had cost the party the New York state elections. Adams, with the support of Federalists in Congress, had ordered the disbanding of the federal army, the establishment of which had been one of Hamilton's priorities. Hamilton retaliated by issuing a pamphlet in which he attacked Adams's character, charging him with "disgusting egotism ... distempered jealousy, and ... ungovernable indiscretion of temper."[58]

But the Republicans soon faced problems of their own when an attempted slave insurrection in Virginia showcased their hypocrisy and vulnerability. The rebellion was organized by a twenty-four-year-old slave, known only as Gabriel, who was a skilled blacksmith and could read and write. Since slaveholders could not keep artisans occupied all the time, they occasionally hired them out to work for pay in nearby Richmond, and there Gabriel found a taste for liberty. Meanwhile, he was caught stealing a pig by a former overseer, Absalom Johnson; Gabriel knocked him to the ground and bit off "part of his left ear." Gabriel was sentenced to death, but he invoked a clause that permitted slaves to escape hanging if they could recite a verse from the Bible and would submit to having a cross branded on their thumb. Afterward, Gabriel became determined to seek freedom for slaves, and he took inspiration from Republicans' embrace of liberty and their justification of protest.

In what became known as Gabriel's Conspiracy, he began to hatch a plan for a slave rebellion. He recruited participants, first from among other slaves like himself who hired out their work. At an organizational meeting on August 10, 1800, these rebels reported that five hundred had promised to take part, and they set a date of August 30 for the assault, which was to include first killing Gabriel's master and then storming the state capitol, killing several white leaders, and taking the governor hostage. Yet when the appointed date arrived, a torrential rainstorm washed out bridges and undermined communication between the rebel groups. They tried to reschedule the uprising for the following night, but then learned that their plans had been revealed by two slaves on a neighboring farm who likely hoped that sharing the information would gain them their own freedom. The terrified Virginia authorities sent out multiple units of militia to round up slaves who had been involved in the plans for the foiled rebellion.

Federalists responded opportunistically to the story of Gabriel's Conspiracy, using it to frighten southerners away from the Republicans. Federalist newspapers had long been spreading rumors that the more egalitarian-minded party, if victorious in the election, would free the slaves, and these events seemed to provide evidence.[59]

But Gabriel had exposed the truth: that the same two parties that had spent years battling over their differences did in fact share substantial common ground after all. Despite the Republicans' avowed belief in equality, they condoned slavery; prominent leaders, even Jefferson and

Madison, owned slaves. And while several northern Federalists opposed slavery, the party itself had not yet embraced an antislavery position. Both parties, in effect, remained committed to upholding slavery.[60] Neither advocated changes to the boundaries of civic membership or alteration in the rigid status hierarchies of their age. On that much, they could agree.

## THE DEADLOCKED ELECTION

Tensions soared as Americans awaited the result of the deadlocked election. Republicans were convinced that the Federalists would resort to force to maintain their power. Some expected that the party would seize forts, arsenals, and arms and enlist a volunteer militia, and that the judiciary—firmly in its control—would permit it. One warned that Federalists intended to burn "the constitution at the point of a bayonet," while others believed that they would have each of them put to death in order to retain power. The Republicans promised to respond with force themselves if the Federalists usurped the presidency. Explained Jefferson, "The day such an act passed, the middle States would arm," because "no such usurpation, even for a single day, should be submitted to." In addition, he noted that the Republicans would call for "a convention to re-organize the government and to amend it," an idea that terrified the Federalists.[61]

Two Republican governors, representing Pennsylvania and Virginia, were already readying their states for military action, making arrangements to call forth the militia. Governor Monroe of Virginia planned to block the federal government should it attempt to take arms from a federal arsenal that was located in the state and to transport them elsewhere. He sent a militia officer on a covert mission to inspect the arsenal, and his fears were confirmed when the federal official on duty told this individual that he had recently received orders that the arms and supplies were to be moved. Clearly the Federalists were already preparing for the need to restore order if need be.[62]

Meanwhile, Hamilton surprised his fellow Federalists by throwing his support to Jefferson. In letters to colleagues he explained that Burr was "the most unfit man in the U.S. for the office of President," for he would use the position to "secure to himself permanent power and with it wealth."[63] Though Hamilton had long despised Jefferson, he thought him worthy of the presidency, and of superior character to Burr—the much lesser of two evils.

The House of Representatives began balloting on Wednesday, February 11, during a severe snowstorm. Under the Constitution, the House voted by states, not individual members. Each state had one vote, and a candidate needed at least nine votes to win. At the outset, at 1:00 p.m., Jefferson received eight and Burr six, while Vermont and Maryland—both internally divided—abstained. Members continued to deliberate and caucus, holding vote after vote through the night. One newspaper reported that it was "ludicrous to see some . . . [representatives] running with anxiety from the committee rooms, with their nightcaps on." By eight o'clock the next morning, twenty-seven ballots later, the impasse remained unchanged.[64] Day after day, vote after vote produced the same results. Exhaustion set in, and tempers flared.

On Saturday, after four more ballots showed the same gridlock, Jefferson had had enough, and he paid a call to President Adams. He warned him that if the Federalists dared to usurp the presidency, it would be considered a coup d'état, and Republicans would oppose it by force. At that point Adams, as Jefferson reported years later, became extremely angry. He told Jefferson that it was within his power to win the outcome: all he had to do was vow to "do justice to the public creditors, maintain the navy, and not disturb those holding office." Jefferson replied that no one should doubt his commitment to the nation, but that he was unwilling to "come into the government by capitulation" and must enter it "in perfect freedom to follow the dictates of my own judgment."[65]

Finally, after a day off on Sunday, once the House reconvened on Monday one individual had changed his mind: Federalist James Bayard of Delaware, who told his colleagues that he intended to switch his support from Burr to Jefferson, which would tip Delaware in Jefferson's favor. His public explanation for changing his mind was that Burr clearly did not have enough support to be elected, and "to exclude Jefferson" would come "at the expense of the Constitution." Other explanations abound. For one, Bayard was known as a maverick, and his support for Burr was never strong. Also, Federalists had just heard that Burr was ready to withdraw from consideration, a change that put pressure on moderates to shift support to Jefferson. Most intriguing, a rumor that circulated in later years suggested that Jefferson had made a deal with Bayard, agreeing to some Federalist conditions in exchange for the congressman's support, though Jefferson denied it to his death and other evidence supports his denial. Whatever the real explanation, Bayard's Federalist colleagues were furious that he was deserting them. When they met in caucus, "the clamor was prodigious" and "reproaches vehement." Outraged New England Federalists "declared they meant to go without a constitution and take the risk of a Civil War."[66] But ultimately Bayard prevailed in breaking the logjam. Ten states voted for Jefferson, four went for Burr, and two did not vote. After five days of deliberation and thirty-six ballots, Jefferson was elected president of the United States. And the young country saw its first peaceful transition of power from one party to another.

It very nearly failed. After his inauguration, Jefferson himself, writing to Governor Thomas McKean of Pennsylvania, said that if the Federalists had usurped power, installing one of their own, the nation would have "end[ed] soon in a dictatorship," and "I was decidedly with those who were determined not to permit it."[67]

Neither did the election bring an end to polarization. Jefferson sounded conciliatory in his inaugural address, when he intoned, "We are all Republicans: we are all Federalists." But he quickly directed his attention to undoing the Federalist accomplishments that had most outraged Republicans, including the Alien and Sedition Acts and much of Hamilton's economic plan, including the tax on whiskey. He commented that he would "sink federalism into an abyss from which there shall be no resurrection for it." Eventually he became known for enlarging executive power and the power of the federal government generally, activities that he and other Republicans had called violations of the Constitution when Federalists had done the same just a few years earlier. Meanwhile, the Federalists of the early 1800s, now that they were in the opposition, appeared to take pages from the Republicans' playbook of the 1790s, calling, for example, for states in the northeast to secede from the Union.[68] In the wake of the election of 1800, the former proponents of nationalism and decentralization seemed to have traded places.

The decade of the 1790s had been fraught with rampant political polarization. It was driven by fierce competition between two emergent parties as well as an upsurge of civic engagement and activism among ordinary Americans. Those on both sides viewed their opponents—other elected officials as well as citizens—not just as political rivals but as enemies, fundamental threats to the nation. Each side believed firmly that their approach would permit the true principles underlying the Constitution to flourish.

## HOW POLARIZATION HARMED DEMOCRACY

It is tempting to think that the Constitution saved the day in the 1790s and the election of 1800, but in fact the nation came precariously close to its first decade being its last.

Of the four potential threats to democracy, only polarization loomed large in the 1790s. The limited boundaries of civic membership and rigid definitions of status remained uncontested by those with political power. This quickly became evident in Republicans' harsh repression of the slave insurrection. Federalists and Republicans had their disagreements over plenty of issues, but challenges to the social order—so strictly defined along lines of race and gender—were not among them. As for economic inequality, Republicans liked to invoke it when they criticized Federalists, but they too represented elites. In fact, free Americans had incomes that differed relatively little from each other's, relative to citizens of other countries at the time and latter-day Americans.[69] Finally, while Republicans charged both the Washington and Adams administrations with executive aggrandizement, and indeed both presidents took measures to amplify the powers of their office, the scope of presidential power was modest compared to what it would become in the twentieth century, and Congress prevailed.

But polarization all by itself wielded the capacity to undermine the fragile beginnings of democracy. Those with political power—throughout most of the decade, the Federalists—used it repeatedly to undermine the legitimacy of the opposition, whether party leaders or organized citizens. They believed the country would be better off if they alone ruled, and so they sought to eviscerate the competition. Neither did they hesitate to curtail civil liberties, convinced that doing so was necessary to quell dissent, whether it was voiced by civic groups or by journalists. On some occasions, their commitment to the rule of law seemed weak, as when presidents used military approaches to put down local rebels or made an end run around Congress. Each time they took such measures, democratic backsliding ensued. Constitutional safeguards proved to be frail in the face of ambitious politicians representing two highly competitive parties.

Nor can the outcome in the election of 1800 be celebrated as a victory for democracy, because ultimately Jefferson won the presidency via a feature of the Constitution that represents its utter antithesis: the three-fifths clause. This feature, the result of a compromise at the Constitutional Convention, meant that for the purposes of representation three out of five slaves counted toward a state's population and therefore greater political power. In 1800, the total population of the northern and southern states was approximately equal. But while northerners were almost all white, more than one-third of southerners were enslaved black people who could not vote. Counting three-fifths of the southern black population toward the region's allotment of House members, in effect, gave the South a bonus of greater representation in Congress and the Electoral College than states without slavery and dramatically enhanced the power of slaveholding southern whites in national politics. As historian William W. Freehling observes, "In an Electoral College where the three-fifths clause gave the southerners 14 extra electors, the Republicans' Thomas Jefferson defeated the Federalists' John Adams, 73–65. Jefferson swept the South's extra electors, 12–2. If no three-fifths clause had existed and House apportionment had been based strictly on white numbers, Adams would have likely squeaked by, 63–61."[70]

In a speech at the Constitutional Convention in August 1787, Gouverneur Morris of New York had articulated most succinctly what the three-fifths clause actually meant: "That the inhabitant of Georgia and S.C. who goes to the coast of Africa, and in defiance of the most sacred laws of humanity tears away his fellow creatures from their dearest connections and damns them to the most cruel bondages, shall have more votes in a Govt. instituted for the protection of the rights of mankind, than the citizen of Pa or N. Jersey who views with a laudable horror, so nefarious a practice."[71]

As the years went by, it became clear that the three-fifths clause provided the South with the means to maintain its commitment to self-government, as practiced under the Constitution, without having to give up on slavery. In addition, it gave the region extra leverage in pursuing any of its other policy goals through domination of each branch of government. Between Washington's election and 1850, slaveholders held the presidency for fifty of those sixty-one years and the Speaker's chair for forty-one, and they claimed eighteen out of thirty-one Supreme Court justices.[72] The nation's commitment to slavery deeply infused government at every level, making for a bizarre hybrid—an egregious form of government that combined some aspects of democracy with elements of sheer authoritarianism.

The final outcome of the election of 1800 was significant in that in an era of pitched polarization, one party did relinquish political power to the other. It happened peacefully, despite all the angst that preceded it. Yet the underlying arrangements that permitted that victory mocked the fundamental democratic principle of equality, a contradiction that would fester and finally erupt a half century later. In the nation's resolution to its first constitutional crisis lay the seeds of its next constitutional crisis, which would come to a head in the 1850s.

# 3

## Democratic Disintegration in the 1850s

At a crossroads on the plains a few miles outside Lebanon, Kansas, just south of the Nebraska border, stands a stone marker indicating the geographic center of the continental United States. When the United States made its last acquisition of contiguous territory on the North American continent in 1853, purchasing southern Arizona and New Mexico from Mexico, it finally matched its modern form. Then as now, Kansas was right in the middle.

Kansas lay in the center of things in more ways than one. It was also at the center of the gathering political turmoil over slavery, which, by the mid-1850s, was already eroding the country's commitment to democracy.

This coincidence of both geographic and political centrality was not lost on Americans in the 1850s. As the great abolitionist orator Charles Sumner observed in 1856 on the floor of the United States Senate:

> Take down your map, sir, and you will find that the Territory of Kansas, more than any other region, occupies the middle spot of North America, equally distant from the Atlantic on the east, and the Pacific on the west; from the frozen waters of Hudson's Bay on the north, and the tepid Gulf Stream on the south; constituting the precise territorial center of the whole vast Continent.

And yet, Sumner lamented, "against this territory, thus fortunate in position and population, a Crime has been so committed, which is without example in the records of the Past." And what was that crime? "The very shrines of popular institutions . . . have been desecrated; . . . the ballot box . . . has been plundered," and "the dearest rights" of American citizens "have been cloven down, while a Tyrannical Usurpation has sought to install itself on their very necks!"

The culprit? Slavery.[1]

❖

Kansas had become a territory in 1854 and was preparing to apply to Congress for statehood, which required that its people adopt a constitution and establish a territorial government. On January 15, 1856, Kansans gathered to elect a legislature according to a new constitution drafted in Topeka the previous fall. But that constitution was in dispute. It had been adopted by a convention made up of delegates committed to excluding slavery from the territory and eventually bringing Kansas into the Union as a free state.

Proslavery Kansans mounted a furious response. They tried to disrupt the ratification of the constitution and ultimately resorted to violence. The result was a series of skirmishes in the fall of 1855 between rival pro- and antislavery militias, including armed proslavery bands who crossed the border from Missouri and threatened to annihilate proponents of a free state.[2] In advance of the vote in January 1856, the fear of further violence was palpable. The mayor of Leavenworth, in the territory's northeast corner, issued a proclamation forbidding voting in the town.

The voters of Leavenworth nevertheless persisted. They postponed the polling by a few days and opted to hold it outside of town at a nearby farm. Despite being harassed by proslavery gangs who threatened to abscond with the ballot box, the men of Leavenworth managed to hold their election without incident. One of those voters was Stephen Sparks, a well-known free-state activist. Sparks brought one of his sons and a nephew with him to the polls, leaving the rest of his family behind at their home.[3]

On the afternoon of January 17, members of a proslavery militia came calling at the Sparks house. They held the Sparkses' younger son at gunpoint and demanded to see Stephen. When his wife replied that he was away on business, they handed her a document demanding that the family leave the territory, and then left.

Around 2:00 a.m. that night Stephen Sparks was traveling home from the polls with his older son and nephew in tow and found himself face-to-face with the proslavery gang. They took Sparks and his nephew prisoner, holding them in a store along the road. Sparks's son managed to run for help, and soon a rescue party of free-staters converged on the store to confront Sparks's captors and secure his release. Leading the rescue posse was Reese Brown, a well-known antislavery figure who had been a candidate on the previous night's ballot. Brown and his crew succeeded in rescuing Sparks, although shooting broke out and Sparks was injured by gunfire.

But the proslavery mob wasn't finished. The next day, a group of them captured Brown and some of his men and brought them back to the store. Brown and his colleagues fought back. In the ensuing fracas, most of the free-staters escaped, but Brown was beaten with a hatchet. Eventually, the proslavery gang left Brown, prostrate and bleeding from his head, outside his own house, where later that morning he spoke his last words to his wife: "They murdered me like cowards."[4] When the votes were counted, Brown had posthumously won a seat in the territorial legislature.

The threats to the election of January 1856 and Brown's murder represented one of the first salvos in the violent conflict over slavery in the territory, which lasted for five years, until the start of the Civil War. What began as a disagreement meant to be solved democratically by the people of Kansas themselves devolved quickly into a cycle of competing constitutions, electoral fraud, conspiratorial fear, and sustained violence. Horace Greeley, the sharp-penned antislavery editor of the *New-York Tribune*, popularized the term "Bleeding Kansas" to describe the episode.

❖

The crisis over slavery that engulfed the nation in the 1850s marked the dangerous reemergence of extreme polarization in American politics, which had been held somewhat in check in the decades following the election of 1800. But in the middle of the nineteenth century, political polarization coalesced around a second critical threat to American democracy: conflict over membership in the political community, specifically the future status of enslaved African Americans. Economic inequality was rising as well as the nation began to industrialize, reaching its highest levels since the beginning of the republic. Moreover, the South was more unequal than the North, reflecting both the exploitative brutality of slavery and the growing difference between the two regions' economic systems.[5] This combination of threats proved even more dangerous to the progress of American democracy than the nearly ruinous polarization of the 1790s.

The political crisis of the 1850s was long in coming. As described in Chapter 2, the settlement of the political crisis of the 1790s that saw Thomas Jefferson elected president had hinged on the three-fifths compromise, which gave the white slaveholding South disproportionate power in American national politics. This was white man's democracy on southern terms. As long as the South retained the ability to protect slavery, the country's two sections could agree on the rules of the democratic game. Southern politicians were happy to adhere to those rules and present themselves as champions of democracy. But the South's practice of democracy among white men depended on a brutal, violent, and dehumanizing system of enslavement of African Americans. For the first few decades of the nineteenth century, most northerners were willing to look the other way in order to promote democracy and shared prosperity for white men throughout the country.

But over the first half of the nineteenth century, African Americans had continued to challenge their exclusion from democratic rights and citizenship, already evident in Gabriel's Rebellion in 1800 and other armed uprisings in the ensuing decades as well as growing legal and political activism. Many white Americans, too, increasingly questioned the wisdom and morality of slavery, some because they came to regard it as wrong, and others because they saw it as a challenge to the North's emerging free enterprise industrial economy. As resistance to slavery grew and the status of African Americans in American society became the central issue in American politics, North and South found themselves on opposite sides of a sharp divide that ultimately could not be bridged by democratic means.[6]

As the conflict grew deeper, national politics gradually decayed. For a half century after the settlement of 1800, American national politics had promoted compromise and mutual accommodation. Elections were hard fought, to be sure, and critical issues such as the tariff and the banking system generated heated debate. But even though the two sides mistrusted each other, they recognized the idea of legitimate opposition.

In the 1850s, however, the South's dominance of national politics began to decline, and as that happened, the region's ability to use the political system to protect slavery eroded. Fundamental disagreement over race, America's formative rift, came to dominate national politics over the course of the decade. The party system reorganized itself around this question, and it drove ruinous polarization.

In this context, national politics devolved into a game of mortal combat, in which the goal of winning overrode the integrity of the democratic process. The notion of legitimate opposition broke down, with each side of the slavery dispute treating the other not merely as an opponent in a political contest but as an enemy to be vanquished. The two sides increasingly talked past each other, conducting their own versions of democracy with as little involvement of the other side as possible. The rule of law broke down, as each side proved willing to go to extreme lengths to prevail—propaganda, rigged elections, and ultimately violence. The integrity of the electoral process deteriorated, and the protection of core democratic rights weakened. In the end, there was no democratic way to resolve the conflict. The result was a widening cycle of mistrust, manipulation, fraud, and violence that finally engulfed democracy and plunged the country into a violent civil war.

## SLAVERY ASCENDANT IN NATIONAL POLITICS

Bleeding Kansas was not the first time new territory provoked conflict over slavery. Earlier in the nineteenth century, Congress had confronted the question of whether to allow slavery in the vast Louisiana Territory, which the United States had purchased from France in 1803. The question arose first in 1819, when Congress began considering the territory of Missouri for statehood. Representative James Tallmadge Jr. of New York proposed prohibiting slavery in Missouri. Tallmadge opposed slavery, but his primary objective was to dampen the impact of the three-fifths clause, which gave extra power to slave states in Congress and in the Electoral College. Southern members of Congress opposed Tallmadge's amendment, leading to an impasse.

The Missouri Compromise broke the logjam in 1820. The measure admitted Missouri as a slave state and Maine as a free state, maintaining a balance between free and slave states in the Union. It also prohibited slavery in the remainder of the Louisiana Purchase north of the 36° 30′ parallel (a line that includes the Kentucky-Tennessee and Missouri-Arkansas borders and the northern edge of the Texas Panhandle). The Missouri Compromise defused the immediate conflict over slavery and effectively postponed the democratic crisis for a generation. But it both reinforced the principle that federal power could ban slavery and taught the slave states that if they stuck together, they could effectively resist this power and, through democratic means, bend the Union to their will.[7]

For the next several decades, national political conflict over slavery was relatively muted, even as resistance and rebellion persisted among enslaved Americans themselves and a movement for abolition germinated and grew, particularly in the North. By then, American politics had been transformed. In the early republic, it had been the province of the wealthy few, although ordinary citizens certainly took sides and became attached to one party or the other. But by the 1830s, politics had become a participatory sport for all American citizens—farmers and fishermen, merchants and shopkeepers, artisans and millworkers, rich and poor alike—as long as they were male and white.[8]

Frequent elections, especially at the local level, made politics a constant presence in the lives of most Americans. Candidates for office increasingly had to appeal to the interests and sensibilities of the common man and try to discern the popular will. In this context, campaigns and elections were often raucous, boozy, and even violent affairs. Campaigns occasionally resulted in riots between rival partisan gangs; in New York City's mayoral election in 1834, thousands of Democrats and Whigs clashed on the lower east side of Manhattan over three days. The mayor himself was beaten, and ultimately the army was called in to keep the peace.[9]

During this period, ordinary citizens came to engage in politics through their political parties. The Republicans and Federalists who had fought out the political conflicts of the 1790s were mostly opposing groups of elite political leaders. But the new parties that developed in the 1830s were mass organizations that spanned the entire country. They mobilized voters and set the terms of political competition at every level of politics, from the local to the national.

Elections everywhere were conducted between the era's two opposing parties: the Democrats (successors to the Jeffersonian Republicans) and the Whigs (who coalesced around opposition to the Democrat Andrew Jackson in the 1830s). Parties held frequent meetings, conventions, rallies, marches, and other events that became part of the country's social fabric. Party rallies frequently featured vast barbecues at which the assembled crowds would feast on whole roast oxen or pigs, accompanied by plentiful ale, hard cider, and whiskey. Partisan newspapers ensured that Americans understood the world in partisan terms. For many citizens, party loyalty became a core part of their identities. Even children got into the act with schoolyard taunts. "Democrats eat dead rats," went one chant. (The inevitable riposte, "Whigs eat dead pigs," was not quite as pointed.)[10]

The parties managed to keep slavery off the national political agenda for a generation. Democrats and Whigs differed on many issues: economic policy, the role of the government in society and the economy, tariffs, and foreign policy, among others.[11] They drew their support largely from different sectors of society. The Whigs appealed on balance to wealthier, more educated, and native-born white Protestant voters, for example; immigrants and Catholic voters were more likely to be Democrats.

But both parties built organizations that competed for white men's votes throughout the country, in both North and South.[12] Elections were hard-fought and competitive, and control of government at all levels swung back and forth between the parties, as did the spoils—jobs, government contracts, and control of public policy—that came along with victory. To remain competitive across regions, the parties were generally silent on the critical issue of slavery; to the extent the parties considered slavery at all, they did not differ dramatically.

White supremacy was the dominant presumption across parties and regions. Even abolitionism, which began in earnest in the 1830s, originated more as a religious and spiritual calling than as a political movement. It did not seriously threaten the South's ability to preserve slavery, nor did it yet challenge the South's disproportionate power on the national scene, owing to the three-fifths rule.[13]

Through the 1830s and 1840s, neither party had a strong incentive to break the silence on slavery. The first party to do so would have lost support in one region of the country or the other and likely paid a severe price at the ballot box. Nevertheless, the truce over slavery was an uneasy one.

In the 1830s, antislavery tracts began to trickle from north to south. The trickle soon became a stream. In 1835, a mob in Charleston, South Carolina, stormed the post office and confiscated antislavery pamphlets that had been sent through the mail by a group of Boston abolitionists to be distributed to the citizens of South Carolina. Once they had seized them, rather than risk circulating antislavery ideas, the mob gathered the pamphlets and made a public bonfire. To prevent repeat performances, the Charleston postmaster began censoring the mail.[14]

Antislavery petitions also started making their way to Congress. These petitions aroused the ire of southern members of Congress, who feared that they would open the door to new attempts to restrict slavery. In 1836, the House of Representatives adopted a "gag rule" on slavery, a procedure by which antislavery petitions were automatically set aside without discussion or consideration. The gag rule was regularly renewed until 1844, when it was finally repealed, largely due to the canny and indefatigable opposition of former president John Quincy Adams, then serving as a representative from Massachusetts. Adams attacked the gag rule not only as a support for slavery, which he opposed, but also—and primarily—as an affront to the rights and liberties essential to democracy, which could not flourish if some ideas were simply ruled out of bounds and could not even be discussed. The gag rule made it clear to many northerners that slavery was not just a southern problem but a potential threat to white men's democracy in the North as well.[15]

Still, it was not petitions but the question of new territories that would bring the clash between slavery and democracy back to the floor of Congress and to the center of national politics.

## THE FAILURE OF COMPROMISE

In the decades following 1820, the United States continued to expand, adding nearly one million square miles to its holdings in North America by the end of the Mexican-American War in 1848. Many Americans opposed the war and the annexation of Texas because they feared it would open up the slavery question, which is precisely what happened. On August 8, 1846, as the war was just under way, the House of Representatives was debating a request from President James K. Polk to provide $2 million toward an eventual purchase of territory from Mexico as a way of bringing the war to a satisfactory close.

As the House deliberated into the evening, Representative David Wilmot, an otherwise undistinguished first-term representative from Pennsylvania, rose to speak. A stalwart Democrat and a reliable supporter of the Polk administration's Mexican war effort and territorial aims, Wilmot surprised no one by adding his voice to the chorus in favor of acquiring territory from Mexico. It was what he said next that shocked his congressional colleagues because it broke the prevailing bipartisan silence on slavery.

Wilmot proposed an amendment to the bill, which became known as the Wilmot Proviso, to ban slavery from any territory acquired from Mexico.[16] With this move he amplified sectional conflict and set the nation on a course that would test American democracy as never before.

The reaction from southerners and their allies was swift and furious. The House, now divided along sectional rather than partisan lines, passed the amendment with ample numbers of Democrats and Whigs on each side of the question.[17] This division on the Wilmot Proviso proved to be a harbinger of a new kind of polarization that broke along sectional lines, with race as its key axis of division, and which would prove extremely dangerous to American democracy in the coming decades.

Although the Wilmot Proviso subsequently died in the Senate, the experience showed the South that its stranglehold on American government was growing fragile. But it also exposed the South's dilemma: if southerners continued to adhere to the democratic process and abide by majority rule in Congress (and in the country at large), slavery's future on American soil would be at risk. The only way to protect slavery was to challenge the democratic legitimacy of the rising antislavery voices in American politics.

The Wilmot Proviso returned to the floor of the House and Senate in various guises in subsequent years, without success. One of its supporters when it came up for consideration in February 1848 was a young lawyer serving what turned out to be his only term as a Whig representative from Illinois: Abraham Lincoln. (Lincoln later claimed to have voted for the proviso "at least forty times" in his short time in Congress.)[18] The proviso never became law, but it had succeeded in kicking off a fierce and increasingly divisive debate that placed the slavery issue front and center.

The drumbeat for rapid statehood for new territories also kept the slavery question in the foreground. Aside from undisputed possession of Texas, the main prize of the Mexican War was California, especially after gold was discovered there just at the war's end in 1848. The prospective admission of California to the Union as a free state alarmed southerners, who wanted the opportunity to extend slavery into the territory newly acquired from Mexico. Banning slavery in California would mean abrogating the Missouri Compromise line of 36°30′. (A good deal of California lies south of that line, which bisects the state just south of Fresno and Monterey.) To southerners, this move seemed to invite further interference and open the door to wholesale abolition.

There were other slavery-related issues simmering. Many northerners wanted Congress to use its control over Washington, DC, to abolish slavery there. The South, in turn, was growing restive over the rising number of enslaved people who were successfully escaping to the North. Frederick Douglass and Harriet Tubman were becoming well-known abolitionist activists after having escaped from slavery in Maryland, and they were not the only ones. The nation's divisions over slavery were widening, and the opposing sides became increasingly hardened as disagreement turned to stalemate.

On March 4, 1850, Senator John C. Calhoun of South Carolina, frail and emaciated from the tuberculosis that would claim his life in less than a month, made his way to the Senate chamber with the help of an associate.[19] For a generation, Calhoun had been the South's most potent voice and slavery's most ardent defender on the national stage, and he came to deliver one last speech. But because he was too weak to make himself heard, his colleague Senator James Mason of Virginia read the speech aloud.

Calhoun believed that the country was at a moment of national crisis over the fundamental sectional disagreement about the South's enslavement of black Americans.[20] The North was growing larger and therefore, in democratic terms, more powerful. He prophesied that without southern resistance, growing northern power would mean the eventual abolition of slavery.

For Calhoun, the conflict over slavery had very nearly moved past the capacity of ordinary democratic politics to resolve. The two sides were enemies, almost beyond reconciliation. As during the crisis of the 1790s, dissent was tantamount to disloyalty—to the Constitution, and ultimately to the integrity of the Union—especially for southerners, who saw growing opposition to slavery as an existential threat. If antislavery agitation continued to grow, the South would be forced to reconsider its allegiance to the United States. In such a circumstance, he warned, "nothing will be left to hold the States together except force." Calhoun concluded with a threat: the slave states, he announced, were ready to leave the Union.[21]

Calhoun's threat did not come to anything immediately. In June 1850, several months after Calhoun's death, delegates from nine southern states met in Nashville, Tennessee, to consider how the South should answer the threat of the proposed slavery ban. Despite forceful arguments for secession, the convention ended inconclusively.

But Calhoun's threat of disunion cast a shadow over a new national compromise over slavery that was taking shape in the summer of 1850. The famed "Great Compromiser" instrumental in the 1820 Missouri Compromise, Senator Henry Clay of Kentucky, worked with Senator Stephen Douglas of Illinois to prepare a framework adopted by Congress and then signed by President Millard Fillmore in September. For the antislavery voters of the North, the Compromise of 1850 admitted California as a free state; split off a large part of the land claimed by Texas, which was already a slave state, into the territories of New Mexico and Utah (in return for a payment of $10 million from the federal treasury to pay off Texas's debts); and banned the slave trade in the District of Columbia. In return, the South claimed a much larger collection of benefits. Slavery would continue in the District of Columbia. Utah and New Mexico would be subject to "popular sovereignty," under which a territory's residents themselves would vote on whether to allow slavery.

Fancying himself Clay's heir as a new great compromiser, Douglas had offered "popular sovereignty" as a potential third way between the extremes of extending slavery across new territory and the Wilmot Proviso ban, which now seemed finally dead. The concept of popular sovereignty seemed to offer a democratic solution, at least for white citizens, to the challenge of the extreme sectional polarization over slavery by subjecting the question of slavery's future to the will of a majority of a territory's voters. But southerners were wary of the idea that slavery could be banned in the territories at all through democratic means. And Abraham Lincoln would later pointedly skewer Douglas's popular-sovereignty position, arguing that popular sovereignty made sense only if one believed that slavery was acceptable.[22]

But the South's great prize in 1850 was the new Fugitive Slave Act, which not only empowered public officials in northern states to arrest former enslaved people but required them to do so. Officials who refused to participate were subject to a fine of up to $1,000 (the equivalent of more than $30,000 today). The act also allowed officials to deputize citizens, even against their will, to aid them in their pursuits. Once captured, alleged fugitives had no right to a trial in court. Instead, they would be brought before a federal commissioner, who decided whether they were to be returned to the owners who claimed them or allowed to remain free. Commissioners received a $5 fee for each person allowed to go free, but $10 for each person returned to the white master who claimed them.

If anything, the Compromise of 1850 inflamed the conflict over slavery. The Fugitive Slave Act, in particular, seemed rigged in favor of the South. The judgment of many contemporaries was swift and harsh. Frederick Douglass saw the compromise as evidence that the country was in the grip of the "Slave Power," a conspiracy of corrupt power and influence that sought to suppress democratic debate on the slavery question and to take over the federal government in order to protect and extend slavery. In the early republic, the North and the South had roughly equal populations, but in the ensuing decades the North grew much faster, and by 1850 the North's population exceeded the South's by 40 percent. How else but by such a conspiracy, many reasoned, could they explain the seemingly perpetual domination of the majority North by the minority South, which seemed like an affront to democratic principles?[23]

At a packed meeting in Boston's Faneuil Hall just weeks after the passage of the compromise, Douglass denounced the Fugitive Slave Act to an overflowing crowd that included some of the city's leading citizens, predicting suffering and bloodshed as a result. Nearly two years later, in a Fourth of July address in Rochester, New York, he was even more withering: "This Fugitive Slave Law stands alone in the annals of tyrannical legislation. I doubt if there be another nation on the globe, having the brass and the baseness to put such a law on the statute-book. . . . The existence of slavery in this country brands your republicanism as a sham, your humanity as a base pretense, and your Christianity as a lie. It destroys your moral power abroad; it corrupts your politicians at home."[24]

Southerners, too, objected to the Compromise of 1850. The ban on the Washington slave trade seemed to many a harbinger of creeping abolition, as did the carving of Utah and New Mexico out of land that had once belonged to Texas, a slave state. Contrary to the northern interpretation, the admission of California as free soil looked to southerners like the fruition of the Wilmot Proviso, as Calhoun had foreseen.[25]

The virulent reaction to the Fugitive Slave Act in the North heightened rather than dampened sectional tensions. Because the act was retroactive, free blacks who had been living in the North for years or even decades were suddenly subject to seizure and forcible return to their former masters with little or no due process. Cases of mistaken identity, in which the wrong person was snatched and delivered up to an "owner," often without any legal process, were not uncommon.[26]

In the eyes of African Americans, and many white northerners as well, the act promoted widespread violations of civil liberties—nothing short of state-sponsored kidnapping—and weakened the already tenuous distinction between enslaved people and free people of color. Resistance to enforcing it was widespread in northern states. After the first fugitive was arrested in New York City, just days after Fillmore signed the act, New York's free black and abolitionist community came together in a mass resistance rally and fundraising campaign.[27]

Southern agents who came north after fugitives often faced stiff and sometimes violent resistance from people of color and their allies. In 1858, for example, the citizens of Oberlin, Ohio, banded together to rescue an alleged fugitive from the custody of a federal marshal and spirit him to safety in Canada.[28]

The Compromise of 1850 may have briefly postponed the conflict over slavery, but it would soon come back in lethal form.

## KANSAS IN THE BULLSEYE

By 1854, Calhoun and Clay were dead. In their place, Stephen Douglas had emerged as the Senate's leading figure—a magnetic orator, canny negotiator, and skillful legislator, widely celebrated for brokering the final deal that sealed the Compromise of 1850. As chairman of the Senate's Committee on Territories, Douglas oversaw the debate over organizing two new territories west of Missouri: Kansas and Nebraska.

These territories became the epicenter of the slavery conflict, and they proved to be the setting for the beginning of the near breakdown of American democracy: the decline of free and fair elections, the erosion of the rule of law, and the disintegration of legitimate opposition. Each of these things happened in Kansas, which became a bellwether for the rest of the nation.

To facilitate building a railroad to the Pacific, Douglas proposed organizing the Kansas and Nebraska territories, which lay directly on the path from the Midwest to California. Southerners, however, saw in Douglas's proposal not just a scheme to promote a transcontinental railroad but, as Calhoun had foreseen in 1850, a plot to attract to the western plains white settlers who would continue to expand the reach and power of free soil and further overwhelm the slaveholding South.[29]

Douglas's principal antagonist in the Senate was David Atchison of Missouri. A fervent proslavery Democrat, Atchison observed that under the Missouri Compromise, the new territory would be free soil because it lay within the original Louisiana Territory and north of the magic 36° 30′ line. Atchison would support the organization of new territories in Kansas and Nebraska only if the region was opened to slavery, effectively repealing the Missouri Compromise.

Douglas proposed to resolve this disagreement by extending the notion of popular sovereignty that he had introduced in 1850. Rather than being bound by the restrictions of the Missouri Compromise, the residents of the newly organized Kansas and Nebraska territories would decide for themselves, through a democratic process, whether to allow slavery. Popular sovereignty again seemed to offer a democratic solution to Congress's dilemma, as long as democracy functioned adequately, with free and fair elections under the rule of law—and with acceptance on both sides of the other side's legitimacy.

Opponents of slavery wasted no time attacking popular sovereignty in Kansas and Nebraska as an antidemocratic sham. In January 1854, a half-dozen prominent members of Congress published a manifesto in a Cincinnati newspaper that was widely reprinted around the country. In what became known as the Appeal of the Independent Democrats, the group assailed the proposed Kansas-Nebraska bill for opening the door to the extension of slavery. The bill, they said, was "part and parcel of an atrocious plot to exclude from a vast unoccupied region immigrants from the Old World and free laborers from our own States, and convert it into a dreary region of despotism, inhabited by masters and slaves."[30]

The Appeal didn't stop at condemning the bill. It also attacked the motives and characters of the defenders of slavery. The measure, they said, was "gratuitous" and "reckless" and had been introduced "without reason and without excuse, but in flagrant disregard of sound policy and sacred faith." The conclusion warned "that the dearest interests of freedom and the Union are in imminent peril. Demagogues may tell you that the Union can be maintained only by submitting to the demands of slavery. We tell you that the Union can only be maintained by the full recognition of the just claims of freedom and man. . . . We entreat you to be mindful of that fundamental maxim of Democracy—EQUAL RIGHTS AND EQUAL JUSTICE FOR ALL MEN."[31]

The Appeal had a galvanizing effect on the slavery conflict. Historian Eric Foner calls it "one of the most effective pieces of political propaganda in our history."[32] It ratcheted up the rhetoric about a Slave Power conspiracy, a notion that had already taken hold in much of the North, and it suggested that the proponents of slavery's extension were betraying the nation's democratic foundations.

Even more consequential, it suggested that Douglas's popular-sovereignty formula, which proposed to use democratic means to decide the slavery question locally, did not, in fact, amount to democracy. Instead, it was despotism in disguise.

The Appeal delayed the passage of the Kansas-Nebraska Act, but it could not prevent it.[33] By the time President Franklin Pierce signed the new law in May 1854, expectations about what would actually happen in Kansas had escalated. Supporters of slavery saw an opportunity to claim new territory for their cause, alarming abolitionists, who saw the gears of the Slave Power conspiracy continuing to turn. At the beginning of 1854, Kansas was home primarily to numerous Native American tribes, many of whom had already been forcibly resettled there from the East in the 1830s. Now once again their land was at risk as the territory was open to white settlers, who rushed in to realize their competing visions for this new territory. Kansas had, finally, become the center of the country politically as well as geographically.

Populating Kansas would be critical to the coming contest. Both sides of the slavery debate began organized campaigns to induce white settlers who shared their views to move there. Even before the Kansas-Nebraska Act was finally passed, Eli Thayer, a Massachusetts schoolteacher and state legislator, organized the Massachusetts (later New England) Emigrant Aid Company to encourage white antislavery New Englanders to move to Kansas. With the company's support, as many as a thousand northeasterners set out for the new territory in the spring and summer of 1854, and several thousand more over the next few years. Migrants from New England founded a number of substantial settlements in Kansas, including the town of Lawrence, named for Massachusetts merchant Amos Lawrence. The company also helped finance infrastructure to help these settlements succeed, including mills, hotels, and, crucially, newspapers.[34]

But the impact of these committed free-soil settlers on politics in Kansas was greater than their numbers. The eastern antislavery press, particularly Horace Greeley's *New-York Tribune*, trumpeted their activities and made the New England contingent seem larger and better organized than it was, arousing fear and anxiety among proponents of slavery. Senator Atchison began to organize his fellow Missourians to cross the border into Kansas—a much shorter journey than the fourteen hundred miles from Boston to Lawrence. Settlers from Missouri regarded the New Englanders (and the midwesterners who soon followed) as alien outsiders who posed a threat to their autonomy. In their eyes, they were agents of a northern abolitionist conspiracy sent south not just to occupy Kansas but also to menace slavery in Missouri and, by extension, the rest of the South.[35] Missourians worried, too, that a free territory next door would make it easier for enslaved people to escape and might embolden enslaved people in Missouri to revolt.

As a territory, Kansas would have a governor appointed by the president, but the citizens of the territory would be responsible for establishing democratic institutions, including electing other officials and adopting a constitution, in preparation for applying to Congress for statehood. As governor, President Pierce appointed Andrew Reeder, a Pennsylvania lawyer with no government experience whose only qualification for the job was that he was a loyal Democrat. It soon became apparent that he was in over his head.

Democracy in the Kansas Territory got off to a bad start. Reeder called an election for a territorial delegate to Congress to be held on November 29, 1854. The election was a fiasco. Only men who had taken up residence in Kansas were supposed to vote, but proslavery Missourians streamed across the border for the day to vote for the proslavery candidate, John W. Whitfield, a veteran of the Mexican war who had been working as a federal Indian agent in Missouri. Inflamed by Senator Atchison's rhetoric and generally disinhibited by drink, these "Border Ruffians," as they came to be known, disrupted the election, stuffing ballot boxes, intimidating free-state voters, and threatening to kill Whitfield's opponent. Whitfield won the election by a very wide margin, outpolling his nearest rival by nearly ten to one. He traveled to Washington and took his seat as a nonvoting delegate in the House of Representatives in December.

In the meantime, another election, this one for a territorial legislature, was held on March 30, 1855. This election, too, was marred by widespread fraud. Again, Atchison and his associates mounted an organized campaign to encourage Missourians to cross the border in order to vote. Hundreds, perhaps thousands, did so, resulting in comically inflated vote totals. At one polling place, five times as many people voted as were listed in the town's voter rolls. A territorial census earlier in the year had counted nearly three thousand eligible voters; more than twice that many votes were counted territory-wide.[36]

Many observers mentioned threats of violence on the part of the often drunk and unruly proslavery forces: knives brandished, guns drawn, voters harassed, election officials intimidated and overpowered. When one antislavery lawyer formally protested the election results, he was captured, shaved, stripped, tarred and feathered, ridden out of town on a rail, and "sold" in a mock slave auction.[37] Not surprisingly in the face of this intimidation, many free-soil voters stayed home.

When the votes were counted, proslavery candidates again won, this time by a lopsided five-to-one margin.[38] Free-soil Kansans protested to Governor Reeder, but the evidently fraudulent results stood. Free-soil proponents challenged the legitimacy of the territorial legislature and began to call it the "bogus legislature." Many simply refused to recognize its authority. Less than a year into territorial governance in Kansas, the idea of a legitimate opposition was faltering.

The legislature proceeded to live up to the free-soilers' fears by adopting a slave code over Governor Reeder's veto. The new code strongly protected the rights of slaveowners and prohibited the circulation of antislavery writings in the territory, reminiscent of the censorship of the mail in South Carolina or the congressional gag rule. The new legislature also refused to seat the few free-soil legislators who had been elected.[39]

A third election was held in October 1855, for a new term for John Whitfield, the territorial delegate to Congress. This time, his opponent was former governor Reeder, who had been fired by President Pierce in August. Despite his partisan loyalty to Pierce and the Democrats, Reeder had become increasingly sympathetic to the free-soil cause. At one point a hotheaded proslavery leader challenged Reeder to a duel after Reeder called him (not inaccurately) a "Border Ruffian." Although Reeder refused the challenge, a fistfight ensued that ended up with pistols drawn before the two men could be restrained. When the October election arrived, free-state Kansans boycotted the voting and held their own election a week later. Not surprisingly, Whitfield won the "official" election, and he resumed his seat in the House when the Thirty-Fourth Congress convened in December.[40]

To advocates of free soil in Kansas, this series of what they saw as stolen elections undermined their own democratic civil and political rights, as free white men, to determine their own fate. These rights, in their eyes, were threatened by despotic outsiders who were bent on subjugating them and undermining their opportunity for self-government.

In reaction to these outrages, a group of free-soil leaders, calling themselves the Free State Party, met in Topeka in late October to formalize their resistance to the proslavery hold on the territorial government and to draft a new constitution for what they anticipated would soon become the state of Kansas. Invoking the sentiments of the Declaration of Independence and the Bill of Rights, the Topeka constitution banned slavery and, just as significantly, conferred voting rights on all white men ("and every civilized male Indian who has adopted the habits of the white man") but required voters to have lived in the state for six months before voting, a clear effort to disqualify the Border Ruffians.

Under the Topeka constitution, the previous year's legislative election was deemed illegitimate, so the territory held yet another election in January 1856. In that election, despite proslavery harassment, free-state voters elected a rival legislature that would meet in Topeka later in the year. It adopted its own laws and even chose prospective United States senators in anticipation of statehood. But statehood was not in the cards because neither side in the slavery contest would give way. Not only were there dueling legislatures in Kansas itself, but escalation of the confrontation to the national stage now seemed inevitable.

## A POLARIZED INVESTIGATION

Events had persuaded antislavery Kansans that elections in Kansas were neither free nor fair and that their democratic rights were imperiled. In addition to challenging the territory's government, they challenged Whitfield's election as congressional delegate and asked the House of Representatives to investigate. In May 1856, a group of free-soilers wrote to Congress complaining about the conduct of elections in Kansas. In strong language, they protested the "invasion of our soil and the usurpation of our rights" by the Missourians. The letter described the tactics used to disrupt the election and impede the democratic process. It alleged that more than three thousand fraudulent votes had been cast in the March 1855 election, and it directly (if probably falsely) accused Senator Atchison of leading the violent Border Ruffians himself, with "bowie knife and revolver belted around him." They concluded with an appeal "not for trivial rights, but for the dearest rights guarantied to us by the Declaration of Independence, [and] by the Constitution of the Union," and asked Congress "to vindicate the sacred doctrines of the government."[41]

In response to the Kansans' letter and other accumulating evidence of election fraud, the House of Representatives convened a committee to investigate the reports of fraud, violence, and proslavery chicanery. Fortuitously for the Kansas free-soilers, the House was under the control of an antislavery coalition of northern former Democrats and Whigs who had broken away from their parties over the slavery issue. Speaker of the House Nathaniel Banks was determined to prevent the extension of slavery to Kansas and promptly dispatched a three-person committee to Kansas to investigate. Two of the committee's members, William A. Howard of Michigan and John Sherman of Ohio (whose older brother, Captain William Tecumseh Sherman, had retired from the army and was working as a banker in San Francisco), were both reliable antislavery men. The third, Mordecai Oliver, was from Missouri, and although he was part of the opposition coalition he was generally inclined to support his fellow Missourians against the charges that had been leveled against them.

Through the spring, the committee traveled around Kansas hearing testimony and gathering evidence, although their efforts were impeded by violence and the intimidation of witnesses. The committee presented its report to the House in July. But it was actually two separate reports, a majority version submitted by Howard and Sherman and a dissenting minority response written by Oliver.

The majority report found substantial and consistent evidence of vote fraud. It concluded unequivocally that territorial elections had routinely been marred by violence and undermined by "organized invasion from the state of Missouri" and that the territorial legislature elected the previous year was illegitimate. Howard and Sherman concluded that Whitfield's October 1855 election to Congress was invalid and consequently that Reeder was entitled to the delegate's seat.[42]

Oliver, for his part, disavowed these conclusions and accused Howard and Sherman of shutting him out of their discussion of the evidence. His minority report reached exactly the opposite conclusions from Howard and Sherman: Whitfield's election was valid, the territorial legislature was legitimate, and the evidence for the supposed Missouri "invasion" was contradictory and overblown.[43]

Tellingly, the majority and minority reports were both selective in their accounts of violence. The two sides could not even agree on a single set of facts, let alone reach a common conclusion—a far cry from the compromising spirit of just a few years earlier and an indication that the belief in the legitimacy of the opposition had deteriorated. On August 1, the House voted, along almost completely polarized sectional lines, to strip Whitfield of his seat and install Reeder in his place.[44]

Reeder would never take up his place in Congress. In April, the territorial supreme court indicted Reeder and several other free-state leaders for treason for daring to defy the proslavery territorial government. He resolved to escape arrest under cover of darkness but was stymied for a time by cloudless, moonlit nights. He recorded in his diary that he had instructed an associate to write a letter addressed to him in Chicago "and to mail it loosely sealed, to induce the belief that I was in the States, by way of Nebraska and Iowa, as we were confident that they [the proslavery authorities] would open it." Eventually Reeder disguised himself as a woodcutter, shouldered an ax, and made his way onto a boat bound for Kansas City, and eventually to St. Louis and then into Illinois.[45]

## BLOODSHED IN KANSAS AND WASHINGTON

The popular-sovereignty experiment in Kansas proved to be a failure; there was, in the end, no democratic solution to the slavery conflict. Rather than bind Kansans together around a common set of principles, goals, and laws, the democratic principle of popular sovereignty had rapidly divided the territory into two factions that were—figuratively and, increasingly, literally—at war over slavery.

Following violent interference with elections, open warfare in the territory began in the fall of 1855. After a series of battles between rival free-state and proslavery militias, the governor managed to negotiate a

truce between the two sides under the threat of federal military intervention. In one notorious incident, proslavery sheriff Samuel Jones of
Douglas County was shot in the back outside Lawrence after he arrested
a group of free-state militia members. Jones survived, but conditions in
the territory grew steadily worse.[46]

In May the conflict came vividly alive on the floor of the United
States Senate. Over two days, on May 19 and 20, 1856, Senator Charles
Sumner of Massachusetts delivered what came to be known as the
"Crime Against Kansas" speech. A fierce abolitionist, Sumner was a
flamboyant orator and an outspoken advocate for civil rights and racial
equality.[47] Sumner's speech was a five-hour broadside, delivered over two
days, against the Kansas-Nebraska Act, the depredations of proslavery
forces in Kansas, and the Slave Power. It filled more than ninety pages
when Sumner, a canny publicist seeking national attention, later had it
published as a book.[48]

In the speech, Sumner singled out two Senate colleagues for special
scorn: Stephen Douglas, the Kansas-Nebraska Act's chief sponsor, and
the widely respected Andrew Butler of South Carolina, one of the Senate's most senior members. Sumner compared them to Don Quixote
and Sancho Panza and proceeded to catalogue their misadventures. They
had, he said, "raised themselves to eminence on this floor in champion-
ship of human wrongs." About Butler Sumner was particularly scathing.
"The Senator from South Carolina," he intoned, following the senato-
rial custom of third-person courtesy, "has read many books of chivalry,
and believes himself a chivalrous knight, with sentiments of honor and
courage. Of course he has chosen a mistress to whom he has made vows,
and who, though ugly to others, is always lovely to him; though polluted
in the sight of the world, is chaste in his sight—I mean the harlot,
Slavery."[49]

Although Butler was not even present while Sumner spoke, his cousin,
Representative Preston Brooks, also of South Carolina, paid careful attention to Sumner's remarks. Exquisitely sensitive to the insult Sumner
had committed against the honor of his family, his state, and his region,
Brooks considered challenging Sumner to a duel but decided against it
because doing so would acknowledge Sumner's status as a gentleman.
Instead, on May 22, Brooks marched into the Senate chamber where

Sumner was sitting at his desk preparing copies of his speech for mailing. He waited until several women present had left and then proceeded to beat Sumner on the head repeatedly with his walking stick. Sumner got tangled in his desk, which was bolted to the floor, and could not escape the blows. Even after his cane snapped in two, Brooks continued his attack until he was restrained by several onlookers. Bloodied and unconscious, Sumner had to be carried out of the chamber. His injuries were so grave that he would be absent from the Senate for nearly three years.[50]

Although violence in Congress rooted in an imagined code of honor was not unusual, Brooks's shocking assault—in the chamber of the world's greatest deliberative body, as the Senate likes to call itself—captured national attention. It drove the wedge deeper between sides in the slavery debate and vividly underscored the growing impossibility of solving the slavery conflict through democratic means. It made Sumner's speech a bestseller and provided ample fodder for the antislavery press. Brooks was convicted of assault in a District of Columbia court and fined $300. Nevertheless, an attempt to expel Brooks from the House failed to achieve the necessary two-thirds vote. Brooks resigned and was defiantly reelected by his South Carolina constituents. Around the South, Brooks was hailed as a hero.[51]

As Sumner was delivering his "Crime Against Kansas" speech on May 19 and 20, a posse of between five hundred and seven hundred proslavery men gathered outside Lawrence under the command of a federal marshal to pursue free-state leaders in town. The marshal came into Lawrence on May 21, the day before Sumner's beating, arrested a few people, had lunch at the Free State Hotel in town, and left. But Sheriff Jones, who had been shot by antislavery forces but had recovered, was hot for revenge. He reassembled the posse and deployed artillery with the intention of laying waste to strategic parts of the town. For an hour they bombarded the Free State Hotel—which the proslavery forces believed to be a fortress, "regularly parapeted and port-holed for use of small cannon and arms"—with cannon fire. When that failed to destroy the hotel, they tried blowing it up with gunpowder. When that failed as well, they set it on fire, then moved on to attack two antislavery newspapers and destroy their printing presses, burn antislavery literature in the street, and loot and burn several houses.[52]

Kansas State Historical Society

3.1 The ruins of the Free State Hotel after the sacking of Lawrence, Kansas, May 1856

Although there was only one fatality, on the proslavery side, the "Sack of Lawrence" (depicted in the engraving above) proved to be a propaganda victory for the free-staters of Lawrence, who gained sympathy because of the proslavery side's extreme and inept military tactics.

But whatever publicity advantage the free-state forces might have had was promptly squandered by a zealous New England abolitionist. John Brown had followed his sons to Kansas in 1855 and was disappointed at the free-staters' inaction and lack of militancy. Incensed by the Sack of Lawrence, Brown assembled a party of raiders and headed toward Lawrence to join the fight—and, he hoped, ignite more concerted and violent resistance to the proslavery forces. On the night of May 24, along the Pottawatomie Creek south of Lawrence, Brown and his band raided the homes of several proslavery settlers and killed five people in particularly gruesome fashion. Some were shot in the head, others hacked almost to pieces with knives and swords.[53]

As Brown probably intended, the Pottawatomie massacre provoked outrage on the proslavery side and ignited a guerrilla war between Brown's forces and the Border Ruffians. The violence provoked by Brown's activity flared around the territory through the rest of 1856, accompanied by the turmoil of war: crops unplanted or left to rot or wither in the field, bands of armed men traveling the countryside, looting, and a fearful population.

Ultimately, violence was quelled by the decisive action of the governor, who mobilized regular army troops to restore order and impose an uneasy truce in the territory. John Brown, who had continued to lead raids and help fugitive slaves through the summer and fall, took advantage of the lull to leave Kansas. He returned east to capitalize on his growing notoriety and raise money for new antislavery ventures.[54]

## CONSTITUTIONAL CRISIS

Bleeding Kansas highlighted democracy's inability to bridge the deepening rift over slavery. Soon the conflict would escalate to Washington, where the same dilemma would play out in the halls of Congress rather than the battlefields of the frontier—a larger and ultimately more dangerous stage.

With violence in the territory abating somewhat, attention returned to the question of how Kansas was to be governed. Rejecting the Topeka constitution, the proslavery legislature called for yet another constitutional convention to be held in 1857, with a clear view toward making Kansas a slave state. In still another election marred by a disparity between the census and the vote count, a boycott by free-state voters, and exceedingly low turnout, Kansans elected delegates to a convention to be held in Lecompton, the territorial capitol, in the fall. When the convention met in September, it adopted a constitution that legalized slavery, incorporated Missouri's brutal slave code, and deemed the property rights of slaveowners "inviolable."[55]

The governor had pledged that the new constitution would be submitted for public ratification and would not go into effect without the approval of a majority of Kansas voters. But the referendum that was actually put before the voters in December did not give Kansans the option of rejecting the constitution; rather, the choices were to approve the constitution as written, with the protection of slavery, or to approve it with an additional clause banning the future importation of slaves into the territory. To the opponents of slavery, this gambit was unacceptable, and they once again boycotted the vote, with the result that the Lecompton constitution passed overwhelmingly in another questionable election on December 21. The free-state contingent responded by holding its own referendum on the Lecompton constitution on January 4, 1858, and this time the constitution was rejected by an even more overwhelming vote.[56]

The Kansas conflict over slavery and democracy now became a full-fledged political crisis on the national stage. While Kansans were considering what to do with the Lecompton constitution, Congress was debating it as well as part of its deliberations over admitting Kansas to the Union as a state. President James Buchanan, a Pennsylvania Democrat who was nevertheless sympathetic to the South, supported the Lecompton constitution. But Stephen Douglas, also a Democrat, vilified it as a mockery of popular sovereignty and as an affront to the principles of democracy. Buchanan's support of the Lecompton constitution provoked a colossal struggle, both in Congress and within the Democratic Party. Buchanan threatened Douglas with political ruin and tried to extract loyalty pledges from wavering Democrats, delaying patronage appointments and dangling lucrative federal contracts in order to win support. "The *thumb screw* is being applied with much force," one observer of these hardball tactics noted.[57]

But Douglas was not deterred and persisted in his opposition. Joining him were senators from the new leading opposition party, the Republicans. The Republican Party was founded in 1854 by antislavery northerners who opposed the Kansas-Nebraska Act. The Whigs had disintegrated along sectional lines, and numerous other parties had formed to fill the political void, including the antislavery Free Soil Party and the anti-immigrant American (or Know-Nothing) Party. But by 1856, northern Whigs, Free Soilers, and antislavery Democrats had coalesced around the new Republican Party. The Republicans, who became the leading opposition party in the 1856 elections, viewed the Lecompton constitution as further evidence of the dominance of the Slave Power in national politics.[58]

In the Senate, the Democrats had a large enough majority that despite opposition by Douglas and three other Democrats from outside the South, the Lecompton constitution was approved by a comfortable margin. The House of Representatives, however, was more closely divided between the parties, and the Buchanan administration stepped up its efforts to flatter, cajole, and bribe its way to victory by retaining the loyalty of Democrats, but without success. Ultimately a "compromise" was reached that sent the Lecompton constitution back to the voters of Kansas. They rejected it once and for all on August 2 by a margin of nearly ten thousand votes.[59]

The defeat of the Lecompton constitution brought the democratic crisis in Kansas to national politics, with largely the same result: extreme polarization to the point of utter political rupture between pro- and antislavery sides. The rupture became increasingly apparent over the rest of the decade as the debate over slavery came to occupy the center of the American political landscape. The Lecompton debate demonstrated to the South yet again that if the future of slavery was to be decided by democratic means, slavery was likely to be defeated. As long as protecting slavery remained the South's highest priority, the key attributes of democracy—free and fair elections, the rule of law, the legitimacy of the opposition—would continue to suffer.

The political violence in Kansas that had claimed, in all, close to sixty lives was beginning to spill over into the rest of the country. John Brown had returned to New England to raise money for new ventures. In October 1859, with financial backing from a group of prominent and wealthy Boston abolitionists, he led a group of several dozen men in a raid on the federal armory in Harpers Ferry, Virginia (now West Virginia). His aim was to "liberate" the weapons stored there, use them to arm slaves in the surrounding area, and incite a general slave revolt that would spread throughout the South. While his band succeeded in capturing the armory, the expected slave insurrection did not occur. Weak tactics and poor planning left Brown and his men trapped in an indefensible position. They were easily defeated by a small force of US Marines combined with local militias under the command of Army Lieutenant Colonel Robert E. Lee and his aide, Lieutenant J. E. B. Stuart. Brown was captured, tried, and hanged. He, too, became a divisive symbol: a martyr to many in the North, a terrorist to southerners, and a symbol to both sides of the menace that lay in a society that clad despotism in the clothing of democracy.[60]

## THE 1860 ELECTION: A POLARIZING CHOICE

As the Lecompton debates in Congress demonstrated, the national political parties that had, a generation before, contained the slavery issue
had now succumbed to the divisions that had convulsed Kansas. There
were no longer two parties that competed nationally on a range of issues.
Rather, there were two sectional parties divided by a single issue: slavery.
The new antislavery party, the Republicans, had outlasted a number of
other new parties that had emerged during the 1850s to supplant the
Whigs. On the proslavery side, the Democrats still aspired to be a national party, but their northern and southern wings were becoming irrec-
oncilably divided. Douglas remained the leading Democrat outside the
South, but his opposition to Buchanan and the Lecompton constitution
made him unacceptable as a national leader of the party.

When Douglas ran for reelection to the Senate in 1858, his opponent
was an emerging leader of the Illinois Republican Party, a former Whig
who had served one term in the House of Representatives. Abraham Lincoln was gaining notoriety as a critic of slavery and of Douglas's popular-
sovereignty approach, which he regarded as a dodge. In their famous
debates around the state that fall, Lincoln continued to attack Douglas
on the meaning of popular sovereignty. Lincoln recognized that popular
sovereignty had failed, and that despite its democratic appearance, it had
become a means to perpetuate and extend slavery. He also understood
that slavery and democracy were fundamentally incompatible, and over
the course of the 1850s he decisively chose democracy. Douglas won
reelection, but the debates, which were widely reported and later published as a book, helped launch Lincoln to national prominence as an
antislavery voice who nevertheless remained committed to the principles
of democracy and the possibility of sectional reconciliation.[61]

Douglas and Lincoln soon faced off again, in the 1860 presidential
election. But this was not the only presidential election held in that year.
In effect, there were two separate elections: one in the North and one in
the South. Douglas entered the Democratic convention as the favorite
for the nomination, but southern delegates rebelled. Meeting in Baltimore, the party split; the northern faction nominated Douglas, while
southern delegates walked out, reconvened across town, and nominated

Vice President John Breckinridge. Lincoln won the Republican nomination, while a group of former Whigs who still held on to the idea of
national unity formed the Constitutional Union Party and nominated
John Bell, a former senator from Tennessee who nevertheless opposed
the extension of slavery.

The election then disintegrated into two contests: between Lincoln
and Douglas in the North and between Bell and Breckinridge in the
South. Lincoln followed a disciplined campaign strategy focused on
northern states, as he might have been expected to do, and he won the
election decisively, winning almost every northern electoral vote, while
Breckinridge swept most of the South and Douglas and Bell divided the
border states. This was the most sectionally divided presidential election
in the country's history to that point, and not even the South's three-
fifths bonus could prevent Lincoln's election.

Even more astonishingly, there were ten southern states in which not
a single vote was cast for Lincoln because he did not appear on any ballot.
Southern states would not even entertain the candidacy of the nominee
of the Republican Party, which was dedicated to opposing slavery (the
same thing had happened to the first Republican presidential candidate,
John C. Frémont, in 1856). It was the first presidential election in American history in which the winner did not receive support from both sections of the country.

When Lincoln's victory was announced, most southerners found
themselves greeting a new president whom they had not participated in
choosing, and about whom they believed the worst—that he was, in the
words of the historian David Potter, "a 'black Republican,' a rabid John
Brown abolitionist, an inveterate enemy of the South."[62]

Southerners feared that the ascendance of Lincoln and the Republicans to national power meant the end of the proslavery influence over the
government that the South had enjoyed since the beginning of the republic. Lincoln would, they assumed, use his office to appoint Republican
judges and law enforcement officials who would erode slavery's edifice
of legal protection. Republican postmasters might decline to stop the
flow of abolitionist literature to the South. The new government might
promote skeptics of slavery, or even African Americans themselves, to
positions of authority.[63]

To the South, Lincoln's impending presidency and his assumption of the mantle of national power was not just an unfortunate but temporary setback; it was a mortal threat to white southerners' most cherished value, and it marked the end of the line for their participation in American democracy.

## THE ROAD TO WAR

Making his way to Washington by train in February 1861, the president-elect received word when he reached Philadelphia of a possible plot to assassinate him in Baltimore, where he would have to change trains and travel through the city from one station to another.

Sectional enmity, long rising, was by then overflowing. Seven southern states had already announced their secession from the United States; delegates from six of them had met in Montgomery, Alabama, to form the Confederate States of America and had chosen former senator and secretary of war Jefferson Davis as provisional president. Once southern Democrats withdrew from Congress, northern Republicans moved quickly to admit Kansas to the Union as a free state.[64]

On the evening of February 22, Lincoln kept to his full schedule of public events in Harrisburg, Pennsylvania. As the evening wound down, he quietly slipped out of the governor's mansion after a testimonial dinner, disguised in a soft cloth cap and shawl and stooping to conceal his height.

He returned to Philadelphia on a special, unscheduled train, and there he boarded the regularly scheduled 11:00 p.m. train to Baltimore rather than taking the train the next day that his public schedule had indicated. On that train he was met by Kate Warne, an operative of the Pinkerton Detective Agency, which had been hired by the railroad to provide security. Traveling as "Mrs. Cherry," one of her undercover identities, Warne greeted Lincoln as her frail brother and escorted him to a sleeping car that she had bribed a conductor to have mostly vacated.[65] Meanwhile, the Pinkerton agency arranged to have the telegraph wires out of Harrisburg cut to make extra sure that no one would learn of Lincoln's change of plans.[66]

When Lincoln's train reached Baltimore, he did not disembark to catch the Washington train as planned. Instead, his sleeping car was detached, drawn through the streets by horses as the city slept, and connected to an early morning southbound train. The crowd of onlookers waiting to greet his scheduled train later that afternoon, possibly including the would-be assassins, was disappointed to find that he was not on board. By then he was already safely ensconced at Willard's Hotel in Washington, around the corner from the White House.[67]

❖

The political crisis of the 1850s was the deepest threat that American democracy had yet faced. Extreme polarization over the question of slavery engulfed the political system and made it impossible for pro  and antislavery sides to engage in productive debate.

The hard-won notion of a legitimate opposition deteriorated and all but disappeared over the course of the decade. Free and fair elections, first in Kansas and then nationwide, were threatened as well, as the two sides held separate elections and each side refused to abide by the results of the other's contest. Civil liberties faded, too, especially as the South repeatedly attempted to stifle antislavery voices. Civil rights, of course, lay at the very heart of the conflict, which fundamentally concerned the injustice of slavery and the boundaries of the American political community. The result was civil war, the ultimate repudiation of the rule of law.

Just over a month after Lincoln's inauguration, Confederate artillery opened fire on Fort Sumter, a US Army installation in Charleston, South Carolina, beginning an armed conflict that would last four years and claim more than six hundred thousand American lives before the ultimate defeat of the South and the abolition of slavery, first by Lincoln's presidential proclamation and finally by constitutional amendment in 1865.

During the war, Lincoln would assume unprecedented executive power: he suspended the constitutional right of habeas corpus in order to imprison suspected rebels and stifle political dissent, declared martial law in parts of the country, and ultimately emancipated slaves by proclamation. But the Union's victory and the triumph of emancipation did not put to rest the question of black Americans' status in the American political community. Far from it. The reconstruction of American democracy after the rupture of war would remain significantly incomplete.

# 4

# Backsliding in the 1890s

In the 1890s, Wilmington was North Carolina's largest urban center and a beacon of progress both for the post–Civil War South and for the nation generally. It boasted the hallmarks of a modern city: electric lights, streetcars, and, most strikingly, a politically empowered and growing black middle class. African Americans made up the majority of the population, and they worked as skilled craftsmen in a wide array of trades and owned numerous businesses, including most of the city's restaurants—which were frequented by whites as well as blacks. Three members of the Board of Aldermen were African Americans, as were numerous public-sector employees. The city possessed a black-owned newspaper, the *Daily Record*, one of only a handful in the nation. President William McKinley appointed an African American named John Campbell Dancy to be the collector of customs for the city's port, making him more highly paid than the state's Democratic governor and other high-ranking state officials, all of whom were white, not to mention most white citizens in Wilmington. Several civic organizations established by the black community flourished. Black literacy rates were growing, as was homeownership; by 1897, more than one thousand African Americans owned some property.[1] Democracy, as indicated by political inclusion as well as the expansion of social and economic rights, appeared to be on the rise.

However, white elites in North Carolina saw in these developments not progress but the demise of the world as they had known it—their "heritage," as they viewed it—and they had grown even more troubled by political developments statewide in recent years. Their party, the Democrats, lost power when the Republican Party, of which African Americans were the core constituency throughout the South, joined forces with the insurgent Populist Party, which included many low- and middle-income whites. In 1894, this multiracial "Fusion" coalition managed to sweep the majority of seats in both chambers of the state legislature, several congressional seats, and even a seat in the US Senate; in 1896, it won even larger victories, including the governorship. It was at that juncture that Democratic Party leaders across the state, together with prominent businessmen, made a decision: it was time to push back, shut out the opposition, and reclaim political power once and for all. Over a period of six months, they hatched plans and chose to make Wilmington the focus of their campaign and the "center of the white supremacy movement."[2] On a single day in November 1898, they would turn back decades of progress in the city.

To lay the groundwork, first Democrats needed to recapture control of the state legislature in the fall elections. In the weeks before Election Day, two white supremacist groups, the White Government Union (WGU) and the Red Shirts, a terrorist arm of the Democratic Party, held rallies and roamed black neighborhoods, armed and on horseback, to intimidate African Americans and prevent them from voting. Newspapers brimmed with white supremacist rhetoric. Gun sales spiked. Republicans feared violence, and Democratic leaders pressured them to withdraw candidates from the ballot if they wanted to be safe. The tactics worked, and Democrats won back the legislature. Now the stage was set for them to retake control of Wilmington.

Two days after the election, early in the morning on November 10, nearly two thousand white men from the WGU and several paramilitary groups, including the Red Shirts, gathered at the city armory, brandishing rifles and pistols. The mob marched into the city, proceeding directly to the offices of the *Daily Record*, where they stormed their way inside, destroyed furniture and the press, then spread kerosene, set fire to the building, and watched as flames devoured it, as shown in the photo.[3]

New Hanover County Public Library

4.1  Burning of the office of the *Daily Record*, a black-owned newspaper,
during coup in Wilmington, North Carolina, November 10, 1898

The paramilitary groups then advanced through black neighborhoods, killing hundreds of individuals as the day wore on. They also dragged several prominent citizens from their homes and banished them from the city. Those expelled were predominantly African Americans, including successful businessmen, the sheriff and chief of police, and open opponents of white supremacy. Some they first threw into jail overnight, while others they took directly to the train station, led by soldiers with fixed bayonets, and forced them to leave town. In addition, they exiled several white Republicans and Populists, mobs jeering at them with cries of "white nigger" and threatening to lynch them.[4]

Later that afternoon, while violence reigned in the city, the white leaders forced resignations—at gunpoint—by members of the biracial Fusionist government. At a mass meeting the evening before, hundreds of white residents, primarily businessmen, merchants, lawyers, doctors, and clergy, had endorsed—with a standing ovation—a "White Declaration of Independence," which included resolutions that the elected leaders must resign. Forced to do so, the mayor and members of the Board of Aldermen relinquished their positions, and a new government of white Democrats—handpicked by those who organized the insurrection—

took power. When the chaos subsided, Josephus Daniels, a leader of the insurrection and the publisher of the *News and Observer*, wrote that the events ushered in "permanent good government by the party of the White Man."[5]

It was a coup d'état, American style. No one came to the aid of those who had been pushed out of power in Wilmington. African American leaders pleaded for help from President McKinley. So did the state's two US senators, Populist Marion Butler and Republican Jeter Pritchard. But the president claimed that he could not act without a request from Governor Daniel Russell. A Republican elected in 1896, Russell faced threats of impeachment from the Democrats and of bodily harm from the Red Shirts, so he made no request for federal intervention. McKinley consequently did nothing, and thereafter took a trip to Atlanta in a show of "sectional reconciliation."[6]

The Democrats quickly took steps at the state level to make their power permanent. Within a few months, they had secured a new constitutional amendment that imposed poll taxes, literacy tests, and other measures that would disenfranchise all African Americans and a good many poor whites for seventy years to come. Democrats in other states throughout the South who also had found themselves challenged by Republicans and Populists now began to replicate these efforts, if they had not undertaken them already. The establishment of racial segregation in all aspects of social life—American apartheid—followed. The multiracial democracy that had been on the rise was vanquished, replaced by white supremacist, authoritarian rule.

This chapter examines how functioning democracy could be dismantled in the United States. While it focuses on developments in the South, it shows that they did not occur in isolation, for they required the acquiescence of national political leaders. Three threats to democracy converged in the 1890s: polarization, racism, and economic inequality. Southern Democrats stoked polarization by effectively using overt racism as a strategy to unify their supporters. Meanwhile, the richest Americans were looking out for themselves; the preservation of democracy was not their concern. Once established, black disenfranchisement and its spiraling effects influenced politics—in the South and at the national level—for decades to come, curtailing all four attributes of democracy.

## ESTABLISHING "PERMANENT GOOD GOVERNMENT BY THE PARTY OF THE WHITE MAN"

In the decades following the Civil War, the United States made strides toward becoming a robust and inclusive democracy. Slavery had at last been outlawed by the Thirteenth Amendment. The ratification of the Fourteenth Amendment and the enactment of the Civil Rights Act of 1875 appeared to nationalize guarantees of civil liberties and civil rights, and the Fifteenth Amendment expanded voting rights to black men. Despite a strong and vocal women's movement that had commenced in 1848 in Seneca Falls, New York, women still remained largely outside of the promises of democracy. A few western states had granted women suffrage, however, providing at least a glimmer of hope that change was possible.

By several measures, the practice of democracy seemed fairly healthy. Voters took part in elections at high rates, surpassing 75 percent in presidential elections and 60 percent in midterms. Most voters were relatively well informed about issues and candidates. Political parties engaged in intense competition, and third parties attracted many followers. Social movements flourished. Yet by the early twentieth century, these trends had reversed themselves. Voting rates plummeted: by 1912, only 59 percent of Americans showed up to vote in the presidential election, and in midterms, turnout dropped to around 40 percent.[7] Other forms of civic engagement declined as well.

Democracy deteriorated not because ordinary Americans grew apathetic nor because political elites passively neglected it. Rather, political leaders actively disenfranchised voters. They engaged in strategic and deliberate mobilization aimed at limiting political competition—overtly undermining both free and fair elections and the legitimacy of the political opposition—by creating new laws and public policies that sharply limited who could participate. In the North and West, "progressives"— who sought to make government more orderly—introduced registration requirements that effectively made voting more difficult for less educated people, the poor, and immigrants. Southern Democrats, meanwhile, deliberately pursued disenfranchisement, both by using legal means and by circumventing the rule of law, and it is the events in the South—along with the actions of national leaders that permitted them—that are our focus here.

Political developments in North Carolina reflected a larger drama that was unfolding across the South, as Democrats saw their political opponents gaining momentum. In state after state, they responded by strategizing about how to crush the opposition permanently. The Wilmington massacre brought into the open efforts on the part of Democratic Party leaders that in most states were typically channeled through a mix of more acceptable means (changing laws and public policies) and covert maneuvering (such as stuffing ballot boxes and miscounting the vote). Through such techniques, Democrats forced state governments across the region to adopt procedures that disenfranchised African Americans as well as many poor whites.

The backsliding of democracy was not inevitable. In fact, several trends in the early 1890s gave some indication that democracy might be strengthening and expanding. Since Reconstruction, African American men in the South had persisted in voting in elections, running as candidates, and winning public office. They were supported and encouraged by northern Republicans, who recognized an opportunity for the party to pick up more seats in Congress.

In addition, highly engaged social movements nationwide offered the potential for allies who could come to the aid of African Americans in the South. Farmers had been suffering from deteriorating prices for commodities in the decades after the Civil War, and they had become active in politics, forming the People's Party, widely known as Populists, in 1892. Industrial workers across the country were also mobilized through labor organizations and strike activity. As the decade unfolded, some signals suggested that these groups could support each other in ways that had the potential to fortify democracy.

Three threats to democracy converged in this era, however—the same ones that had come together in the 1850s and helped give rise to the Civil War—and they made democracy vulnerable once again. Political polarization escalated to historically high levels in the late nineteenth century; in fact, the percentage of congressional votes in which one party voted against the other was even higher than in our own polarized era. It was not that the two parties held particularly divergent views on policies, but rather that they were fiercely competitive in elections and therefore party loyalty ran high, even on nonideological matters such as the distribution of government benefits. Conflict over membership and status occurred in plain sight, through loud, rampant, and violent white supremacy. Earlier in the nineteenth century, economic inequality had already grown sharply, and while it did not continue to increase overall, the wealth of those at the very top of the income distribution, the top 1 percent, continued to soar and they pulled sharply away from everyone else.[8] Yet threats alone do not determine what transpires; political choices and contingencies can make all the difference.

Tragically, the national political support that might have aided African Americans in the South either evaporated or failed to materialize. Federal officials and northern Republicans did advocate for black voting rights early on, but ultimately they lost interest, attracted to political opportunities elsewhere. The possible unity between farmers, workers, and African Americans that might have provided resistance to backsliding failed to coalesce. The wealthiest Americans, industrial elites, did unify themselves, coordinating their political involvement around Republican candidate William McKinley and bankrolling what remains to this day the most expensive presidential race in US history. The subsequent deterioration of democracy in the South was of little concern to them. African Americans were abandoned and isolated in what became "authoritarian enclaves," states that governed as authoritarian regimes, situated within a nation that was regarded as democratic.[9]

To this day, the United States remains the only functioning democracy in Western history ever to have taken away voting rights from such a large number of citizens who had been exercising them previously.[10] By the same stroke, white southern elites regained extra political power—not only to rule in their own states as autocrats but also to exercise an outsized voice in national politics for the next seventy years.

## THE RISE OF MULTIRACIAL DEMOCRACY IN THE SOUTH

Once the Civil War ended, the enfranchisement of black men in the South occurred with striking speed and efficiency. In 1867, the Reconstruction Congress ordered that for states of the former Confederacy to be readmitted to the Union, they must write new constitutions that guaranteed black men the right to vote. Congress divided the South into

five military districts and sent in military commanders to implement
the newly inclusive suffrage rules. Recently liberated African Americans
embraced voting as the means to pursue civil rights and public policies
that would facilitate their social and economic mobility. They found willing partners in the Republican Party, which was eager to strengthen its
political capacity by recruiting supporters among a potentially vast group
of new voters.[11]

As early as the summer of 1867, the Republican Party initiated a major registration drive across the South. It sent upward of 120 organizers
to tour the region, promoting registration, and it mobilized military-
appointed registrars—many of them black—to travel to every county in
ten states in the region to enroll eligible voters. Black churches and other
local organizations joined the efforts. In some localities, on the first day
that registrars were available, huge groups of men would arrive ready to
register to vote. These efforts produced remarkable results: by the end of
the year, voter registration rates among black males surged, surpassing
75 percent in Arkansas and reaching nearly 100 percent in Alabama,
Louisiana, Texas, and Virginia.[12]

These new voters swiftly took advantage of their capacity to change
the face of government. Over the course of Reconstruction more than two
thousand African Americans won election to public office. The majority
served at the local level, as city councilors, county commissioners, justices of
the peace, sheriffs, and a vast number of other roles. Eighteen gained high-
ranking positions at the state level, including Governor P. B. S. Pinchback
of Louisiana and the lieutenant governors of Louisiana, Mississippi, and
South Carolina. Hundreds served in state legislatures, and sixteen in the
US Congress, including two in the Senate—Blanche K. Bruce and Hiram
Revels, both of Mississippi.[13]

Many of Reconstruction's promises for African Americans vanished quickly. The Ku Klux Klan had emerged in Tennessee in 1866 and
quickly became established in all southern states. Its members used vigilante tactics to terrorize black elected officials, among others. When the
1876 presidential election produced no candidate with enough electoral
votes to declare victory, the Compromise of 1877 broke the logjam, but
at a huge political cost. An electoral commission appointed by Congress
agreed that Republican Rutherford B. Hayes of Ohio would become

president, but only on the condition that he would withdraw federal troops from the South and leave the Civil Rights Act of 1875 unenforced. The Supreme Court soon made it clear that it understood the Fourteenth Amendment only in the narrowest of terms, not as guaranteeing national rights of citizenship to African Americans or other individuals. By these indicators, the national government seemed to be deserting not only African Americans in the South but also the possibility of a more robust democracy for all.

Less well known, however, is that Reconstruction did not end in a single stroke. Although black voter turnout and officeholding declined from their high initial rates, African Americans continued to be a political force in southern politics for the next couple of decades. To be sure, Democrats in the region used violence and other means to try to discourage blacks from voting, and in some states and localities they engaged in fraud to rig the outcome of elections. Yet although black voter turnout in presidential elections fell sharply in some states, such as Florida, where it plummeted from 84 percent in 1880 to a mere 14 percent in 1892, in most other states it declined only modestly or held steady. In Alabama, for example, black turnout persisted at 55 percent over those same years, and in Virginia, it barely dropped at all, from 59 to 58 percent. Similarly, the number of black officeholders fell from 162 in the region in 1876 to 74 just two years later, but after that it declined more slowly, with 35 still remaining in office in 1890.[14]

African Americans remained highly committed to using their new political rights through the 1880s. Despite the Supreme Court's weakening of the Fourteenth Amendment, the Fifteenth Amendment remained a potent force. In 1884, the Court heard a case brought forward by Jasper Yarbrough and a group of seven other white men in Georgia who had sought to intimidate a black man, Berry Saunders, by trying to prevent him from voting in the 1882 election. The men had been convicted under the Enforcement Act of 1870, in which Congress forbade groups of people from banding together to interfere with African Americans' voting rights; the law aimed to crack down on Klan violence. Yarbrough argued that the act was unconstitutional, but the Court disagreed. In its unanimous *Ex parte Yarbrough* decision, it clarified that the Fifteenth Amendment conferred a right to vote on citizens, the federal government could intervene to protect that right, and the Congress could legislate rules to ensure its implementation. Bolstered by stronger voting rights, Republicans seized the opportunity to promote black voter turnout in the South, to their political advantage. They ran against a Democratic Party that played up racism, calling itself the "white man's party" and stoking fears of "Negro domination" if the opponents won.[15]

The political parties competed intensely with each other in the high-turnout elections that were typical in the South in the 1870s and 1880s. In presidential elections, voter participation often reached 63 percent; Democrats netted votes from approximately 37 percent of adult males, and Republicans were the choice of a respectable 25 percent. In guber-natorial races in most states in the 1880s, Republicans and independents typically attracted at least 40 percent of those who voted. In six out of seven states, more than 70 percent of the electorate turned out for these contests. Blacks voted primarily for the Republican or independent can-didate in most southern states, and their support could swing elections.[16] This became clear in 1883, when Democrats lost power in both Virginia and Tennessee. Black voters in the South therefore constituted a durable political force, one that national Republican Party leaders appreciated and were not ready to sacrifice, at least not yet.

Multiracial democracy thus continued in the South even after Re-construction ended, and African Americans found that their votes could make a crucial difference in electoral outcomes. If the federal government could ensure stronger enforcement of the Fifteenth Amendment, pro-tecting voting rights, African Americans' political involvement would be even more effective. Their allies in the Republican Party pursued that goal in Congress.

## PARTISAN BATTLES IN CONGRESS OVER VOTING RIGHTS

Black voter suppression concerned northern Republicans for numer-ous reasons. Some were troubled because they valued human rights and sought to undo the injustices caused by racism. Still more worried about the political consequences: they were convinced that were it not for fraud on the part of southern Democrats, their own party would enjoy more victories and have a better chance of gaining the majority in the

House of Representatives. This was a reasonable assumption, given that black-majority areas made up one-third of House districts in the South, and absent ballot stuffing and intimidation by white elites, Republicans would likely typically triumph in those areas. Put differently, the party was effectively "cheated" out of at least fifteen seats in each Congress. In the Republicans' 1888 platform, therefore, they called for "effective legislation to secure the integrity and purity of elections." They charged that the president, Democrat Grover Cleveland, and the Democratic majority in the House "owe their existence to the suppression of the ballot by a criminal nullification of the Constitution and laws of the United States."[17] Republicans thus set out to strengthen voting rights, and whatever their motives, accomplishing such reforms would bolster democracy.

They found a political opening when they gained unified control of both chambers of Congress and the presidency from 1889 to 1891, for the first time since 1883. Senator George Frisbie Hoar and Representative Henry Cabot Lodge, both of Massachusetts, introduced the Federal Elections Bill of 1890 into their respective chambers. The bill proposed that federal judges, if petitioned by citizens, could appoint supervisors to oversee congressional elections and make their own tallies; a federal board of canvassers could issue decisions in the case of contested outcomes, and a federal judge could do so if the decision was challenged. The House, furthermore, could override federal judges' decisions.[18]

Hoar had conceived of the bill years before. In 1884, speaking to the Commonwealth Club of Boston, he vowed to "consecrate" himself to the "cause" of creating a "system of laws, institutions, and administration under which . . . millions of men will represent the Black race in the manhood and citizenship of this republic." Hoar was concerned about racism, convinced that, "in all these race difficulties and troubles, the fault has been with the Anglo-Saxon. . . . The white man has been the offender."[19] When it came to electoral laws, moreover, Hoar knew of what he spoke: he had served on various commissions in Congress to oversee election-related matters, including the one charged with resolving the 1876 presidential election crisis.

The Federal Elections Bill of 1890 had the potential to upend southern politics. Southern Democrats clearly recognized this and began calling it the "force bill." They viewed it as what an Arkansas newspaper

termed the "gleam of a half-concealed bayonet." White southerners recognized the threat and gave voice to their rage first on editorial pages.
The *Richmond Dispatch* declared, "Not for twenty years has the public
mind been so much disturbed." A Mississippi paper commented, "The
South stood one reconstruction. It remains to be seen whether it will
submit to another."[20] Republicans in Congress had thrown down the
gauntlet, spurring appeals to white solidarity in the South.

In the House, the bill passed quickly—not surprisingly, along party
lines—but it came to a halt in the Senate. There, the Democrats filibus-
tered the bill for thirty-three days—enough time for Republican unity
to fracture. While the older generation of Republicans championed
the cause of black voting rights, the party's younger leaders were more
focused on issues such as a strongly protectionist tariff bill that would
safeguard emerging industries. This would appeal to voters in the West,
whom young Republicans were more eager to court than southerners.
The tariff appealed to these lawmakers also because it would generate
a surplus of federal revenues, funds they were keen to direct to their
spending priorities. In anticipation of such largesse, they enacted the
Dependent Pension Act of 1890, which granted pensions to Civil War
veterans when they could no longer perform manual labor. Meanwhile,
antimonopolists—particularly in the West—pressed for monetary reform, specifically by replacing the gold standard with the free coinage of
silver. The Federal Elections Bill languished as the filibuster continued,
losing support and momentum. One day when several Republican senators were absent from the chamber, a free-silver advocate moved that
the body consider new business—essentially forcing a vote on whether
the debate over the elections bill could continue or if it would be left to
die. At this point the Republicans fractured, with six of them joining
all the Democrats in favor of moving on to other business; support for
continuing debate over the bill failed by just one vote, 34 to 35, effectively
killing it.[21]

The Republicans' failure to enact the Federal Elections Bill of 1890
would turn out to be vastly consequential. Its immediate effect was to
produce what political scientist Richard Valelly terms a "boomerang."
Once Republicans had lost on their gambit to strengthen voting rights,
Democrats came roaring back with a vengeance. In 1892, in a campaign

that hinged on the regulation of federal elections, the party won unified control of the national government for the first time since before the Civil War. Up until 1890, northern Democrats had taken a racially moderate stance, but the conflict over the elections bill had spurred southern Democrats to proclaim white supremacist arguments unabashedly. Enticed by the prospect of winning back the White House, northern Democrats and candidate Grover Cleveland fell in line behind the southerners, using race-baiting tactics to stoke fears among white voters of what would occur if Republicans succeeded in altering election procedures.[22]

Once the Democrats triumphed at the polls and gained control of both chambers of Congress, they swiftly proposed the repeal of all Reconstruction-era federal election statutes. They aimed to abolish specific parts of the Enforcement Act of 1870 that outlawed poll taxes, literacy tests, election fraud, and interference by state and local officials of those voting in national elections. They also wanted to terminate statutes that mandated federal supervision of national elections. A House report calling for such repeals demanded that "every trace of reconstruction measures be wiped from the books."[23]

The House passed the repeal, and the Senate followed suit a few months later—without the Republicans even mounting a filibuster. Democrats were willing to make electoral regulation the central issue in American politics indefinitely, it seemed, leaving Republicans to choose between fighting that battle unceasingly and turning instead to the other issues that concerned their supporters. Given that choice, as Valelly puts it, "they called off the fight. African Americans were now on their own."[24] Northern Republicans had proven to be fickle political partners. Once the cause of voting rights no longer suited their needs, they effectively abandoned it, making this key feature of democracy vulnerable, along with the civic status of millions of African Americans.

## THE WORKERS' AND FARMERS' STRUGGLES INTENSIFY

While drama over voting rights unfolded in Washington, DC, a flurry of social movements was on the rise among ordinary Americans in far-flung parts of the nation. Perhaps there has been no other era in American history in which so many citizens from different corners of the polity became as mobilized to strengthen democracy. If only they could unite their efforts, they stood a fighting chance of overwhelming the powerful interests that dominated the political system.

The growing ranks of industrial workers emerged as one powerful force that might have helped to prevent democratic backsliding. In the decades after the Civil War, Americans had witnessed the transformation of their agrarian economy into a modern industrial powerhouse. New forms of economic inequality grew starkly apparent, evident in the rise of large corporations led by magnates such as Andrew Carnegie, Jay Gould, J. P. Morgan, John D. Rockefeller, and Cornelius Vanderbilt, each of whom wielded the capacity to control the wages and working conditions of huge numbers of workers. Trade unions, such as the National Labor Union in 1866 and the Knights of Labor in 1869, arose to represent the needs of this new class of industrial workers.

Yet workers' status remained among those aspects of American life that signified the limits of democracy and the slow pace of democratization. Workers were effectively governed under the old "master-servant" code of common law, an aspect of "belated feudalism" that lingered up until the 1930s, when courts finally permitted legislatures to endow workers with rights. In the late nineteenth century, therefore, labor activism still received no protection from government, and the courts viewed "freedom of contract" as a broad right of employers, while interpreting the commerce clause of the US Constitution narrowly to forbid attempts at regulating the workplace.[25]

Yet even without legal protection, workers pursued their goals aggressively. In the Great Railroad Strike of 1877, employees of the Baltimore and Ohio Railroad in Maryland walked off their jobs; railroad workers in several cities across the country subsequently followed their lead, paralyzing the nation's transportation system. Railroad executives pressured public officials to put down the uprising with the use of local police, state militia, and even federal troops. In 1886, more than six hundred thousand Americans walked out of their factories and other workplaces in a general strike organized by the Knights of Labor; it peaked on May 1 in a call for the eight-hour workday.[26]

The 1890s emerged as the era of greatest labor militancy in the nation's history—as well as of repressive responses on the part of government, which quickly made clear its alliance with the titans of industry. In 1892, steelworkers in Homestead, Pennsylvania, went on strike to protest deep wage cuts by their employer, Andrew Carnegie. Armed with rifles and dynamite, they engaged in a violent battle with three hundred Pinkerton detectives who had been hired by the company to defend it. After some of the Pinkertons died, their surviving colleagues surrendered. The events backfired for the workers: the Pennsylvania governor responded by ordering 8,500 militia to take possession of the mill, and to hire scabs in place of the workers.[27] That same year, workers in Idaho mines went on strike to demand union recognition. When management sent in strikebreakers, the strikers blew the mine up. Federal authorities and state militia subsequently swooped in and took charge.

Economic conditions worsened as the nation entered a depression, and conflict mounted between workers, on one side, and management and federal authorities, on the other. Following the Panic of 1893, thousands of businesses failed and unemployment rates surpassed 10 percent for the next five or six years, making it the worst downturn in American history aside from the Great Depression of the 1930s. In 1894, some 4,000 members of the American Railway Union employed by the Pullman Company protested their working conditions, and eventually they were joined by the support of 125,000 workers across the nation—from Ohio to California—who boycotted any trains carrying a Pullman car. The federal government intervened and President Grover Cleveland sent in the army to halt the strike, while the union's leader, Eugene Debs, was arrested and eventually served time in prison. The Supreme Court ruled in the government's favor, arguing that federal authorities could halt strikes if they interfered with interstate commerce.[28] It was one of the era's several high court decisions that solidified the alliance between government and big business.

Meanwhile, farmers were organizing as well, growing even more politicized than workers. Because of rising competition in grain and textile production both in the United States and abroad, as well as monetary issues, they faced sharply falling prices for their products. Many shouldered heavy debt burdens. Those in the West were subject to high interest rates and found themselves persisting precariously, typically just one bad harvest away from foreclosure and the loss of their independence.

In the South, nearly half of all farmers—disproportionately African Americans—worked as sharecroppers or tenants, typically on terms that made their debt to the landowner inescapable. As political scientist Elizabeth Sanders points out, for farmers the enemy was not an employer, as it was for workers; rather, they faced an entire system—including the terms of credit, supply, transportation, and marketing—that increasingly seemed to be rigged against them.[29]

Growing desperation among farmers made it all the more obvious that they should unite their efforts, particularly because neither of the two major parties took up their concerns. They organized first through the Grange, or Patrons of Husbandry, a reform-oriented fraternal organization begun in 1867 that was not overtly political but spurred engagement in a new proliferation of third parties.

Increasingly, people in the predominantly agricultural regions of the country—the West, the Plains, and the South—perceived themselves as deeply disadvantaged by the monetary system, which was based on the gold standard. This meant that the amount of money in the economy was tied to the amount of gold held by the government and was therefore fixed. With the money supply artificially constrained while farmers' productivity was high, prices for agricultural goods were prone to fall. Falling prices were particularly bad for debtors, namely farmers in this era, and a boon to creditors, namely the eastern financial elites, those who ran the banks, trusts, and railroads that set the terms under which the farmers had to operate. Farmers' livelihoods depended on their ability to borrow, both to take out mortgages on their land and for annual expenses such as seeds for planting their crops, but low prices for farm products meant that they often lost money and could not repay their debts.[30]

Farmers, therefore, viewed the gold standard as a source of oppression that left them perpetually hovering near financial crisis and destitution. Some agrarians, those belonging to the National Independent Party, championed a return to the circulation of "greenbacks," meaning US government-produced notes not backed by gold that had been issued during the war. The "greenbackers," as they became known, believed that this strategy would make it easier for farmers to pay their debts and would also raise prices. Once the cost of silver dropped, moreover, they began to call for replacing the gold standard with silver coinage; the

"Free Silver" proponents called for a "bimetallic" approach based on both gold and silver. These alternatives to the gold standard would each have expanded the money supply.[31]

Mobilization among farmers intensified in the 1880s. The Farmers' Alliance originated in Texas in the 1870s, but its growth took off in 1884, spurred by an organizational model composed of locally based suballiances of individual members. It sent forth "lecturers," modest rural professionals from the ranks of its members, who traveled to remote areas and, through impressive oratory, spread the "gospel" about the need for economic collective action. The Farmers' Alliance quickly proliferated across states and by 1890 boasted 1.3 million members. Most threatening to middlemen who charged the farmers steep prices, the alliance promoted economic cooperation, through tactics such as boycotts of goods sold by cartels and the creation of commodity-processing plants run by farmers themselves. It grew increasingly political, first using state conventions to articulate farmers' policy demands, and by 1890 endorsing candidates running for office if they supported its platform.[32]

The years of agrarian organizing led to the creation of the Populist Party, forged by Farmers' Alliance leaders who wanted to build on their success at the state and local levels by mounting a national political campaign. While they share a name with the twentieth-century and contemporary political movements that seek to upset the political order, they differ from them in many other respects. Latter-day populists are indifferent, at best, to democratic norms; they tend to embrace demagoguery; and they seek to construct and appeal to widely shared grievances. Nineteenth-century American populists, by contrast, sought to build a broad coalition. Unlike the Farmers' Alliance, which had excluded African Americans (who had in turn forged the Colored Farmers' Alliance), the People's Party, at least among national leaders, pursued a biracial movement. Its 1896 platform highlighted the dangers to democracy in the South, stating: "The People's party condemn the wholesale system of disenfranchisement adopted in some of the States as unrepublican and undemocratic."[33]

The Populists also aimed to build a coalition that transcended occupational lines, by working together with the labor movement and embracing the priorities of the Knights of Labor. The party platform, endorsed in Omaha in July 1892, heralded a "union of labor forces" to redeem democracy from unchecked capitalist powers. It called for a wide array of progressive policy reforms, including free and unlimited coinage of silver, a graduated income tax, government ownership of railroads, the eight-hour workday, and the end of government subsidies to private companies. Finally, it declared, "We believe that the power of government—in other words, of the people—should be expanded . . . to the end that oppression, injustice, and poverty shall eventually cease in the land."[34]

These disparate groups of farmers and workers were poised in the 1890s to unite in pursuit of greater democratization in the United States. Each of them, independently, generated organizing power that threatened to unsettle "politics as usual" and challenge the dominance of elites. The Populist Party aimed to bring them all together and indicated a willingness to work across racial lines as well. Meanwhile, the party gained momentum in a region ripe for the expansion of democracy: the South.

## SOUTHERN DEMOCRATS FACE RISING OPPOSITION

Populists managed to make serious enough inroads in the South to scare Democrats in the region. In the 1892 presidential election, these agrarian insurgents performed well for a third party: their presidential candidate—James Weaver of Iowa, who had served as a general in the Union Army—won 8.5 percent of the national vote and carried four states in the plains and mountain West. They also netted three governorships, eleven seats in the US House, and three in the Senate.[35]

Although Populists did not secure victories in the South, they made a good showing in several races there. In the official results in the race for president, for example, Weaver came in second to Democratic candidate Grover Cleveland in both Alabama, where he earned 37 percent of the vote, and in Texas, with 24 percent. In fact, the Democrats' well-known use of election fraud in the region casts doubt on whether the Populists actually lost those races. In Alabama, where the Democratic gubernatorial candidate, Thomas Jones, was declared the victor over Populist candidate Reuben Kolb, even the state's Democratic Party–affiliated newspaper reported, "The truth is that Kolb carried the state, but was swindled out of his victory by the Jones faction, which had control of the

election machinery and used it with unblushing trickery and corruption."
The strong levels of support for the Populists indicated that at least some
southerners had turned against the Democrats, which, as historian C.
Vann Woodward explains, was no small thing: "Changing one's party
in the South of the nineties involved more than changing one's mind.
It might involve a falling-off of clients, the loss of a job, of credit at the
store, or of one's welcome at church. It could split families, and it might
even call in question one's loyalty to his race and his people."[36]

The threat to the southern Democrats intensified in the 1894 midterm elections. The appeal of the Populists had grown as the depression
set in, unemployment rose, and support for a greenback/silver approach
rose higher and higher. In some states, moreover, savvy politicians had
noticed in the 1892 results that Populists and Republicans, in combination, could outperform Democrats. They seized the opportunity to
fashion a new strategy of electoral coordination, the Fusionist approach.
Through it, African Americans and struggling white southerners joined
forces to defeat Democrats.

In North Carolina in 1894, Republican and Populist leaders combined ranks to create a Fusion slate of candidates that achieved stunning
success. The Fusionists took the majority in both chambers of the state's
General Assembly and sent Marion Butler to the US Senate and several representatives to the US House. Unlike the Democrats, who had
starved public services, the new state legislators immediately enacted a
reform agenda that included increased funding for public schools from
elementary through higher education, established institutes for training
teachers, and limited the legal interest rate. They also sought greater fairness in elections, for example by ordering ballots to be designed using
colors to indicate different parties so that individuals who could not read
would still be able to vote and forbidding employers to fire or threaten
employees regarding their political preferences.[37]

Voters in other southern states were also demonstrating a readiness
for the same sort of political change. Tennessee elected Populist governor
John Buchanan in 1891, and Georgia and Alabama each sent Populists
to the US House of Representatives. Several states elected numerous
Populists to their state legislatures; in 1894, Alabama elected thirty-four

to the lower house of the legislature, Georgia forty-seven, and Texas twenty-two.[38]

In 1896, the Fusionists won even bigger victories in North Carolina. Their candidate for governor, Republican Daniel Russell, had announced on the campaign trail, "I stand for the Negroes' right and liberties. . . . They . . . demand, and they ought to have it, every right a white man has." It was estimated that 87 percent of African Americans turned out to vote, helping ensure the Fusionist victories of not only Governor Russell but all other statewide offices as well, and eight out of nine House seats in Congress. The Fusionists also gained larger majorities in the state Assembly, leaving the Democratic Party nearly decimated. it retained only 26 seats out of 120 in the House and only 7 out of 50 in the Senate.[39]

The 1896 election results in North Carolina meant that Democrats' worst fears had been realized. For several years, Democrats throughout the region had been dreading such an outcome in their own states. Several had already determined that the time had come to push back, using a bold and forceful new strategy. What ensued would deal severe damage to democracy.

## SOUTHERN DEMOCRATS TAKE CHARGE TO SHUT DOWN THE OPPOSITION

Democratic political leaders throughout the South gradually concluded that the strategies they had been using since the Civil War were no longer sufficient for maintaining political control. For years they had routinely stuffed ballot boxes and rigged the vote count, and they had not infrequently resorted to intimidation and violence. They had tried to ignite racism and white supremacy as a means to foster solidarity among whites and to appeal especially to lower-income people. Yet their opponents appeared to be relatively unscathed and persisted still. Some Democratic leaders decided that it was time to try a different and more permanent approach: changing the rules for how elections were run, in ways that would cripple the political opposition once and for all.[40]

Leaders in the Mississippi Democratic Party had already begun to chart a new course. In 1889, they had faced threats both from within their state—where Republicans nominated a full slate of candidates for the first time since 1875—and from Washington, DC, where Republicans in Congress were aiming to pass the Federal Elections Bill. US senator James Z. George, a Democrat, sought a means of keeping his party in power, and called for a constitutional convention for the purpose of restricting voting. The main support for the convention came from white Democrats in black-majority counties, who were most fearful of losing power. They trusted George. As a colonel in the Confederate Army, he had been captured by the Union Army on two occasions and had spent two years as a prisoner of war. In 1875, he had orchestrated the state's violent overthrow of Republicans in power, using the white supremacist Red Shirts to intimidate African Americans.[41] Meanwhile, for a few years Democrats in white-majority counties had wanted a convention to deal with unrelated issues, so they went along with the plans.

While the procedures followed by the convention abided by formal rules, they neither emanated from grassroots pressure nor received widespread popular support. Existing Mississippi laws made it easy for a small number of well-organized political elites to call a convention, because only a bare majority of the legislature needed to approve it (62 percent of Democratic lawmakers did so), while the electorate had the opportunity neither to approve the call for a convention nor to ratify its results. The public was permitted to vote for the delegates, but a mere 15 percent of the electorate turned out in that election, selecting 130 Democrats and only 4 members of the opposition parties.[42]

Under George's leadership, the convention sought ways to limit the franchise legally, without violating the Fifteenth Amendment, thus diminishing Democrats' need to resort to ballot-stuffing and violence. Or, as the *Jackson Clarion-Ledger* put it, the meeting's aim was to "render [the Federal Elections Bill] largely nugatory" by expelling from the electorate those who could not read. The most important restrictions included poll taxes, set at $2 per voter per year statewide and with local officials permitted to charge an additional dollar, and literacy tests. Election workers were empowered to evaluate a prospective voter's literacy according to an "understanding clause," meaning that a person had to be "able to read any section of the Constitution of this State; or . . . able to understand the same when read to him, or give a reasonable interpretation thereof." Individuals also had to provide evidence that they had paid all required taxes in the previous two years. Residence requirements mandated that voters had to have lived for at least two years in the state and one year in the locality; these restrictions were expected to affect the black population— which was known to move more frequently—more than whites. Finally, voters had to have registered at least four months in advance.[43] The opposition delegates voted against the restrictions on suffrage, but they were vastly outnumbered.

The new rules proved to be ruthlessly effective. Black turnout in Mississippi elections plummeted from about 40 percent in 1888 to almost nothing by 1890 and beyond. The restrictions also harmed support for the Populists by diminishing voting rates among poor whites. Registrars could exercise their judgment, though, in deciding who met the standards of the "understanding" clause of the literacy tests; delegates had intended for this ambiguous language to appease illiterate whites, on the assumption that white election officials would use their discretion to approve them. A political scientist from the Brookings Institution described what happened when a black attorney, a Harvard graduate, attempted to register to vote in the state. The registrar, a blacksmith, asked him to explain the meaning of the due process clause, "which he did with a considerable amount of learning and ability." The registrar ruled, however, that the explanation was not "reasonable" and refused to register the man. At the 1890 convention, in fact, one delegate had professed that "if every Negro in Mississippi was a graduate of Harvard, and had been elected as class orator . . . he would not be as well fitted to exercise the right of suffrage as the Anglo-Saxon farm laborer."[44] The discretion embedded in the "understanding clause" relied on registrars' racism to perceive things similarly.

In the American system of federalism, states have been called "laboratories of democracy," meaning that some may adopt progressive reforms and test them out, and then other states can emulate them if they wish. In the 1890s, Mississippi became a laboratory—not for democracy, but rather for its dismantling. Other states in the region soon followed its example and also pursued disenfranchisement, typically using poll taxes and literacy tests to achieve it. By 1894, five additional states had adopted restrictive voting procedures. Subsequently, the record showed that Democrats suppressed the opposition far more effectively in states that had already erected barriers to voting than in states that were slower to do so. Among the states that pursued disenfranchisement early on, the Republican or Populist opposition at its peak gained an average of only 33 percent of the vote, whereas in the states where voting rights remained more robust, the opposition parties netted a more formidable 45 percent. The more restrictive states also featured much lower voter turnout: an average of 42 percent of the electorate voted, compared to 73 percent elsewhere.[45] Democrats in states that had not yet pursued disenfranchisement could not help but notice these results, particularly as the political challenges of the decade intensified. As the initial assault on voting rights in Mississippi prompted Democrats across the region to replicate such efforts, democratic backsliding gained momentum.

## THE PIVOTAL ELECTION OF 1896

In the 1896 presidential election, the promise of the Populist Party suddenly became channeled into the Democratic Party at the national level, making for a profound opportunity to expand and deepen democracy. Democratic candidate Williams Jennings Bryan aspired to be the voice of the people, representing farmers and workers alike, taking on the mantle of populism.

Unlike their southern brethren, Democrats elsewhere in the nation did not position themselves as leaders in repression; to the contrary, they often allied with Populists in their quest to gain political advantage in the North and West, where Republicans tended to dominate politics. Within the Democratic Party, moreover, a battle raged between the reform-oriented free-silver proponents versus the conservative defenders of the gold standard, which included President Grover Cleveland and other pro-business forces.

These two developments and the Populists' political momentum culminated in the 1896 Democratic convention. Beforehand, Populists had hoped that the Democratic Party might implode and that their own would replace it. Yet when delegates convened, reformists predominated and they wrote a bold platform that not only advanced the free and unlimited coinage of silver and agrarians' other policy priorities but also condemned the federal government's role in repressing strikes, lambasting it as "government by injunction." In addition, they called for stronger railroad regulation, a constitutional amendment to restore the income tax (which had been invalidated by the Supreme Court in 1895), and a public works program to combat unemployment.[46]

Then candidate William Jennings Bryan—a Populist in all but name—delivered his electrifying "Cross of Gold" speech. He galvanized and united the party's Free Silver proponents with Populist advocates of the working masses. His speech concluded: "Having behind us the producing masses of this nation and the world, supported by the commercial interests, the laboring interests and the toilers everywhere, we will answer their demand for a gold standard by saying to them: You shall not press down upon the brow of labor this crown of thorns, you shall not crucify mankind upon a cross of gold." On the convention floor, impassioned delegates nominated Bryan on the fifth ballot.

With Bryan running against Republican candidate William McKinley, American voters faced a genuine choice between two divergent alternatives. For years, the parties had quarreled only over the tariff, a topic that engaged few Americans; now the fundamental role of government in an industrializing society was in question. Bryan himself, an ardent spokesperson for what he called the "toiling masses" of farmers and industrial workers, barnstormed the country. In three months, he traveled eighteen thousand miles. In northern cities he tried to reach out to organized labor. He argued that government existed not to serve monied elites but rather to harness economic power and put it to the service of the public.[47]

Powerful interests—affluent individuals and major companies—reacted with terror. They envisioned the Democratic Party under Bryan's leadership as an uprising of the masses against them. They were particularly horrified at the prospect of abandoning the gold standard, which they feared would promote inflation and weaken their economic dominance. They allied as never before. Cleveland industrialist Mark Hanna, who believed that the dominance of the Republican Party was essential for the success of business and had been raising money for the party since 1880, became a "kingmaker" for McKinley. At his urging, corporations and wealthy individuals contributed vast sums to the McKinley campaign, more than $4 million—or 6 percent of GDP—making it the most expensive campaign in American history to this day. They outspent the opposition five to one. Businesses sought to convince their employees and customers to support the Republican ticket. Newspapers, including those that typically endorsed Democrats, lined up in support of McKinley as well. All argued that Bryan's leadership would decimate the northern industrial economy. Hanna also excelled at organization, sending forth fourteen hundred paid workers to barrage the country with pamphlets that promised that McKinley would bring prosperity.[48]

Meanwhile, Bryan himself faltered. Speaking to voters, he ignored most of the party's progressive platform and focused primarily on the monetary system. He failed to attract support among industrial workers, who ultimately decided their fate was better protected by the party of their employers. Working-class radicalism was on the wane, which was hardly surprising, given the repression workers had endured for years— not only from employers but from government as well, not least at the hands of a Democratic president. Under the newly emergent model of unionism, advanced by the American Federation of Labor, workers took up their workplace issues on the shop floor rather than through political action. Some northern workers supported Democrats at the state level who pursued eight-hour-workday legislation and policies that would sanction unions. But when it came to national politics, they remained loyal to the Republican Party.[49] In short, the alliance between workers and farmers that Populists had envisioned—and which could have provided national support for democracy in the South—failed to materialize.

McKinley's 1896 victory, meanwhile, held troubling ramifications for the cause of democracy in the former Confederacy. Republicans emerged emboldened by their newfound support in disparate corners of the nation. McKinley triumphed because he won states not only in the industrial Northeast and Midwest but also along the borders of those regions, from Maryland to Iowa and Minnesota, as well as California and Oregon. These results carried a crucial lesson for the Republicans: they could get by without the South. Younger Republicans saw neither a need nor a political purpose in continuing the uphill battle of party-building in the South, for they had plenty of supporters elsewhere.[50] The national party would soon abandon the region altogether.

The 1890s had presented several opportunities for the emergence of a concerted, national effort to protect democracy, not least voting rights in the South. Yet one by one, the political allies that African Americans might have had in this quest vanished. Republicans lost interest in the region as they found political fortunes elsewhere. As wealthy people steered the party's ascent in the 1896 campaign, their priorities dominated, and democracy was not among them. With Bryan's defeat, Populists nationally saw their dreams wither, though they managed to remain competitive in some states and localities for a while longer. Farmers' potential alliance with workers had not borne fruit. African Americans were left abandoned and isolated in the South, and now Democrats in the region seized the opportunity to reclaim and consolidate their power, starting in North Carolina.

## STAGING A COUP D'ÉTAT IN NORTH CAROLINA

"This is a white man's country and white men must control and govern it."[51] So stated the "Democratic Hand Book" of North Carolina's State Democratic Executive Committee in 1898. By that time, tensions were growing between the Republicans and Populists, who shared little in common aside from their Fusionist electoral strategy. The state's Democrats, now operating without pressure from elsewhere, took advantage of the opportunity to plot their return to power. Racial antagonism provided a means of attracting voters across party lines, and the Democrats embraced it as their path back to power. When the state's Democrats held their convention that year, they denounced the Fusionist legislatures as part of "Negro Domination," and vowed to restore "rule by the white men of the State."[52]

Party leaders developed a campaign strategy rooted in appeals to white supremacy. They quietly enlisted the support of the state's business community, vowing that if they won, they would not raise its taxes, while they also stoked the racist inclinations of many whites. They selected as party chair Furnifold Simmons, who had been born on his father's plantation in 1854, graduated from Trinity College (which later became Duke University), became a lawyer, and served in Congress for one term, 1887 to 1889.

4.2 "A Serious Question—How Long Will This Last?"
white supremacy cartoon, published in the *News and Observer*,
Raleigh, North Carolina, August 13, 1898

Prominent Democrat Josephus Daniels praised Simmons as "a genius in putting everybody to work" for the party by employing a three-prong strategy: "men who could write, men who could speak, and men who could ride—the last by no means the least important." For the "men who could write," Simmons recruited newspaper editors throughout the state to the party's cause. Daniels himself, as editor of the *News and Observer*, became the "militant voice of White Supremacy," and many of his newspaper's articles and cartoons (one of them shown above) were also published elsewhere in the state and beyond. For the "men who could speak," Simmons established what was essentially a speakers' bureau, with renowned orators in the party—such as prominent lawyer Charles Aycock; Alfred Moore Waddell, a former lawyer, a lieutenant colonel for the Confederate Army, and four-term congressman; and others ready to travel the state during election season—addressing audiences.[53]

The third prong, "men who could ride," included the paramilitary Red Shirts, who often appeared on horseback, brandishing weapons as they sought to intimidate African Americans from voting. Simmons also spurred the creation of the White Government Union (WGU), managed by the Democratic Party, with the aim of bringing supporters of the

Populists back into the fold. The preface to the WGU's handbook read, "Our State is the only community in the world, with a majority of white voters, where the officers selected to administer the Government are the choice of negroes and not of the whites. This condition has been brought about by an unfortunate division among the white people; and it is likely to continue until that division is removed."[54]

The Democrats chose Wilmington as the focus of their efforts. Aycock proclaimed the city to be "the center of the white supremacy movement."[55] A group of prominent businessmen known as the "Secret Nine" were rumored to have been laying the groundwork for the eventual coup for six to nine months beforehand, while coordinating with the statewide white supremacy campaign. They divided Wilmington into sections, assigned ward captains to be in charge of the areas, and organized militias to patrol them. Another clandestine group, the "Group of Six," supplemented those efforts. The Chamber of Commerce came out against the Fusionist city government, claiming it to be bad for business, and promised white workers that with political change, they would be given jobs currently held by blacks. Meanwhile, local leaders organized White Government Union clubs among white residents of the city. The county Democratic Party provided the red shirts to the bands of men, WGU members and others, who were armed and instructed to use intimidation, including to "announce on all occasions that they would succeed if they had to shoot every negro in the city." The office of a Democratic congressional candidate provided whiskey to the men to "fire them up, and make them fiercer and more terrorizing in their conduct."[56]

On October 24, Waddell delivered a fiery address to sixty prominent citizens of Wilmington. He pronounced that it was "best and wisest for both races" that white people, whom he credited with making the United States the "grandest country on the globe ... [,] should alone govern it as a whole in all its parts." A diatribe against African Americans followed, as Aycock told the audience, "The greatest crime that has ever been perpetrated against modern civilization was the investment of the negro with the right of suffrage." Then he leveled blame at the Fusionists, particularly Governor Russell, and proclaimed, "The salvation of society depends on the outcome of this election." In his closing argument, Aycock reminded his listeners that they were descended from the Americans who had won the Revolutionary War and fought for the South to preserve their "heritage." Then he threatened violence against African Americans: "We maintained it against overwhelming armies of men of our own race, shall we surrender it to a ragged rabble of negroes led by a handful of white cowards who at the first sound of conflict will seek to hide themselves from the righteous vengeance which they shall not escape? No! A thousand times no! Let them understand once and for all that we will have no more of the intolerable conditions under which we live. We are resolved to change them, if we have to choke the current of the Cape Fear with carcasses." With his parting words, Waddell thundered, "Negro domination shall henceforth be only a shameful memory to us and an everlasting warning to those who shall ever again seek to revive it. To this declaration we are irrevocably committed and true men everywhere will hail it with a hearty Amen!"[57]

Waddell's speech reportedly "electrified his hearers," and it was praised as "the most remarkable delivery ever heard in a campaign here in the memory of this generation." The entire speech was published in the *Wilmington Messenger* and was widely circulated.[58]

Then the editor of the black newspaper, the *Daily Record*, published what white supremacists considered to be an inflammatory editorial, and they became further enraged. During the summer, the *Wilmington Messenger* had published a speech delivered the previous year at the Georgia farmers' convention by Rebecca Latimer Felton, a prominent social reformer and an ardent white supremacist. She blamed postbellum white men for the circumstances of white rural women, many of whom lived in poverty. In particular, she lambasted them for failing to respond adequately to what she claimed was a problem of rape of white women by black men. Alexander Manly, the editor of the *Daily Record*, responded with a bold editorial in which he blamed whites for hypocrisy and pointed out that white men often raped black women. In the highly charged environment, these charges amounted to dynamite.[59]

On Election Day, Democrats stuffed ballot boxes, ensuring their victories. At a mass meeting of whites the next day, businessmen and professionals affirmed the White Declaration of Independence. It read, "We . . . do hereby declare that we will no longer be ruled, and will never again be ruled by men of African origin." A set of resolutions followed, including the demand that Manly must leave Wilmington and cease publication of the *Daily Record*. If this demand was not agreed to by the Committee of Colored Citizens (CCC) within twelve hours, the declaration promised, it would be followed up with force.[60] The CCC did respond, but not within the time required.

When the morning of November 10 dawned, the paramilitary forces made it their first order of business to destroy the offices of the *Daily Record*; afterward a massacre ensued throughout the city. The Wilmington Light Infantry paraded two rapid-firing machine guns on horse-drawn wagons, dragging them through the city to intimidate residents. White paramilitary units on horseback roamed black communities and shot African Americans throughout the day. No definitive body count was ever conducted, but African Americans believed that some three hundred perished, while fourteen hundred fled the city.[61]

By 4:00 p.m., the Republican mayor, Board of Aldermen, and chief of police—none of whom were up for election for another year—had resigned and been replaced by white Democrats. The new board chose Waddell as mayor. The Democrats then fired all black municipal employees and permanently closed down a firehouse serving a black neighborhood. Some months later, the board would secure a new charter for the city from the legislature and hold new elections, in which Waddell and Democratic aldermen prevailed. The white supremacists who had seized control—mostly prominent, wealthy residents—were now in charge, in Wilmington and throughout much of the state.[62]

## DEMOCRATS TAKE ACTION "TO SETTLE THIS QUESTION ONCE AND FOREVER"

Any lingering hopes that the federal government would act to protect democracy in the South were put to rest when the Supreme Court, also in 1898, handed down its decision in the case of *Williams v. Mississippi*. The decision declared that the restrictions on voting established in Mississippi in 1890 did not violate the Fifteenth Amendment because—at least ostensibly—they applied to all citizens. Disenfranchisement withstood judicial scrutiny—by the same Court that two years earlier had handed down *Plessy v. Ferguson*, upholding Louisiana's system of segregated railroad cars as within the police powers of its legislature.[63]

Democratic leaders throughout the South grew convinced that restrictions on voting offered them the best means to dominate politics
permanently, effectively shutting down the opposition. Said one Democrat in Alabama, "Now we are not begging for 'ballot reform' or anything
of that sort, but we want to be relieved of purchasing the Negroes to carry
elections. I want cheaper votes."[64] The solution that was more efficient
than ballot-stuffing, this logic implied, was disenfranchisement.

One month after the Wilmington massacre, Josephus Daniels traveled to Washington, DC, to consult with representatives of states that
had already disenfranchised. On his return to North Carolina, he gave
a speech in Laurinburg, where the first white supremacy rally had been
held the previous spring. "What shall be the permanent memorial we
grateful people shall erect to commemorate the mighty revolution of
1898?" he asked. Then he provided the answer: "A constitutional amendment that will disfranchise the mass of negro voters. There is no half-
way ground in a revolution such as we have passed through. No election
law can permanently preserve white supremacy." He continued, "As long
as 120,000 negroes stand united, with their names on the registration
books . . . they present a constant temptation to the demagogue to ride
into office by a division of the white vote added to the solid negro vote."[65]

When the state's Assembly met in January 1899, before overturning
Fusionist legislation it took action to solidify the disenfranchisement of
African Americans—or, in the words of the speaker of the North Carolina House, "to settle this question once and forever." Following Mississippi's example, it approved the adoption of literacy tests and poll taxes,
to be ratified by the electorate as a constitutional amendment. And like
Louisiana, which had acted one year earlier in its own effort to defeat
Fusionists, it changed election laws in ways that would limit Republican
participation when the citizens went to the polls to vote on the amendment. As one Democratic state senator put it, he favored "a good square,
honest law that will always give us a good Democratic majority."[66]

In the 1900 election, the Red Shirts groups, which included as many
as one-quarter of whites in some counties, came out in full force to intimidate opposition voters. The night before, Waddell told a crowd to "go
to the polls tomorrow and if you find the Negro out voting, tell him to
leave the polls and if he refuses, kill him, shoot him down in his tracks."[67]

Those who made it past the vigilante forces faced registrars newly empowered by the change in electoral laws to deny the vote to all African
Americans. The state ratified the constitutional amendment by a 59 to
41 percent margin and elected the white supremacist orator Aycock as
governor.

In North Carolina, the process was now complete: Democrats had
managed to secure their power for seventy years to come by limiting suffrage. No longer would they need to resort to extralegal procedures in one
election after another: they had enacted "reforms" that would deliver the
election to them year after year. Turnout declined, falling from 75 percent
in 1900 to under 50 percent in 1904. As a result, both the Democratic
and Republican parties became more conservative, because neither had
any motivation to represent those who couldn't afford the poll tax or
couldn't read. Democrats, who held control, kept taxes low and provided
few public services, while Republicans abandoned African Americans
and cast their lot with business.[68]

Over the next decade, the remaining southern states followed suit,
each adopting similar procedures that permitted Democrats to rule, un-
challenged, by denying African Americans the right to vote. The most
contentious issue that emerged revolved around whether such measures
should disenfranchise not only blacks but poor whites as well. The white
planter elites in black-majority counties were unconcerned about such
consequences, while whites in counties where they were in the majority
resisted a rollback of their democratic rights. Public officials in Louisiana
rejected the approach Mississippi had used to protect poor whites, the
"understanding" clause, convinced that it engaged election administrators
in fraud. They adopted instead the "grandfather clause," which exempted
from literacy and property tests people who were entitled to vote on
January 1, 1867, along with their sons and grandsons—a clear inclusion
of whites and exclusion of African Americans.[69] That approach subsequently became more common.

As these changes stripped millions of their voting rights and effectively terminated political competition in the South, the federal government sat on its hands. The remaining states in the region disenfranchised
African Americans during the presidency of Theodore Roosevelt, who did
not interfere. His successor, William Howard Taft, made the Republicans'

new stance on black voting rights explicit, saying in his 1909 inaugural address, "I look forward with hope to increasing the already good feeling between the South and the other sections of the country. My chief purpose is not to effect a change in the electoral vote of the Southern States. . . . While the fifteenth amendment has not been generally observed in the past, it ought to be observed, and the tendency of Southern legislation today is toward the enactment of electoral qualifications which shall square with that amendment. . . . [I]t is clear to all that the domination of an ignorant, irresponsible element can be prevented by constitutional laws which shall exclude from voting both negroes and whites not having education or other qualifications thought to be necessary for a proper electorate."[70] With those words, President Taft—and the Republican Party—sanctioned the disenfranchisement measures that had been put in place under southern Democrats. The demise of democracy was not simply a function of regional uniqueness in the South: it occurred because the federal government of the United States permitted it and, indeed, approved of it.

## DEMOCRACY DERAILED

From 1890 to 1910, the entire South transformed itself from a functioning democracy to a region of authoritarian enclaves. In the 1880s, adult males in the region typically voted at rates of 64 percent. In the early 1890s, turnout averaged 73 percent in states that had not yet adopted disenfranchisement, while it hovered at 42 percent in the states with such rules. By the early twentieth century, turnout plummeted across the region to an average of merely 30 percent. African Americans were almost completely excluded from voting, and voting among whites fell sharply as well, to only about half of previous levels.[71]

Disenfranchisement produced the effect its white southern elites intended: it put an end to meaningful electoral competition, thus granting them uncontested political power. In the 1880s and early 1890s, the South had featured actual contests for power, with one in four adult males voting for Republican or third-party candidates. By the 1910s, not only had the electorate shrunk, but also party competition had been almost entirely eradicated, with only one in ten voters choosing alternatives to the Democrats.[72] The Democrats had effectively shut down the political opposition, and that change would produce far-reaching consequences for citizens' lives.

From Reconstruction up until disenfranchisement, African Americans had served as public officials throughout the South. From 1869 to 1901, every Congress except one had included African Americans, and hundreds had served in state legislatures and thousands as local officials. After disenfranchisement, all were gone. In the years that followed, only through federal patronage did any blacks gain positions in government, and the power of southern Democrats in the federal government—paired with the loss of Republicans' commitments to civil rights—sharply reduced the political will to promote such appointments.[73]

Such exclusion carried severe repercussions. At the most obvious level, African Americans were barred from a basic form of standing or civic status in society. Beyond that, their lack of political power produced ripples of effects for public policy. States typically allocated funding for schools on the basis of population, leaving it to local officials to distribute funds, but this meant that in black-majority areas, white elites who held all the political power could channel resources toward the schools their children attended while starving those serving black children as well as hill-country whites.[74] Political inequality fostered and perpetuated economic and social inequality.

At a more fundamental level, when people are denied the right to vote, they are easily deprived of basic protection under the rule of law. African Americans became powerless to stop the upsurge of lynchings that had been taking place across the South since Reconstruction. Anti-lynching crusader Ida B. Wells-Barnett explained, "With no sacredness of the ballot there can be no sacredness of human life itself. . . . The mob says, 'This people has no vote with which to punish us . . . therefore we indulge our brutal instincts.'" As late as 1922, one lynching took place *every week*, and crowds gathered to watch, treating it as a form of entertainment.[75]

Political disenfranchisement also permitted the full establishment of formal segregation, as southern states developed and entrenched a vast array of Jim Crow laws. Certainly these policies had already begun previously and had been sanctioned by the federal government when the Supreme Court had handed down *Plessy v. Ferguson*. Yet once African

Americans were excluded from voting, these legal strictures proliferated, segregating all aspects of life, from schools to restrooms and water fountains. The federal government, too, adopted such restrictions, including in the military. In short, "disenfranchisement was like the locomotive of a train," Valelly explains; attached to it were the perpetuation of lynching, the rise of de jure segregation, and the demise of educational opportunities.[76]

Once in place, disenfranchisement and the system of American apartheid it promulgated would endure for seventy years. While these apartheid arrangements lasted, they endowed white southern elites with extra political power in national politics, similar to the extra power they had exercised from the founding through the Civil War owing to the three-fifths compromise. Now that power accrued to the Democratic Party, giving it the extra Electoral College votes that permitted Woodrow Wilson to win the presidency in 1912—at which point he thoroughly segregated the civil service. In addition, Democrats gained about twenty-five extra seats in Congress between 1903 and 1952—a difference that had the impact of altering some 15 percent of roll-call votes. One-party rule in the South meant that once a member was elected to Congress, he served for years, gaining seniority and with it top committee assignments and leadership posts.[77] These officials who held their positions because of authoritarian structures were able to hold sway over national politics, influencing the shape of the legislation that made it to the floor in each chamber and determining which bills would never see the light of day. White supremacy prevailed, and democracy was beaten to a pulp.

## A FORMIDABLE CONFLUENCE OF THREATS

By the end of the 1890s, all four characteristics of democracy had suffered harm over the course of the decade. Southern Democrats not only refused to recognize the legitimacy of the political opposition, but they also went further, deliberately seeking to terminate it once and for all. They succeeded in doing so by eviscerating the voting rights of African Americans. As they pursued their goal of consolidating power, they ran elections in ways that were anything but free and fair, and they did not hesitate to thwart the rule of law. As the result of these body blows to democracy, more harm ensued: once blacks lost political power, their civil liberties and civil rights became vulnerable as well and were taken from them. All three branches of the federal government and both major parties condoned these developments.

Democratic backsliding in the 1890s was hardly inevitable. It followed a few decades during which a multiracial democracy was on the rise in the United States in local, state, and federal government. From the late 1890s onward, by contrast, race became a more rigid and legally enforced dividing line in American society than it had been in those decades since Reconstruction. How did it happen?

The 1890s featured ambitious politicians in both of the two major parties, as well as in the insurgent Populist Party. In the course of their competition for political power, three threats to democracy—polarization, racism, and rising economic inequality—coalesced in ways that led to severe backsliding.

That racism drove democratic backsliding was plain to see. White supremacy energized southern whites, infused them with anger, and spurred their participation. For those motivated by it, destruction of democracy mattered little, for they believed they were restoring the rightful order of society, in which the boundaries of membership and definitions of status were defined by race. This was articulated blatantly by the White Declaration of Independence, which was endorsed by hundreds of people in Wilmington in 1898.

But while racism was undoubtedly the most overt threat to democracy in the 1890s, it did not occur in isolation; in fact, its presence helped obscure other threats in the era that also proved consequential. Southern Democrats sought to gain and hold power, to wrest it from Republicans and Populists who had become increasingly competitive. To do so, they embraced white supremacy not least because it was a political strategy that produced powerful results, engendering political unity among whites supporting their party and sanctioning disenfranchisement of their political opponents, easing their path to political dominance. Put differently, while southern Democrats were clearly racists, racism was not just a goal but also a means to an end, and that end was political power.[78]

Meanwhile, polarization and racism drove deep cleavages in politics that helped to obscure the profound and growing influence of affluent

Americans on politics. The role of economic inequality in the deterioration of American democracy during the 1890s can easily be missed, in part because economic elites did not cluster in one party. The nation featured distinct regional sections, each with its own political economy, and elites in each region held different priorities. Rather than unifying in one major party against the masses, therefore, they dominated both of the two major parties, where they advocated different positions on key issues. Industrialists allied themselves with the Republican Party, while planter elites in the South cast their lot with the Democratic Party.[79] The fierce competition between the parties obscured the profound inequality in society that leaders of both condoned.

As a candidate, William Jennings Bryan was an exception to the rule, and if he had succeeded in making his case to ordinary Americans nationwide, a new politics might have emerged that could have challenged the role of powerful elites in both regions. Yet his campaign faced a highly mobilized Republican Party, galvanized by the unsurpassed campaign contributions of wealthy industrialists and by effective on-the-ground organization. In the face of such mobilization and a highly polarized politics, industrial workers in the North perceived themselves to be better off by allying with the party of their own employers rather than the Democratic Party, as it seemed to represent mostly farmers, not people like them.[80]

Meanwhile, economic elites in the South dominated the Democratic Party as well, and it was they who primarily planned and supported white supremacy campaigns: the impetus for black disenfranchisement emanated from them, not from poor southern whites. In fact, many ordinary white southerners worried that they themselves would be disadvantaged by the new voting restrictions. Wealthy planters living in black-majority areas provided the driving force behind such efforts as they sought to consolidate their power. Similarly, the coup d'état in Wilmington came to pass because political elites and business elites worked tirelessly at it and coordinated their efforts. The *Charlotte Daily Observer* credited the business community: "The business men of the State are largely responsible for the victory. Not before in years have the bank men, the mill men, and the business men in general—the backbone of the property interest of the State—taken such sincere interest. They worked from start to finish, and furthermore they spent large bits of money in behalf of the cause."[81] In each case, economic and political elites mobilized ordinary people on behalf of the cause, from voters through Red Shirts. Race-baiting served their purposes in that process, but it would be inaccurate to identify racism among ordinary people as the primary cause of the disenfranchisement that ensued.

The United States entered the twentieth century with democracy dramatically restricted. Conflict over the formative rift of race, which divided the parties in those decades, had given rise to backsliding. Democrats who sought to consolidate their power in the South had done so, through appeals to white supremacy, while Republicans in the North and West found they could get by without black voters. As a result, African Americans were stripped of voting rights, civil liberties, and civil rights, and would remain so for more than a half century.

The political settlement of the 1890s meant, moreover, that economic inequality would persist. Elites in both parties foreclosed the possibility of the more widespread reforms for which Populists had hoped, though they did in time manage to achieve some key reforms in Congress.

Subsequently, political polarization would begin to decline. The next decade when democracy would once again stand on the brink was the 1930s.

# 5

## Executive Aggrandizement in the 1930s

In 1932, as the Great Depression entered its third year, millions of Americans were out of work and desperate. People needed jobs so that they could feed their families, but for many there was no work to be found. One group, however, thought they saw a lifeline from the federal government. But to tap it, they would have to confront the government itself.

Nearly four million veterans had survived World War I. In 1924, Congress had overridden President Calvin Coolidge's veto to approve compensation averaging approximately $1,000 for each one of them. The catch: the payments were not to be made until 1945.[1] As the Depression worsened, many of these veterans of the Great War began demanding advance payment of their "bonus" as a way of alleviating the misery of joblessness.

In the spring of 1932, a group of several hundred veterans set out for Washington from Portland, Oregon, to demonstrate for immediate bonus payments. Led by a man named Walter Waters, who proved to be a canny publicist, their cross-country journey generated headlines as they neared their destination.

They reached St. Louis in May and crossed the Mississippi River into Illinois, hoping to ride freight cars of the Baltimore and Ohio Railroad to Washington. But the B&O's management saw them not as honorable veterans but as "agitators" and was determined not to let them ride its cars. The governor of Illinois, however, was facing reelection that fall and feared taking action against the veterans, who aroused public sympathy. So he ordered the Illinois National Guard to transport the veterans to the Indiana border by truck. Other governors to the east followed his lead, and on May 29, the Oregon contingent completed the final leg of its journey with an assist from the Maryland National Guard.[2]

Inspired by the publicity, veterans from around the country streamed to Washington to join the Oregonians, and by mid-July more than twenty thousand veterans had congregated in the capital. With the help of the sympathetic chief of police, retired army general Pelham Glassford, they organized themselves into the "Bonus Expeditionary Force" (BEF), a group whose name was a deliberate play on the American Expeditionary Forces, as the US Army had designated its World War I battle troops.[3]

In an improvised camp in Anacostia Flats, across the Anacostia River from downtown Washington, thousands of veterans took up residence in temporary shelters, some accompanied by their wives and children. Others occupied vacant land and abandoned buildings around the city. They survived mostly on private donations that came in from around the country, as well as some equipment that Glassford was able to cadge out of a reluctant War Department. Glassford also arranged for a "Bonus Clinic," staffed by medics from the Marines, to provide health care.[4]

To keep order in the camps, the BEF formed a tight military-style organization, complete with a loyalty oath and a corps of "military police," to keep out nonveterans and radical agitators such as communists. Roy Wilkins, a young reporter for *The Crisis*, the National Association for the Advancement of Colored People's monthly magazine, noted that the BEF was racially integrated, with black and white veterans living peacefully side by side.[5]

As the Bonus Army assembled, Representative Wright Patman of Texas introduced legislation to meet the veterans' demands for early payment of their bonus. When the Senate defeated the bill on June 17, the announcement of this result stunned the crowd of veterans assembled outside the Capitol into a tense silence. One journalist, parroting the Hoover administration's fears of revolution, perceived echoes of "the mobs of the French revolution; the crash of the Kerensky Government in

Russia; the Spanish uprising." But the crowd simply sang "America" and the veterans returned quietly to their billets around the city.[6]

The veterans gathered in the BEF did not disperse, however. They remained in Washington and continued to demonstrate, even with no hope that Congress would grant their request. Although Glassford believed that the veterans would eventually leave peacefully, the administration of President Herbert Hoover grew increasingly uneasy.

While this group of desperate citizens remained orderly and peaceful, the administration saw them as a band of menacing radicals. Fearing an uprising—or, worse, a coup d'état—the administration began mobilizing the army and prepared to implement the "White Plan," the standing set of military orders for quelling an insurrection in the capital.[7]

On the morning of July 28, the District of Columbia police began to move in to evict the protesters from government buildings they were occupying in downtown Washington. For the most part, they met little resistance, but in the early afternoon, one group fought back with bricks and stones, and the police responded harshly, fatally shooting two of the veterans.

At around 1:30 p.m., Hoover ordered in the army. Commanding the operation was the army chief of staff, General Douglas MacArthur, assisted by his chief aide, Major Dwight Eisenhower.

At 4:00 p.m., with MacArthur leading the way, a column of some six hundred soldiers marched from the Ellipse, just south of the White House, toward an encampment of veterans on Pennsylvania Avenue southeast of the Capitol. The force included infantry with bayonets fixed, tanks, and two hundred mounted cavalry brandishing sabers. Commanding the Third Cavalry as they rode through the streets of Washington was Major George Patton.

Through the day and into the night, the army fought the BEF as if they were confronting a riotous mob. The soldiers donned gas masks and rolled through the downtown camp, flattening shanties, threatening protesters with bayonets, and liberally lobbing tear gas canisters to disperse the crowd. Many veterans turned and ran, but others remained and resisted, hurling bricks and stones at the troops. By nine o'clock that night, the veterans had retreated, and MacArthur ordered his troops to continue on to Anacostia to clear the BEF encampment there.

Courtesy of the National Archives (photo no. 111-SC-97532)

5.1  Federal troops burn the Bonus Army camp, Washington, DC, July 28, 1932

As they approached the Eleventh Street Bridge over the Anacostia River, MacArthur received direct orders from President Hoover, who was by then anxious to avoid escalation, not to continue across the river. But MacArthur ignored the order and the troops moved on. After pausing to allow the remaining BEF members to evacuate, MacArthur's soldiers put torches to the Anacostia encampment, leaving it burning in the shadow of the US Capitol (as seen in the photograph above), forcing veterans and their families to scramble away from the rubble and smoke. The Bonus Army was broken, and most of the veterans, who had come to Washington looking for help in their distress, left the city with no bonus and dashed hopes.[8]

Hoover and MacArthur would insist that the Bonus March was motivated by radicals bent on overthrowing the government. At a press conference the day after the operation, MacArthur reported that "that mob down there was a bad looking mob. . . . It was animated by the essence of revolution." He claimed "beyond a shadow of a doubt" that the BEF were "insurrectionists" bent on taking over the government. Grandiosely he compared his triumph to the liberation of communities "which had been held in the grip of a foreign enemy."[9]

But not all observers saw the incident this way. Others regarded Hoover's response and MacArthur's attack as an excessive and unconscionable exercise of power. "If the army must be called out to make war on unarmed citizens," wrote the *Washington News*, "this is no longer America."[10]

The veterans would eventually get their bonus, though it would take four years. Not until 1936 did Congress finally override President Franklin Roosevelt's veto and authorize immediate payments. But meanwhile the Bonus Marchers, and particularly the federal government's response to them, exposed the coming challenge of American democracy—how to respond vigorously and effectively to the unprecedented economic crisis without compromising democracy.

## CRISIS OF DEMOCRACY AND CAPITALISM

Uncertainty about the future of democracy in the 1930s stemmed principally from the collapse of the global economy, which caused Americans to question the effectiveness of their system of government. Many Americans had already been living on the edge of destitution even during the Roaring Twenties, and the epidemic of joblessness during the Great Depression, which affected as many as one in four members of the workforce, left them with little hope. Yet with the crash of the financial markets, the richest Americans lost much of their wealth, reducing the gap between them and everyone else. As economic inequality diminished, it receded as a threat to democracy, although widespread economic distress remained.

Political polarization was also entering a period of decline in the 1930s. Since the 1890s, the Republicans had dominated national politics and Democrats struggled to contend. Consequently, the fierce partisan battles that characterized the late nineteenth century subsided. The Democratic Party, moreover, was increasingly divided between white southerners, who strenuously defended segregation and white supremacy in the South, and urban northerners, who advocated a progressive program of social welfare and labor rights. Thus, divisions over policy often did not break down along party lines. On many economic issues, southern and northern Democrats would combine to oppose Republicans, but particularly on issues involving race or labor, southern Democrats and Republicans would often join together.[11] Although the parties still represented distinct and often opposing segments of society, these shifting coalitions meant that parties tended not to act as "teams" that were always and unalterably opposed to each other but rather as more fluid and cooperative coalition partners.

This three-legged party system also tended to push conflicts over membership and issues of race off the national agenda. Race still remained a crushing rebuke to the claims of American democracy; Jim Crow, disenfranchisement, and white supremacy reigned in the South, and segregation and discrimination were rampant in the North as well. Challenges to white supremacy continued through the work of organizations such as the National Association for the Advancement of Colored People and the ultimately unsuccessful fight to make lynching a federal crime.[12] Overt conflict over the boundaries of membership, however, was not a defining feature of the political system in the 1930s, as it had been in the 1850s and 1890s, although racial exclusion remained a key feature of American democracy.

As the events of the 1930s unfolded, the threat to democracy that emerged most visibly in the 1930s was executive aggrandizement. The presidency had until then been a relatively weak office. Although presidents had occasionally exerted great force, Congress remained the primary center of power in American politics. For much of American history, executive power was mostly a latent threat until the Great Depression and the global crisis of capitalism and democracy in the 1930s brought it to the surface and ultimately made it into a weapon that presidents could wield for a variety of purposes, both good and ill.

Unlike the 1850s and the 1890s, when multiple threats combined to push American democracy to the brink, the 1930s, like the 1790s, saw one overriding threat to democracy. And once again, even if the nation avoided the dramatic backsliding of the nineteenth-century crises, a single threat proved unsettling enough.

❖

By the time Franklin D. Roosevelt became president in March 1933, having defeated Hoover by a landslide in the 1932 election, the American economy had fallen into ruin. More than 24 percent of American workers were unemployed. Between 1929 and 1933, the total output of the American economy shrank by roughly 40 percent.[13] An explosion of homelessness led to the construction of shantytowns—derisively named Hoovervilles—where hundreds of thousands lived in flimsy shacks. Local welfare agencies and private charities were stretched to the breaking point, and millions were left without any resources to cope.

The banking system neared collapse. Bank runs, in which depositors rush to withdraw their funds all at once (think Frank Capra's film *It's a Wonderful Life*), were common sights in cities and towns around the country. Many banks went out of business, leaving their customers with nothing. Prices for agricultural products dropped, leaving farmers destitute and unable to pay their mortgages, further deepening the banking crisis.

In the face of this emergency, the Hoover administration seemed paralyzed, unable to muster a response that could prevent a downward spiral. And it was not alone. Around the world, both economic distress and political crises proliferated. The 1930s were suffused with the fearful sense that capitalism was crumbling and liberal democracy was under threat.[14]

To make matters worse, competing forms of government had arisen across the ocean that seemed destined to outperform or overpower democracy in the United States. Fifteen years after toppling the czar in 1917, the Russian Revolution had produced a totalitarian dictatorship under the iron will of Joseph Stalin. Meanwhile, in Italy under Benito Mussolini, followed by Germany under Adolf Hitler, an alternative form of totalitarianism, fascism, was also on the rise.

As American society seemed to be sliding toward some kind of collapse, many Americans thought these totalitarian regimes seemed better able to maintain social order, protect at least some of their citizens from the ravages of economic collapse, and avoid the fecklessness that seemed to afflict the United States. Public figures such as Charles Lindbergh, the famous aviator, and Henry Luce, the founder and publisher of *Time*, expressed sympathy and even support for Hitler and Mussolini. Nicholas Murray Butler, the president of Columbia University and a Nobel Peace Prize winner, observed that "there is no question but that we must accept the demonstration that Fascism is a form of government of the very first order of excellence." Totalitarian societies, Butler contended, tended to produce "men of far greater intelligence, far stronger character and far more courage than the system of elections."[15]

Homegrown populists of various stripes were also stirring the pot. Governor Huey Long of Louisiana brought much-needed development to his state but, as historian David Kennedy notes, "he closed his grip over the state's political apparatus, making Louisiana the closest thing to a dictatorship that America has ever known."[16] Elected to the Senate in 1930, Long amassed millions of followers for his "Share Our Wealth" movement, which promised prosperity under his leadership. Father Charles Coughlin, a Catholic priest whose radio sermons reached tens of millions of listeners, spouted antisemitic vitriol while expressing support for fascism and disdain for what he saw as the weakness and moral bankruptcy of both capitalism and democracy.

Into this maelstrom stepped Roosevelt. The new president acknowledged and sought to assuage national anxiety in his inaugural address on March 4, 1933, when he proclaimed that "the only thing we have to fear is fear itself—nameless, unreasoning, unjustified terror which paralyzes needed efforts to convert retreat into advance."[17]

As Roosevelt took office, fear prevailed, and the fate of democracy—in the United States and around the world—seemed to hang in the balance. Roosevelt's challenge was to offer the commanding leadership that was needed to put Americans back to work and preserve American capitalism, without sacrificing democracy in the process.

Against the odds, Roosevelt succeeded, but not without a significant cost. In averting the crisis of democracy in the 1930s, Roosevelt advanced executive aggrandizement and set himself and future presidents up to exert much more direct, individual, and unfettered power. In some instances the exertion of presidential power came at the direct expense of Americans' rights, as in the expansion of domestic surveillance in the interest of national security and most egregiously in the incarceration of more than a hundred thousand Japanese Americans during World War II. And Roosevelt also accepted the existing racial limits on American democracy, frequently capitulating to southern demands to preserve segregation even as federal power grew.

## FRANKLIN ROOSEVELT: AMERICAN DICTATOR?

The dual aims of securing the economy and safeguarding democracy were central to Roosevelt's presidency. Through the 1930s, he devoted himself to the New Deal, an evolving program of reconstruction and reform. The New Deal had two critical components. First, it aimed to promote Americans' economic security, both by meeting the immediate crisis of the Depression and then by restructuring the economy to prevent a recurrence of the misery the Depression caused.

Second, and at least as important for its impact on American democracy, the New Deal sought to restructure the government. Roosevelt saw the Depression as a national emergency, and he thought the government's response under Hoover was disorganized and anemic. He sought to empower the executive branch—and particularly the president—to enable the government to act more vigorously, not just in the face of future emergencies but also as a matter of routine.

This evolution of presidential power under Roosevelt would drastically alter the conventional understanding of the separation of powers under the Constitution. From the time of the founding of the republic, Congress, which represented the nation's broad diversity of outlooks and interests, had been the dominant branch of government; it had the power to make laws, determine government spending, and declare war.[18] The president, by contrast, had limited authority; in designing the presidency, the framers of the Constitution took pains to try to prevent it from becoming a dictatorship by embedding it in a system of separated powers with checks and balances. Presidents in the early twentieth century had begun to expand the powers of the office and gained new control over a growing and more capable executive branch. Yet even with these changes, presidents remained secondary to Congress through the 1930s: empowered to execute Congress's decisions but not to govern on their own except in an extraordinary circumstance. And the Great Depression, Roosevelt asserted, most assuredly was such an exceptional moment.

The New Deal began with an extraordinary exercise of power. The day after his inauguration, Roosevelt issued a proclamation calling Congress into an immediate unscheduled session. The day after that, he issued another proclamation that shut down the country's banks for four days in order to calm public fears about the soundness of the banking system and buy his new administration some time to respond.[19]

Congress convened its special session at noon on March 9 to consider Roosevelt's hastily written Emergency Banking Act. Only a handful of copies had been printed, so Representative Henry Steagall, chairman of the House Banking and Currency Committee, read the bill aloud. On the Senate floor, Huey Long and Senate banking chairman Carter Glass almost came to blows as Long tried to raise objections about the bill's potential impact on small local banks. Both the House and the Senate passed the bill within hours, and by early evening Roosevelt had signed it into law.[20]

He now wielded unprecedented power over the country's financial affairs. "Roosevelt Gets Powers of Dictator," proclaimed a headline in the pro-FDR *New York Times* two days later, reporting on both the banking act and the anticipated Economy Act, which eventually passed on March 20. "When Mr. Roosevelt has put his signature on the economy bill," wrote the *Times*'s Arthur Krock, "he will be in possession of more arbitrary authority than any American statesman has had since the Constitution was framed. . . . No head of a nation, operating under a popular form of government," he went on, "will have even a goodly percentage of this authority."[21] As Krock reported, some members of Congress were privately uneasy about this, but by and large Congress, and the rest of the country, acquiesced quietly.

Some observers were not so quiet. Many Americans cheered Roosevelt's move to assume control because it seemed as though someone was finally taking charge at a time of desperate need. "The situation is critical, Franklin," the formidable liberal columnist Walter Lippmann told Roosevelt privately a month before he was inaugurated. "You may have no alternative but to assume dictatorial powers." He repeated this theme in his column. "Popular government is unworkable except under the leadership of a strong national executive," he wrote. The assumption of "'dictatorial powers,' if that is the name for it—is essential." Lippmann's paper, the *New York Herald Tribune*, generally the voice of mainstream, respectable Republicans, titled an approving editorial "For Dictatorship, if Necessary." *Barron's*, the business magazine, wrote that "a mild species of dictatorship will help us over the roughest spots in the road ahead."[22]

In a lighter vein, the humorist Will Rogers captured the country's mood well shortly after Roosevelt's inauguration:

> Now Mr. Hoover didn't get results because he asked Congress to do something. There's where he made a mistake. . . . This fellow Mr. Roosevelt, he just sends a thing up every morning, says "Here, here's your menu, you guys, sign it, you know what I mean, right here." Now Mr. Roosevelt, he never, you know, he never scolds them. Congress is really just children that never grew up, that's all they are. . . . Now Mr. Roosevelt, we've turned everything over to you. We've given you more power than we've ever given any man . . . in the history of the world. We don't know what it's all about. We tried to run the country individually and along democratic lines, but boy, we gummed it up, so you take it and run it as you want to, you know.[23]

For ordinary Americans, Roosevelt himself personified the drastic change they desperately wanted. Many of the thousands of letters that streamed into the White House implored him to take action, which is precisely what he had promised in his inaugural address:

> This nation asks for action, and action now. . . . We do not distrust the future of essential democracy. The people of the United States have not failed. In their need they have registered a mandate that they want direct, vigorous action. They have asked for discipline and direction under leadership. They have made me the present instrument of their wishes. In the spirit of the gift I take it.[24]

Roosevelt's actions in the earliest days of his presidency tended to be relatively restrained compared to the predictions that he aspired to dictatorship. Still, the sense that the constitutional structure of American democracy was deficient remained in the air through the 1930s.

## THE NEW DEAL AND THE ECONOMIC CRISIS

After its eventful opening months, Roosevelt turned to address the nation's deep economic distress. The New Deal tackled problems that had never before been considered the responsibility of the federal government: joblessness and poverty, economic security, labor rights, and housing, among others. In taking on these challenges, Roosevelt oversaw a broad expansion of the federal government's powers and responsibilities that largely succeeded in stabilizing the economy and forestalling more dramatic and radical approaches such as socialism or fascism. But they also set the stage for executive aggrandizement.

Initially, the government sought to provide immediate relief for the unemployed, mostly by establishing work programs that provided people with jobs. Many of these programs had bewilderingly similar names and involved large-scale government spending on public works projects: the Public Works Administration, which built bridges, dams, and airports; the Civil Works Administration and the Works Progress Administration (WPA), which undertook smaller-scale building projects in communities around the country and supported the arts; the National Youth Administration, which provided training and jobs for young people; and the Civilian Conservation Corps, which focused on projects in rural areas. Millions of workers got jobs through these programs; the WPA alone employed nearly two million people each year until World War II and spent a total of more than $10 billion.[25]

Next, the New Deal sought to create longer-term protection for American workers and their families from what Roosevelt called the "hazards and vicissitudes of life." The Social Security Act of 1935 created systems of old-age pensions and unemployment insurance for American workers in order to provide some protection against the risks of an industrial wage economy. The National Labor Relations Act guaranteed workers the right to form unions and engage in collective bargaining. The Fair Labor Standards Act of 1938 set up a structure of minimum wages, maximum hours, and other protections to help ensure fair treatment in the workplace. And a series of laws sought to attack homelessness and improve housing standards by making mortgages, and thus homeownership, more affordable and promoting the construction of public housing and the improvement of urban neighborhoods.[26]

Though these programs brought much-needed economic stability and confidence to citizens, they also extended new social rights in divisive ways that elevated some Americans (particularly white male industrial workers) while further marginalizing others (largely many women and African American men). Policies such as Social Security and fair labor standards, for example, excluded large categories of workers (particularly domestic and farm workers), which meant that women and black male workers tended not to be covered by the new national umbrella of social protection.[27] And federal housing programs discriminated against African Americans through practices such as redlining (systematically rating heavily black neighborhoods as high risk for mortgages) that promoted discriminatory lending, reinforced local segregation, and amplified inequality.[28] For all these programs did to shore up the foundations of the American economy, they excluded many based on race and gender from the full meaning of American democratic citizenship.

Having provided immediate relief and longer-term protections to at least some Americans, the New Deal moved on to restructuring and regulating the economy in order to prevent future economic collapses. Some of these attempts would be short-lived, struck down by the Supreme Court as exceeding constitutional limits on the federal government's authority. But others would become the foundation of the modern administrative and regulatory state. For example, the Banking Act of 1933 (known as the Glass-Steagall Act, after its chief congressional sponsors) prohibited banks from engaging in especially risky and speculative investments and created the Federal Deposit Insurance Corporation to insure depositors' funds in case of bank failures. The government also moved to regulate the stock market and established the Securities and Exchange Commission (SEC) to enforce new financial market rules.[29] Together, these and other policies would help stabilize the economy and put the country on the road to recovery. Yet they came at a cost to the underpinnings of American democracy, as they advanced and helped to consolidate the presidency's expanding power.

## EXPANDING PRESIDENTIAL POWER

The New Deal also set in motion a process of executive aggrandizement that would make FDR and future presidents significantly more powerful than their predecessors and more able to resist challenges from the opposition.

To be sure, a number of earlier presidents—Jefferson, Jackson, Lincoln, Theodore Roosevelt, Wilson—had enlarged the power of the office. But few took this strategy as far as Franklin Roosevelt. He even previewed his intentions in his inaugural address. The kind of action the country needed, he said, "is feasible under the form of government which we have inherited from our ancestors. Our Constitution is so simple and practical that it is possible always to meet extraordinary needs by changes in emphasis and arrangement without loss of essential form."[30] He had every intention of enlisting Congress and the states in his plans for relief and recovery, according to the customary understanding of the constitutional order and the president's role in it.

But he was wary of Congress's tendency to dither and delay. "It is to be hoped," he said, "that the normal balance of Executive and legislative authority may be wholly adequate to meet the unprecedented task before us. But it may be that an unprecedented demand and need for undelayed action may call for temporary departure from that normal balance of public procedure." Should Congress not step up to its responsibilities, he declared, "I shall not evade the clear course of duty that will then confront me. I shall ask the Congress for the one remaining instrument to meet the crisis—broad Executive power to wage a war against the emergency, as great as the power that would be given to me if we were in fact invaded by a foreign foe."[31] Roosevelt leaned on the specter of a national emergency to assert his right, indeed his duty, to assume commanding power in the interests of protecting democracy, a move that might be recognizable to democratically elected leaders elsewhere with autocratic aspirations.[32]

Roosevelt did not seize power as a dictator might, with military force. Rather, he dramatically expanded the power of the presidency through the regular constitutional processes of legislation. This expansion happened in three ways.

### DIRECT PRESIDENTIAL AUTHORITY

First, Congress granted the president direct policymaking authority. An important example of the expansion of presidential policy authority is trade policy, a realm in which Congress had utterly failed in the years before Roosevelt took office. In 1930, Congress had passed the disastrous

Tariff Act, better known by the names of its chief sponsors, Senator Reed Smoot of Utah and Representative Willis Hawley of Oregon. After the Depression began, pressure rose on the government to raise tariffs on imports in order to protect American agriculture and industry from foreign competition, which Smoot, Hawley, Hoover, and their allies believed would promote economic recovery. But as the bill moved through Congress, the inexorable logic of congressional policymaking took hold. Members of Congress, eager to promote the economic interests of their constituents, began advocating for tariffs to protect favored industries that were concentrated in their districts. The benefits of a tariff are highly concentrated on the industry it protects, while its costs—for example, in higher prices—are widely dispersed and thus almost invisible.

Following this logic, many industries large and small lobbied Congress for tariff protection, from the "humble buckwheat industry" of New York (they were successful) to the producers of live goldfish and canned sardines (they were not). Congress loaded up the Smoot-Hawley bill with very precise and sometimes comical tariffs—not just on major industrial and agricultural products such as steel, automobiles, soybeans, and wheat but also on products as diverse as fountain pens, pencil lead, combs, toothpicks, and violins and other stringed instruments (but only those made after 1800). In all, Smoot-Hawley raised tariffs on nearly nine hundred products and increased tariff levels an average of 20 percent.[33]

Many recognized that Smoot-Hawley would restrict trade and limit economic growth. More than one thousand economists signed a letter to Hoover imploring him to veto the bill; Thomas Lamont, the influential J. P. Morgan partner, recalled that he "almost went down on my knees to beg Herbert Hoover to veto the asinine Hawley-Smoot Tariff."[34] Hoover signed the bill anyway.

To many, including Roosevelt, Smoot-Hawley represented not just an economic calamity but also a profound political failure. Hoover's inability to control Congress or stand up to special interests provoked particular scorn. "For some reason, which is beyond the scope of ordinary explaining," wrote Walter Lippmann, "he surrendered everything for nothing. He gave up the leadership of his party. He let his personal authority be flouted. He accepted a wretched and mischievous product of stupidity and greed."[35]

The lesson Roosevelt learned was that Congress could not be trusted with critical policy areas where their parochial tendencies to promote local interests would undermine the national interest. Instead, he sought a way to make trade policy that would stymie Congress's ability to resist his choices. To replace Smoot-Hawley, he promoted the Reciprocal Trade Agreements Act (RTAA), which he signed into law in 1934. This law, whose principles remain the basis of national trade policy today, empowered the president to negotiate tariff agreements with other countries without congressional approval and gave him unilateral power to adjust tariffs as he saw fit. The RTAA utterly flipped the trade script by taking Congress almost entirely out of the tariff-writing game and giving the president direct authority over a critical area of policy, authority that Roosevelt—and most subsequent presidents—regularly used, usually (but not always) to lower tariffs and liberalize trade.[36]

Roosevelt's opponents regarded the RTAA's expansion of presidential power as dangerous not just to trade policy but also to American democracy. None was more excoriating than Republican representative Hamilton Fish (who represented Roosevelt's home in Hyde Park, New York). "Thomas Jefferson would turn in his grave," Fish said, "at the thought of transferring such autocratic and despotic taxing powers to the Chief Executive. . . . President Roosevelt evidently is not concerned with either the Constitution or our representative form of government."[37] This move was the essence of executive aggrandizement: perfectly legal and proper, and designed to make the president's power more secure and less susceptible to opposition.

## CONGRESS DELEGATES AUTHORITY TO THE PRESIDENT

Besides granting direct policymaking authority to the president, the New Deal dramatically expanded presidential power by increasing the size and scope of the federal bureaucracy as well as its independence from Congress. The policy challenges facing the federal government were increasingly complex. Previously, Congress itself had tended to write detailed policies to address these problems and then rely on the executive branch to carry out its instructions, as in the case of Smoot-Hawley. But as the federal government became increasingly involved in complex relief, recovery, and regulatory issues on a previously unimaginable scale,

Congress quickly reached the limit of its ability to prescribe and manage these policies with any precision.

Instead, Congress began to *delegate* its authority to the president. Instead of writing detailed specifications into law, Congress would authorize an executive branch department or agency to take control of the policy within Congress's guidelines. (This was not as complete a grant of authority as in trade policy, where the president was essentially given carte blanche.) The agency could then write precise rules and regulations that had the force of law and make key decisions about important policy matters, all of which could directly affect the lives and livelihoods of citizens, and all without explicit congressional approval. As the political scientist Theodore Lowi described this system of delegation: "Modern law has become a series of instructions to administrators rather than a series of commands to citizens."[38]

Not only was the executive branch supposed to do more, but there was much more of it. The everyday administrative work of the executive branch soon dominated the federal government, and the basic routines of individual and corporate life came increasingly to involve encounters with the federal bureaucracy. Individual citizens claimed new unemployment or Social Security benefits, public corporations made regular financial disclosures to the new SEC, and labor unions applied for recognition to the National Labor Relations Board.[39] For the first time, almost all Americans found that the federal government had a direct and visible impact on their lives. As the New Deal unfolded and Congress approved a host of new policies and programs, the size of the executive branch grew dramatically. In 1933, when Roosevelt assumed office, there were fewer than 600,000 civilian employees of the executive branch; by 1941, on the eve of American entry into World War II, there were more than 1.4 million. Federal government expenditures nearly tripled during the same period, from $4.7 billion in 1933 to $14 billion in 1941.[40]

STRENGTHENING PRESIDENTIAL MANAGEMENT

Finally, the president acquired greater capacity to control what the government does. As the bureaucracy grew, so did the president's managerial responsibilities. But when Roosevelt assumed office, the White House staff consisted of only three assistants along with several dozen clerks and secretaries who managed schedules, document flow, and the like.[41] Roosevelt managed to augment this staff with another hundred or so people he borrowed from other federal agencies, but it quickly became clear that without substantial changes, the White House staff would be a stumbling block for the president as he struggled to manage the exponentially growing business of the federal government.

At the same time, Congress seemed equally unable to manage the government's affairs. Congressional management seemed prone to the kind of highly localized representation and "logrolling" that characterized the Smoot-Hawley tariff. In place of direct congressional management, Roosevelt sought a more streamlined executive-led approach, which would both give him greater control and allow the government to be run according to the emerging standards of scientific management, which were supposed to stand above the dirty business of politics and apart from representative democracy.[42]

In 1936, Roosevelt appointed a Committee on Administrative Management to make recommendations about how to improve the management of the executive branch and in particular how to ensure that the president had the resources, information, and advice he needed to run the government effectively.[43] The Brownlow Committee (so called after its chairman, Louis Brownlow, of the University of Chicago) issued its report in January 1937. "The President needs help," the report famously began. It recommended that the president be given a more ample staff, starting with up to six executive assistants, who should be people "in whom the President has personal confidence and whose character and attitude is such that they would not attempt to exercise power on their own account. They should be possessed of high competence, great physical vigor, and a passion for anonymity." The Brownlow Committee also recommended a number of sweeping reforms to give the president more concentrated authority over the executive branch and its increasingly far-flung activities, at Congress's expense, including the authority to reorganize the executive branch.[44]

Around the same time, Roosevelt also advanced a scheme to expand presidential control of another key government institution: the Supreme Court. For four years, the Court had frustrated his attempts at reform by declaring key New Deal enactments unconstitutional. In one critical decision, Chief Justice Charles Evans Hughes declared outright that "Congress cannot delegate legislative power to the President to exercise an unfettered discretion to make whatever laws he thinks may be needed or advisable."[45] This blow threatened the entire New Deal agenda, which depended on the ability to expand executive power through precisely this approach.

In the 1936 election, Roosevelt won reelection in an even bigger landslide than his 1932 triumph. (His opponent, Governor Alf Landon of Kansas, won only two states, Maine and Vermont, for a total of eight electoral votes.) Exasperated with the Supreme Court's obstructionism, Roosevelt and his allies began to refer to the justices derisively as "nine old men" and began casting about for a solution to the Court problem.[46] They were not altogether wrong in their characterization; the justices' average age was seventy-one, and six of the nine were older than seventy. He could not force these older justices to retire; under the Constitution, their appointments were for life.

Instead, he proposed a plan to "pack" the Court. Court-packing—filling courts with political loyalists—is a notorious "constitutional hardball" tactic. While often perfectly legal, it enables leaders to stack the political deck in their favor and solidify their power. In February 1937, Roosevelt asked Congress to pass a bill that would have empowered the president to appoint an additional justice for each sitting justice who remained on the Court after reaching age seventy. This would have allowed him to appoint six new justices immediately, which would certainly have unblocked the Court's obstruction of the New Deal. But the firestorm of criticism to Roosevelt's plan was swift and furious; it came from both parties and across the political spectrum. Roosevelt eventually backed down, which was an easier pill for him to swallow after the Court changed its tune and upheld a state minimum wage law in March, signaling a new receptiveness to the New Deal approach to law and policy.[47] (Justice Willis Van Devanter, one of the "four horsemen" of the Court's hard-core conservative wing, retired in June, further advancing the Court's pro–New Deal drift. By the time Roosevelt died in 1945, he had appointed eight of the Court's nine members because of deaths and retirements.)

The Brownlow Committee issued its recommendations for greater presidential capacity in the middle of the court-packing controversy, and

OLIVER TWIST

5.2  Franklin Roosevelt, as Oliver Twist, asks Congress for more power, 1937

taken together, the two proposals looked to many of Roosevelt's opponents like a presidential power grab. Roosevelt's opponents, emboldened by the court-packing fight, tore into the Brownlow proposal, likening Roosevelt's desire to consolidate presidential power to the spirit driving the fascist regimes in Europe. "We have just witnessed, in Europe, what happens when one man is permitted too much power—Hitler in Austria," wrote one critic. Harold Ickes, the secretary of the interior and a close advisor, warned Roosevelt that the American public was increasingly inclined "to unconsciously group four names, Hitler, Stalin, Mussolini and Roosevelt." Roosevelt's offhanded public statement that "I have no inclination to be a dictator" only fanned the flames of opposition.[48] An editorial cartoon published in the *Chicago Tribune* (see above) depicted Roosevelt as Oliver Twist asking for more power, which a bedraggled Congress willingly dishes out.

In late March 1938, Father Coughlin, the right-wing radio priest, roused his millions of listeners to oppose the reorganization plan, and tens of thousands of telegrams flooded members of Congress, overtaxing both the Post Office and Western Union, which struggled to keep up with the flow of messages. Not satisfied with the telegram campaign, Coughlin then urged groups of his followers to travel to Washington "like modern Paul Reveres whose business will be to . . . rouse from slumber their respective Representative and Senator" and insist that they oppose what he portrayed as President Roosevelt's power grab. On April 5, twenty-five hundred opponents of the bill gathered for a rally in the Hippodrome in New York City, and by April 7, a delegation of several thousand (which included Paul Revere's actual great-great-granddaughter) assembled in Washington to lobby members of Congress against the reorganization bill.[49]

Congress defeated the full Brownlow Committee reorganization proposal, but in 1939 it passed a scaled-back Reorganization Act. The act gave Roosevelt his six assistants as well as broad (but limited) presidential authority to reorganize the federal government. Under this authority, Roosevelt promulgated several reorganization plans that rationalized and consolidated some of the administrative sprawl that had occurred over the previous six years. Most significantly, he created the Executive Office of the President, which brought the influential Bureau of the Budget out of the Treasury Department and directly under presidential control. Together, these reforms paved the way for much more active and intrusive presidential control over the federal government's day-to-day activities than had ever been possible before.

## A NEW PRESIDENCY?

The expansion of both the size and scope of government raised the American people's expectations about what the government could and would do for them. However, the growing powers of the president also focused attention on Roosevelt as the one figure in the political system able to deliver what the American people needed. This meant that Roosevelt alone would either win credit or shoulder blame.[50] This shift planted the seed for another important dimension of executive aggrandizement: under these circumstances, opposing the president could be seen as tantamount to confronting the people themselves.

Roosevelt himself was thoroughly in his element as the embodiment of the federal government and the center of public attention. He was an extraordinary communicator and a master of using new technology—radio, in his case—to reach the mass public and create a personal connection with them, unfiltered by the press.[51] Roosevelt was not the only popular leader of his era to master the radio as a tool of popular communication. Hitler and Mussolini, too, used the radio airwaves very effectively to build their mass constituencies and project themselves as the voice of their people (although with very different effects).

This skill was especially apparent in his fireside chats. Beginning in the second week of his presidency and continuing through the week after the D-Day invasion in June 1944, Roosevelt gave regular radio addresses to the American people. He spoke simply and directly, as if he were gathered with family or friends around the fire. "As he talked," recalled Frances Perkins, a longtime aide who served as secretary of labor, "his head would nod and his hands would move in simple, natural, comfortable gestures. His face would smile and light up as though he were actually sitting on the front porch or in the parlor with them."[52] Roosevelt's skill at conveying intimacy over the airwaves created an unusual sense of affectionate familiarity between him and the public.

An estimated forty million Americans listened to the first broadcast. Citizens responded by flooding the president with letters in unprecedented numbers, reflecting both their sense of intimacy with the president and the depth and scope of their hopes, needs, and expectations.[53]

But this apparent personal connection between the president and the public, coupled with the presidency's growing power and institutional resources, can create dangers as well. It amplifies demands on the presidency. Presidents, especially since Roosevelt, enter office with the enormous weight of public expectations on their shoulders. Even with the growing resources of the presidency, presidents repeatedly find themselves unable to measure up to the demands of citizens, and they find it increasingly appealing to look for ways to bypass the normal routines of government and act unilaterally. Finally, such a connection encourages the public to look to a single leader for salvation in hard times, and it further emboldens presidents to think of themselves in this light.

## ROOSEVELT, NATIONAL SECURITY, AND THE TOOLS OF PRESIDENTIAL POWER

Nowhere was the temptation to take on this role of national savior greater, for Roosevelt and his successors alike, than in the realms of foreign policy and national security.

A long history well predates Franklin Roosevelt of presidents asserting vigorous and often unchecked power in foreign and military affairs. The conflict over slavery in the territories in the 1850s, for example, arose largely because President James K. Polk deployed both the army and the diplomatic corps under his direction to maneuver the country into a war of conquest with Mexico. During the Civil War, President Lincoln used his war powers to emancipate slaves, but also to declare martial law and suspend the right of habeas corpus in order to suppress wartime dissent. (The latter two acts were ultimately invalidated by the Supreme Court, although not until the war was over and Lincoln was dead.)[54]

Presidential concern about domestic dissent only grew in the twentieth century. During and after World War I, and especially after the Bolshevik Revolution in Russia in 1917, President Woodrow Wilson was particularly worried about subversion at home. In April 1919, a series of several dozen mail bombs targeting government and business leaders were intercepted, setting off a "Red scare" and providing a pretext for a crackdown on suspected radicals. Attorney General A. Mitchell Palmer ordered a series of raids on radical individuals and organizations. The raids—led by a twenty-five-year-old Justice Department lawyer named J. Edgar Hoover—were carried out on January 2, 1920. They were concentrated in the teeming industrial cities of the East, and particularly in immigrant communities. Several thousand people were arrested and hundreds were deported. The newly formed American Civil Liberties Union later published a widely read "Report on the Illegal Practices of the United States Department of Justice" that carefully documented unlawful tactics and improper detention, among other problems. President Wilson ultimately admonished Palmer, who was hauled before a Senate subcommittee to testify about "illegal practices."[55] But the episode marked a substantial step forward for the government's capacity to harm its perceived political opponents.

The government took another step in this direction in the early 1920s during the administration of Warren G. Harding. In what became known as the Teapot Dome scandal, Secretary of the Interior Albert B. Fall received large bribes from several oil companies in return for authorization to drill on federal land. Once the scheme was exposed in 1922, the Senate began an investigation, led by Senators Robert La Follette Sr. (a Republican) and Thomas Walsh (a Democrat). Attorney General Harry Daugherty was a close political associate of Harding's (part of the "Ohio Gang," a group of cronies, many corrupt, who surrounded Harding through his unlikely political rise). Under Daugherty's direction, Bureau of Investigation director William J. Burns deployed his agents to "investigate" Senators La Follette and Walsh, among others, mostly as a pretext for blackmailing them into curtailing their own investigations of Fall and company.[56]

Fall, who became wealthy with his ill-gotten oil money, was ultimately convicted of bribery. After the resulting scandal and following Harding's death in 1923, both Daugherty and Burns resigned. Burns opened a private detective agency, which was subsequently hired to "investigate"— that is, harass—the jurors in the trial of one of the oil company executives who had bribed Fall, in order to try to secure his acquittal. The man who replaced Burns at the head of the Bureau of Investigation on May 10, 1924, was J. Edgar Hoover, then twenty-nine. Hoover, of course, went on to serve as director of what later became the Federal Bureau of Investigation under eight presidents until he died in 1972.

Building on the experience the government had gained in operations such as the Palmer Raids and the Teapot Dome investigation, Franklin Roosevelt inherited a growing security and surveillance capacity in the executive branch. During his presidency, he explicitly joined presidential authority to this emerging national security apparatus. The story of how this happened begins with a bootlegger.

Roy Olmstead, a former Seattle police lieutenant, was convicted during Prohibition of importing illegal liquor into the United States from Canada. The basis for his conviction was evidence obtained through wiretaps installed, without a warrant, on his home and office telephones. Olmstead appealed his conviction on the grounds that the wiretap evidence violated his constitutional rights to be protected from unreasonable searches and self-incrimination. In 1928, the Supreme Court upheld

Olmstead's conviction, ruling that government wiretapping was constitutional because listening to a conversation, even clandestinely, was not the same as a "search."[57]

Wiretapping technology had emerged in the mid-nineteenth century as a means to intercept telegraph communication, and it was used during the Civil War as a tool of military intelligence. As the telephone came into widespread use in the late nineteenth century, the technology proved useful for covertly listening in on phone conversations, and its effectiveness for both law enforcement and monitoring politically suspect activity soon grew clear. But wiretapping also sparked controversy. Civil liberties advocates objected that it was a violation of privacy, while law enforcement officials countered that the ends justified the means. In 1924 Attorney General Harlan Fiske Stone prohibited the Justice Department from using it; the Bureau of Investigation's rules specifically called it an "unethical practice." By the time Olmstead's case reached the Supreme Court in 1928, Stone, by then a justice, dissented along with Justice Louis Brandeis, whose sharply worded opinion stated that "in a government of laws, existence of the government will be imperiled if it fails to observe the law scrupulously."[58]

In 1934, Congress passed the Communications Act of 1934, which regulated the telephone business and established the Federal Communications Commission (FCC) as the federal government's watchdog over the relatively new telecommunications industry. Among other things, the act protected unsuspecting telephone users from wiretapping by making it a federal crime to "divulge or publish" the contents of any intercepted telephone conversations, which would render wiretapping useless as a law enforcement tool. Under this provision of the new law, the evidence that had been used to convict Roy Olmstead would not have been allowed.

Roosevelt, meanwhile, who was increasingly worried about the threat of Nazi (and, to a lesser extent, communist) subversion in the United States, desperately sought intelligence about fascist activities. FBI director J. Edgar Hoover was willing to provide the intelligence the president sought, and Attorney General Homer Cummings reversed Stone's prohibition on wiretapping.[59]

But twice, in 1937 and 1939, the Supreme Court ruled that evidence obtained through wiretapping was inadmissible in court and that in ordinary circumstances wiretapping amounted to a violation of civil liberties. (It was in the second of these decisions that Justice Felix Frankfurter coined the phrase "fruit of the poisonous tree," familiar to watchers of television crime dramas today, to describe any evidence obtained as the result of an illegal act.)[60]

In 1940, in the wake of these decisions, Roosevelt's new attorney general, Robert H. Jackson, grew queasy about the continuing use of wiretapping by the government, whether for political intelligence or criminal evidence. In March 1940, Jackson reinstated the Justice Department's ban on wiretapping.[61]

At that moment, the United States sat uneasily on the sidelines of the European war that had begun the previous fall. Roosevelt's appetite for intelligence had only grown more voracious. And J. Edgar Hoover was not at all happy with the shackles that Jackson's order placed on his agents. Hoover approached Secretary of the Treasury Henry Morgenthau, Roosevelt's close friend and neighbor in upstate New York, and asked him to intercede with the president. A member of a leading Jewish American family, Morgenthau was especially concerned with stopping Nazism in Europe and undercutting Nazi activity in the United States.[62]

When Morgenthau carried Hoover's concerns to Roosevelt, the response was swift and crystal clear: "Tell Bob Jackson to send for J. Edgar Hoover and order him to do it and a written memorandum will follow."[63]

The next day, May 21, the president signed a secret memorandum to the attorney general authorizing wiretaps for political purposes. "I am convinced," the memo stated, "that the Supreme Court never intended any dictum in the particular case which it decided to apply to grave matters involving the defense of the nation. It is, of course, well known that certain other nations have been engaged in the organization of propaganda of so-called 'fifth columns' in other countries and in preparation for sabotage, as well as in actual sabotage." In light of this danger, Roosevelt authorized the attorney general (and, through him, the FBI) to wiretap the communications of people suspected of subversive activity.[64] Finally, the memo "requested" (but did not demand) that such investigations be kept to a minimum and focused primarily on non-Americans rather than on American citizens.

The Roosevelt memo gave Hoover explicit authorization from the president of the United States to spy almost without restraint on politically suspect Americans.[65] The burgeoning national security apparatus, which would grow by leaps after the United States entered World War II and then faced off against the Soviet Union in a decades-long cold war, was now intimately tied to the president's power.

## CONCLUSION: TOWARD THE IMPERIAL PRESIDENCY

That the political turmoil of the 1930s brought the perpetuation of democracy marked a considerable achievement in a dark decade that saw the destruction of democracy elsewhere in the world. We rightly remember Franklin Roosevelt as a leader who effectively steered American democracy through two major crises. He did so by pursuing the expansion of executive power as an answer to the crises of democracy and capitalism. Roosevelt's firm assertion of executive power helped democracy flourish, both globally and at home; in many ways, the New Deal deepened democracy, as the federal government began to protect social rights and labor rights more vigorously than before.

But along with these accomplishments, Roosevelt's presidency brought with it the burgeoning of a new threat to democracy's future: the power of the presidency itself. Judiciously used, the tools of executive power can help presidents manage complex problems of governance and respond quickly to emergencies. But they can also become weapons that enable a president to wield executive power on his own behalf or for partisan gain.

Unlike Lincoln's wartime powers, Roosevelt's expansion of presidential power would prove to be not just durable but also further expandable. Roosevelt's skillful leadership and crisis management reveal how effective executive power can be at solving real problems and overcoming representative democracy's tendency toward paralysis. But it also opened the door not only to heightened conflict between the president and Congress but also to the temptation on the part of presidents to use their growing power to stifle the opposition and undermine democracy.

And, as in the 1790s and the 1890s, the outcome of the crisis came at the expense of progress toward a more inclusive society and by perpetuating exclusion along the lines of American society's "formative rift": the color line.

As executive power was expanding, the other three threats were at relative low points. Polarization continued to abate as the economy revived, the United States fought and won a world war, and the Democratic Party surged to a generation of political dominance. Economic inequality began to diminish when the Great Depression set in, and it continued its decline as the New Deal took hold, the war stimulated the economy, and prosperity resumed. And conflict over the boundaries of membership remained relatively muted (mostly because white supremacy ruled).

For the remainder of Roosevelt's presidency, he directed his newfound power almost entirely to fighting World War II, which the United States entered after the Japanese attack on Pearl Harbor in December 1941. The war brought about an even more dramatic expansion of the federal government than the New Deal, both to direct the war effort and to regulate the civilian economy and society through rationing, price controls, taxation, and sales of war bonds, among other things.

In some instances, Roosevelt put his presidential power to use in ways that advanced democracy. For example, in 1941, Roosevelt established by executive order the Fair Employment Practice Committee (FEPC) to promote equal opportunity and combat racial discrimination in war industries; two years later, he strengthened the FEPC's mandate and brought it into the White House, directly under presidential control.[66]

But Roosevelt's power also took the country in more ominous directions during the war. Just months after Pearl Harbor, Roosevelt ordered the removal of people of Japanese ancestry from large swaths of the country, mostly on the West Coast, on the grounds that many were likely to be agents of an enemy nation and potential spies or saboteurs. As a result of Roosevelt's order, more than one hundred thousand people, most of them American citizens, were forcibly evacuated from their homes and confined to euphemistically named relocation centers for the duration of the war.

Roosevelt and his advisors were well aware that this order was constitutionally dubious; some, such as Attorney General Francis Biddle and even FBI director Hoover, opposed it as unnecessary and ill-advised. But Assistant Secretary of War John J. McCloy expressed Roosevelt's view: "If it is a question of safety of country or the Constitution of the United States, why the Constitution is just a scrap of paper to me." Unlike Lincoln's wartime declaration of martial law, Roosevelt's order was upheld by the Supreme Court in a decision that was not repudiated until 2018.[67]

When the war ended in the summer of 1945, the Allies, mostly a coalition of democracies, had defeated the fascist regimes of the Axis powers and succeeded in keeping the world safe for democracy. Many of the core attributes of American democracy had been preserved; free and fair elections, the legitimacy of the opposition, and the rule of law all survived.

Yet the New Deal and World War II simultaneously imperiled the integrity of rights, even while defending them. The internment of Japanese Americans overtly and directly violated civil liberties and civil rights. The burgeoning national security apparatus gave the federal government new capacity to monitor ordinary citizens in ways that curtailed their civil liberties. New social rights underscored the administration's repeated compromises on racial and gender inclusion. Moreover, African Americans who had fought for their country against the racist regimes of Germany and Japan returned home to a country that remained segregated.

And when Franklin Roosevelt died, just three months into his unprecedented fourth presidential term, he left behind a transformed presidency that now possessed immense power, which his successors would wield to combat the totalitarian ally-turned-antagonist, the Soviet Union, in a cold war that would dominate the rest of the century.

But that new executive power represented not only a weapon against a foreign adversary. It would also prove to be a threat to democracy at home.

# 6

## The Weaponized Presidency in the 1970s

Shortly after midnight on June 17, 1972, an overnight security guard named Frank Wills noticed something amiss in the Watergate office complex in Washington, DC. While making his nightly rounds, he came upon a series of doors to the parking garage that had been propped open with paper. At first he thought nothing of it—he locked the doors, recorded the incident in his logbook, and moved along. But when he returned shortly before 2:00 a.m., he found the doors unlocked again, this time with tape used to prevent them from locking.

Now suspicious, Wills called the District of Columbia Metropolitan Police. The nearest uniformed officers responded to the police dispatcher that they were busy putting gas in their squad car (although they were, in fact, drinking at a nearby bar), so three plainclothes officers soon arrived on the scene in an unmarked car, without lights or sirens.

At the same time a man named Alfred Baldwin was sitting in room 723 of the Howard Johnson's Motor Lodge across Virginia Avenue. He had been posted there as a lookout while his accomplices inside the Watergate finished their job. But he had become too absorbed in a late-night TV broadcast of *Attack of the Puppet People* to notice the officers' arrival.

The officers climbed to the sixth floor, found more doors taped open, and drew their guns. Not until they made their way onto a balcony directly across from his room did Baldwin notice their presence. Confused by the sight, he radioed his accomplices inside the Watergate to ask if their team was wearing "hippie clothes." No, the answer came back; they had on suits and ties. Were they carrying guns? asked Baldwin. Again the answer was no; the burglars were unarmed. In that case, Baldwin concluded, they had a problem.

It was too late. Within minutes, the police officers arrested five men for breaking into the headquarters of the Democratic National Committee (DNC). Indeed clad in business suits, the burglars were carrying wiretapping equipment, tear gas canisters, film, large amounts of cash in consecutively numbered bills—and an address book containing the telephone number of E. Howard Hunt, a former CIA operative who was working as a consultant for the White House. Hunt had recruited the burglars from among his former CIA associates; several had connections to anti-Castro forces in Cuba and the ill-fated 1961 Bay of Pigs invasion. At the moment the five men were arrested, Hunt was personally directing the operation, on behalf of President Richard Nixon's reelection campaign, by walkie-talkie from the adjacent Watergate Hotel. (It is still not known who ordered the burglary.)

On Monday morning, June 19, White House press secretary Ron Ziegler dismissed the break-in to reporters as a "third-rate burglary attempt." But Hunt and his burglars were so closely connected to the president's reelection campaign that by the next morning, emerging links between the break-in and the White House were headline news on the front page of the *Washington Post*. Soon the FBI was investigating as well.

President Nixon grew increasingly alarmed by what might be uncovered. On June 23, Nixon's chief of staff, H. R. Haldeman, told him that the FBI had traced the money used to pay the Watergate burglars back to Nixon's reelection campaign and that this trail of evidence could lead straight to the president's closest circles. Even worse, L. Patrick Gray, the inexperienced Nixon loyalist who had been named acting director of the FBI after J. Edgar Hoover's recent death, was proving unable to steer the bureau's investigation away from the White House.

Desperate to conceal White House involvement with the break-in, Haldeman and Nixon concocted a scheme in which the CIA would ward off the FBI from investigating further by claiming that it was a matter of national security, citing the burglars' Cuban connections to give the claim an air of plausibility. Yet as Nixon and Haldeman plotted, their every word was captured for posterity by an automatic recording system that Nixon had had installed in the Oval Office the previous year. Even though the recording would remain concealed from the public for more than two years, Watergate soon metastasized into a scandal of unprecedented proportions.

At the heart of Watergate was President Nixon's sustained pattern of attempts to rig the political system in his favor. He sought nothing less than to "weaponize" the presidency: to wield its power and the resources of the national security state to punish his enemies and advance his own political fortunes. When Nixon took office in 1969, he found a large and powerful executive-branch apparatus at his disposal. Between the beginning of World War II and 1969, the executive branch doubled in size (from 1.4 million employees to 2.9 million) and federal expenditures grew fivefold, even when accounting for inflation (from $35 billion to $185 billion in 1969 dollars).[1] In particular, World War II and the Cold War saw the creation of a large and seemingly permanent national security state, including a consolidated Department of Defense, expanded intelligence services (encompassing the Central Intelligence Agency and the National Security Agency, among other agencies), and the National Security Council, which enabled presidents to consolidate and expand their control over defense and intelligence activities.

Nixon did not hesitate to use this apparatus as his own personal political weapon, often through criminal means. Frank Wills's discovery on the night of June 17, 1972, set off a chain of events that not only engulfed what remained of Nixon's presidency but also precipitated a constitutional confrontation that threatened free and fair elections, civil liberties, and the rule of law. Above all, Watergate revealed the dangers to a democracy of unchecked executive power.

❖

The Watergate affair signaled the maturation of the weaponized presidency, which grew out of the expansion of executive power that had begun in the early twentieth century, taken shape in Franklin Roosevelt's presidency, and accelerated since World War II. In the latter part of the twentieth century, the weaponized presidency bolstered and reinforced the idea of politics as mortal combat—the idea that political rivals were not just opponents but enemies to be vanquished. What reemerged was the antidemocratic notion—reminiscent of the 1790s, the 1850s, and the 1890s—that disagreement equaled disloyalty and that compromise meant defeat.

Since the earliest years of the republic, presidents have sought to use their power for political advantage; Franklin Roosevelt certainly did so even as he was stretching presidential power during the Depression. But the presidency's new powers have raised the stakes of this game and increasingly enabled presidents to act in dictatorial ways.[2] And in the last half of the twentieth century this lethal combination raised the very real specter of American authoritarianism.

In particular, the perceived risks of espionage and subversion during the Cold War dramatically expanded the president's authority in the realm of national security and led the government to expand its efforts to attack political dissent. These efforts ranged from the scare tactics of Senator Joseph McCarthy and the efforts of the House Committee on Un-American Activities to the FBI's extensive COINTELPRO (government-speak for COunter INTELligence PROgram) project, which used a range of suspect and downright illegal clandestine activities to target supposedly subversive elements in American society. COINTELPRO's targets famously included Martin Luther King Jr., who in 1964 received an anonymous letter, actually written by an FBI agent, threatening to reveal his extramarital activities and urging him to kill himself.[3]

When Richard Nixon ran for president in 1968, the Republican Party was on the ropes. Nixon and his supporters hoped that he could lead his party back to competitiveness in national elections, and in order to do this he pursued a political strategy aimed at sharpening the perceived differences between the parties and expanding electoral opportunities for Republicans.

Nixon's challenge was that his election came at a low ebb for both political polarization and economic inequality in the United States. Americans were more economically equal in the late 1960s than at any other time in the twentieth century, the result of a postwar era of shared prosperity. And although Republicans were generally the party of business and Democrats the party of labor, low inequality tended to mute political conflict.

Political polarization also hovered at historically low levels in the post–World War II decades. Democrats remained divided between a more conservative, white supremacist southern wing and a more liberal northern wing, while Republicans were also more ideologically diverse than today. In 1950, an expert panel of political scientists lamented that there was not enough polarization in American politics—that American parties offered voters very little real choice and frustrated attempts to hold parties accountable for the actions of the government. And because the Democrats were the clear majority party, Republicans often followed a strategy of accommodation rather than partisan confrontation.[4]

But the politics of partisan compromise became more perilous during the 1960s. In the wake of the advances of the civil rights and women's movements of the 1960s, the United States had evolved, as least formally, into a more egalitarian democracy than ever.[5] At the same time, many Americans saw these changes as a threat to an older era of segregation and white male dominance, a threat that was underscored for them by a wave of violence in cities around the country as African Americans protested decades of segregation, inequality, and ill-treatment.

In campaigning and governing, Nixon set out to exploit these growing divisions over race and provoke confrontations on issues that could divide voters along racial lines. He stoked these grievances to win over white voters around the country. He actively pursued a "southern strategy," appealing to southern white voters on issues such as "law and order" and opposition to school busing, to signal that he was sympathetic to their resentment over national action on civil rights. He launched a "war on drugs" that would wreak decades of havoc and destruction on communities of color. Nixon aide John Ehrlichman spelled out this stance bluntly decades later. The Nixon administration, he said, "had two enemies: the antiwar left and black people.... We couldn't make it illegal to be either against the war or black, but by getting the public to associate the hippies with marijuana and blacks with heroin, and then criminalizing both heavily, we could disrupt those communities."[6]

Nixon also channeled many middle American voters' resentment toward cultural elites. In a nationally broadcast speech on November 3, 1969, he explicitly appealed to what he called the "silent majority" of Americans who did not demonstrate or protest but embodied a different set of values that seemed to be under attack by cultural and political currents. Nixon's strategy of tapping into and amplifying racially charged resentment against suspect elites worked. Following the speech, letters and telegrams streamed into the White House by the thousands and Nixon's approval rating spiked to the highest point it would reach in his entire presidency.[7]

## DOMESTIC DISSENT AND GOVERNMENT SURVEILLANCE

When Nixon took the presidential oath in January 1969, the Vietnam War was going badly, and it would soon get worse. Nearly forty thousand Americans had already been killed in the conflict, and it was becoming apparent that the United States could not win. As public opinion increasingly favored peace, the administration's bloody escalations of the war were met with a rising tide of protest at home. Primary challenges from antiwar candidates Senators Eugene McCarthy and Robert Kennedy had driven President Lyndon Johnson into retirement. Now, antiwar protests grew in scope and scale. Unrest on campuses increased as well, posing broader challenges to the establishment. The American invasion of Cambodia in the spring of 1970 provoked even more vociferous protest that was occasionally met with violence. On May 4, the Ohio National Guard shot and killed four unarmed student protesters at Kent State University, escalating the cycle of outrage, protest, and reaction.

The antiwar movement's militancy alarmed Nixon, but the administration felt constrained in its efforts to meet this challenge. Five years earlier, in response to increased public and congressional scrutiny of the FBI and its methods, longtime Bureau director J. Edgar Hoover had imposed severe restrictions on intelligence operations. At a 1965 Senate subcommittee hearing on questionable government surveillance, Hal Lipset, a private detective from San Francisco, had demonstrated the latest advances in bugging technology: Lipset sat at the witness table with what looked like a martini, only to reveal at the end of his testimony that the pimiento in what appeared to be the drink's olive was actually a listening device, while the toothpick that skewered the garnish contained a copper antenna. The incident drove home the government's growing technological capacity as well as the threat that new eavesdropping capabilities posed to Americans' civil liberties. The right to privacy and the idea of freedom from government intrusion had gained currency since the 1930s, and several Supreme Court decisions during this period also set limits on surveillance, striking down a New York law that allowed broad and unrestricted government wiretapping and directing that authorized wiretapping required a search warrant.[8]

Responding to heightened public attention to government intrusion during the 1960s, Hoover, always protective of the FBI's reputation, sought to reduce opportunities for public criticism. He curtailed COINTELPRO activities, prohibited break-ins, and limited interagency cooperation so that the FBI could not be held responsible for the illegal practices of other agencies. All CIA requests for FBI intelligence would now require approval from the attorney general. Alongside the implementation of these new policies, Hoover appointed William Sullivan, the FBI's head of domestic intelligence (the godfather of COINTELPRO and the purported author of the Martin Luther King Jr. "suicide letter"), to represent the FBI concerning FBI-CIA cooperation. But Sullivan and other top FBI officials—including Assistant Director W. Mark Felt— were frustrated by these new restrictions, which they felt hamstrung the bureau just as domestic radicalism was rising to dangerous levels.[9]

Nixon knew from his own campaigns, in which he had routinely smeared his opponents as radicals and communists, that surveillance and political espionage were highly useful tools to gather information about protest activities, provide evidence for disloyalty claims, and chip away at the democratic legitimacy of the opposition by insinuating that they were un-American. In Nixon's mind, and in the minds of many Americans, the line between antiwar protesters and agents of communist subversion was a fuzzy one. Nixon deliberately sought to exploit this presumed (but mostly imaginary) linkage to promote the idea that protesters were not a legitimate opposition but enemies of American power and values.

Soon the combination of Nixon's contempt for protesters, his appetite for intelligence, and the ambitions of two bureaucrats would lead to efforts to subvert the FBI's own safeguards against unlawful surveillance. A document that came to be known as the Huston Plan, ostensibly aimed at coordinating the government's intelligence activities, would propose a vast expansion of the president's power to attack those he perceived as

political enemies, and it set in motion a train of events that would ultimately consume Nixon's presidency and threaten the stability of American democracy.

## THE HUSTON PLAN: JOINING THE NATIONAL SECURITY STATE
## TO PRESIDENTIAL AMBITION

In April 1969, only three months into his first term, Nixon was already
frustrated by the growing power of student protest movements and paranoid about leaks coming from within his administration. Fed up with
a domestic intelligence apparatus that was unwilling to investigate student protesters with sufficient gusto, Nixon asked White House counsel
John Ehrlichman to prepare a report on "foreign Communist support of
campus demonstrations." A few weeks later, when the *New York Times*
revealed the covert American bombing campaign in Cambodia based
on information leaked from inside the administration, Nixon and his
national security advisor, Henry Kissinger, ordered the FBI to wiretap
dozens of government officials to try and find the leaker. Hoover assented, but demanded that the White House's requests for wiretaps be
documented in writing so that the FBI could avoid blame if the scheme
was revealed.[10]

As this was occurring, a young Nixon White House staffer, Thomas
Charles Huston, joined forces with Sullivan to expand the executive
branch's ability to conduct domestic surveillance. Although Huston
served formally on the speechwriting staff, one of his first White House
assignments, which came directly from the president, was to prepare a
report about radicals in the antiwar movement.[11] Huston met with Sullivan at the FBI and followed up with a memo requesting as much information as could be obtained about student protests. As he delved into
the subject, Huston learned more about the things that were stymieing
Nixon's goal of suppressing dissent, including long-standing rivalries and
conflicts among various intelligence agencies as well as Hoover's caution
in the face of public concerns.

Though united in their effort to reshape executive power, Huston and
Sullivan could hardly have made a more unlikely pair. Sullivan was rumpled and messy, unusual qualities in a bureau whose agents were required

to conform to punctilious standards of dress and grooming. "He looked," one journalist observed, "more like a farmer come to town for the day, uncomfortable in his city clothes and anxious to get back home." Unlike most agents, who came to the FBI steeped in law and criminology, Sullivan had aspired to be a professor and taught high school English in his Massachusetts hometown before joining the FBI from graduate school in 1941. As he rose through the ranks and took command of domestic counterintelligence, Sullivan developed a reputation as something of a renegade: a bit of a cowboy, an intellectual, even a liberal—the last a political anomaly in the largely conservative bureau.[12]

Huston, on the other hand, was a buttoned-down midwesterner. A lawyer who had led campus conservatives at Indiana University in the early 1960s and later served as an army intelligence officer, he was a committed acolyte of the conservative movement growing around figures such as William F. Buckley Jr. and Barry Goldwater. In 1965, Huston had been president of Young Americans for Freedom, a conservative activist organization that had been instrumental in buoying hard-liners like Goldwater over the Republican Party's moderate wing represented by Dwight Eisenhower, Nelson Rockefeller—and Richard Nixon. From there, Patrick Buchanan (described by one commentator as Nixon's "rottweiler") recruited him into Nixon's 1968 presidential campaign, overcoming Huston's skepticism about Nixon's conservative bona fides. Nixon's victory ushered Huston into a post at the White House, where his fierce anticommunism and his background in military intelligence set him up to serve as Nixon's point man on domestic counterintelligence—the new president's "favorite young dirty trickster," one historian has called him. One of Huston's functions was to oversee Internal Revenue Service investigations against organizations perceived as hostile to the administration; use of the IRS to harass people and organizations seen as politically suspect had, in fact, predated Nixon, but Nixon and Huston deployed the power of audits and investigations on an unprecedented scale.[13]

In spite of their divergent backgrounds and styles, Huston and Sullivan forged an alliance over their shared belief that domestic radicalism had reached dangerous levels and that the demands of national security outweighed legal concerns and constitutional restraints—a belief that Franklin Roosevelt had shared a generation earlier. In April 1970, Sullivan began to explore ways to increase the government's domestic intelligence capacity and relax Hoover's operational limitations.[14]

Around the same time, on Sullivan's recommendation and Huston's endorsement, the administration organized a meeting on June 5 between the president and the heads of the FBI, CIA, National Security Agency, and Defense Intelligence Agency (DIA), for the purpose of conveying Nixon's displeasure with the current state of domestic intelligence and spurring the agency heads into action. This high-level effort presented Huston and Sullivan with a golden opportunity to press their case for loosening the restrictions on government intelligence gathering. But in order to achieve this goal, Sullivan and Huston—and the president—faced a formidable adversary: J. Edgar Hoover himself.[15]

At the meeting, in remarks that were largely drafted by Huston, Nixon railed against "revolutionary terrorism" and told the chiefs in stark terms that he was unhappy with their collective work and wanted them to step up their domestic intelligence game. "We are now confronted," Huston's draft stated, "with a new and grave crisis in our country—one which we know too little about. Certainly hundreds, perhaps thousands, of Americans—mostly under 30—are determined to destroy our society." One of the agency participants, General Donald Bennett, director of the DIA, recalled that "the President chewed our butts."[16]

Following the June 5 meeting, the president appointed a committee of representatives from each intelligence agency to examine the surveillance challenge and make recommendations about how to improve domestic intelligence gathering. Although Sullivan had hoped to chair the committee, Nixon announced instead that Hoover would do so, and Huston would direct its staff.

The interagency committee met for the first time on June 8. As Huston had done for Nixon three days earlier, Sullivan prepared an opening statement for Hoover to read aloud. True to form, Hoover abandoned Sullivan's remarks and followed his own script. Taking a position very different from what likely was outlined in Sullivan's written statement, Hoover explained that the committee's purpose was to draft a "'historical summary' of domestic unrest" at the president's request. Following his opening remarks, Hoover invited additional comments. Sullivan spoke up. He directly contradicted the director, a formidable presence who did not brook insubordination inside the FBI. The president, Sullivan said, wanted more than a historical account; he actually wanted a much more comprehensive report that included "a review of 'intelligence gaps'" and an evaluation of intelligence "collection methods."[17] Emboldened by Sullivan's impertinence, the other intelligence bureaucrats at the meeting agreed with Sullivan, and Hoover backed down—for the time being.

The committee members emphasized that they would not make recommendations, but instead would present the president with a list of options. But Sullivan, with Huston's connivance, worked to steer the committee toward a more direct approach. For the purposes of secrecy, most meetings took place at CIA headquarters in Langley, Virginia. Huston and Sullivan often drove together between Washington and Langley, giving them ample opportunity to strategize. Most committee discussions focused on Hoover's restrictions and potential changes to existing investigatory practices, rather than enumerating current domestic threats. Some of the changes that the committee considered included broadening wiretap authorization, expanding NSA opportunities to surveil American citizens, the establishment of a permanent interagency committee, and permitting domestic break-ins for surveillance purposes. In effect, these proposals would have meant a massive restructuring of intelligence community procedures.[18]

As the meetings continued through the month of June, Sullivan attended as Hoover's representative and reported regularly to the director on the committee's progress. Sullivan's memos, however, became increasingly misleading, implying that the committee was following the director's script. This approach, Sullivan thought, gave him the latitude to pursue his actual goal, one he shared with Huston and Nixon: the removal of Hoover's shackles on FBI agents.

Sullivan portrayed his actions purely as following directives from the president. This institutional method for surveillance practice authorization would, he hoped, allow him to sidestep Hoover.[19] Ironically, this was the same tactic that Hoover had used to sidestep Attorney General Jackson and persuade President Roosevelt to authorize wiretapping in 1940, though now with Hoover cast in Jackson's role as the impediment to wiretapping and other suspect tactics. But Hoover, a veteran of more than five decades in the federal government, was not so easily outmaneuvered.

The committee's forty-three-page report, submitted at the end of June and drafted largely by Sullivan, outlined a series of internal security threats and assessed the strengths and limitations of current intelligence coverage of each: "militant new left threats," the "black extremist movement," foreign intelligence services, and "other revolutionary groups." It then assessed the legal and operational restraints on several forms of intelligence collection, including electronic surveillance, surreptitious entry, opening mail, and the infiltration of student groups on college and university campuses. In each case, the report laid out several options, ranging from leaving the restrictions in place to removing them entirely. Although the committee did not make explicit recommendations about whether or not the restrictions should be lifted, it did note that "the President has made it clear that he desired full consideration be given to any regulations, policies, or procedures which tend to limit the effectiveness of domestic intelligence collection."[20] In essence, the report pointed the way toward a dramatic and unprecedented expansion of the government's ability to spy on American citizens without the usual legal and constitutional restraints.

Hoover was livid when he finally read the report, and he threatened to withhold his signature. He did not downplay the risks of domestic subversion, nor did he object to aggressive surveillance. Rather, he feared that if the plans outlined in the report were implemented, the FBI would be subject to much more intensive scrutiny and oversight. He assented only after Sullivan allowed him to add a series of footnotes detailing the risks of the committee's proposals and expressing the FBI's disapproval. When the other committee members learned, shortly before the signing ceremony for the report on June 25, that Hoover alone had been allowed to register his personal opinions in the report and the other agency heads had not, the entire effort almost fell apart. Huston managed to assuage their anger by promising to present their views clearly to the president, and the signing went on as scheduled.[21]

Huston sent the report to the president with a cover memo recommending that Nixon approve its most drastic options, even those tactics he acknowledged to be illegal, such as intercepting mail and surreptitious entry. He also belittled Hoover's objections as "inconsistent and frivolous," equivocating about the full extent of the FBI director's opposition. He encouraged the president not only to sign the report but also to convene the interagency committee to express his approval directly, an action that he supposed would effectively neutralize Hoover's objections. Huston was in effect asking Nixon to directly authorize the "recognizably illegal activities" that the plan proposed. Nixon gave his approval, although without the showmanship Huston recommended. Huston sent a memo on July 23 to the intelligence agencies instructing them to put the plan into place.[22]

A day or two later, Hoover went on the warpath. He told Attorney General John Mitchell, who was among Nixon's closest confidants, that the FBI would seek prior authorization from the attorney general for any illegal surveillance practice, which would insulate Hoover himself and prevent the White House from shirking responsibility for illegal activity.[23]

Nixon and Mitchell now recognized that the risks of pursuing the Huston Plan were simply too great. Haldeman instructed Huston to recall his memo from the intelligence agencies; copies came back with the staples removed, indicating that the agencies had likely kept copies to provide their own political cover. Huston would engage in a month-long campaign inside the White House to get Nixon to reconsider, but he failed. Hoover, the master bureaucrat, had prevailed.[24] Nevertheless, the Huston Plan provided arguments for activities previously deemed beyond the pale. Building on decades of developed governmental capacity and the assumption of presidential authority, the plan presented a template for the weaponization of presidential power to an unprecedented degree, posing a substantial threat to civil liberties and the rule of law. It would set the stage for the gravest constitutional conflict the country had endured since the Civil War.

## THE PENTAGON PAPERS, THE PLUMBERS, AND THE ORIGINS OF WATERGATE

Though it is often associated with the infamous break-in and wiretapping of DNC offices in the eponymous office complex, the name "Watergate" itself is actually shorthand for a broader set of interlocking scandals that accumulated over time and ultimately engulfed Richard Nixon's presidency.

The Watergate story truly begins just about a year after the development of the Huston Plan when, on June 13, 1971, the *New York Times* began publishing excerpts from a long-secret Defense Department study of American involvement in Vietnam that became known as the Pentagon Papers.[25] Secretary of Defense Robert McNamara had commissioned the study in 1967 as the Vietnam War was becoming increasingly costly, intractable, and controversial. Through a critical analysis of the war, the study revealed poor decision-making by government officials dating back to the Truman administration, systematic government lies to the public, and hitherto secret military operations, including American bombing in Cambodia and Laos. After compiling the study, Defense Department analysts worked hard to keep it confidential; not even President Johnson or President Nixon knew about its existence. One of these analysts was a young economist and former Marine officer named Daniel Ellsberg. Increasingly incensed by what he regarded as an unjust war, Ellsberg began to photocopy the Pentagon Papers—a herculean task, considering that the study was roughly 7,000 pages long and amounted to more than forty volumes. Ellsberg shared the documents with Neil Sheehan of the *Times*, who had already distinguished himself for tough, skeptical reporting from Vietnam, and the paper sent the findings into print.

Nixon initially saw in the Pentagon Papers an opportunity to embarrass his opponents by revealing the mistakes and misconduct of previous Democratic administrations.[26] But as stories continued to appear, the president and his advisors became concerned that further leaks might compromise national security and reveal some of Nixon's own clandestine war efforts, most notably his intervention to sabotage peace talks with North Vietnam in the days before the 1968 election.

The administration's first move was to sue the *Times* (and the *Washington Post*, which had also begun publishing articles based on the material) to halt publication, but within weeks the Supreme Court ruled in favor of the newspapers, and the revelation of the material continued. Meanwhile, the administration became determined to prevent further leaks and to punish the leakers. By the time the Supreme Court ruled, Ellsberg had revealed himself as the man who gave the papers to the press. He became a prime target for the administration, though he was not the only one.[27]

The White House next grew concerned about reports that analysts at the Brookings Institution, a left-of-center think tank in Washington, had more secret material about Vietnam in their files. Morton Halperin and Leslie Gelb, both principal authors of the Pentagon Papers, were by then senior fellows at Brookings. (Halperin's home telephone had already been tapped by the FBI, at Nixon and Kissinger's direction, because he had been suspected of leaking information about the war to the press.) Incensed, Nixon was bent on retaliation. He meant to use every tool at his disposal—even those that had been dismissed as unwise, if not outright illegal, just a few years earlier. "Bob? Now you remember Huston's plan?" Nixon said to Haldeman just days after the initial publication of the Pentagon Papers. "I want it implemented on a thievery basis. Goddamn it, go in and get those files. Blow the safe and get it." Here was the president of the United States urging his subordinates to commit burglary and arson in the service of a political vendetta.

Astonishingly, some of Nixon's staff took the bait. One aide, Charles Colson, whom Haldeman described as the president's "hit man," actually devised a plot to firebomb Brookings.[28] The idea was to start a fire big enough to trigger the fire alarm and then, in the ensuing chaos, send operatives into the building to retrieve whatever classified or damaging material might have been there. When White House counsel John Dean got wind of the plot, he got on a plane and went to California to see John Ehrlichman, who was part of Nixon's inner circle and was traveling with the president. Ehrlichman called the operation off.

Although more sensible heads prevailed and the scheme was never carried out, the president's demand for action whatever the cost was clear. As he told Kissinger, "I don't give a goddamn about repression, do you? I don't think we're losing our soul. If we do, it'll come back." White House operatives also concocted other plans for similar operations that never came to fruition: conducting black-bag surveillance jobs against antiwar protesters or hiring "thugs" to provoke antiwar protesters to violence.[29]

In July 1971, Nixon established a "Special Investigations Unit," which operated out of a basement office in the Executive Office Building (EOB) next door to the White House. The group's task was to stem the flow of secrets to the press and the public and "investigate other sensitive security matters." One member of the team, David Young, recounted a conversation with his grandmother when she learned what he was doing at work. "Your grandfather would be proud of you," she told him, "working on leaks at the White House. He was a plumber." He put a sign on the door of Room 16 of the EOB that said, "Mr. Young—Plumber." The sign eventually came down to preserve the covert nature of the group's work, but the name stuck: the Plumbers.[30]

The Plumbers assembled a team of operatives that included Howard Hunt, the former CIA agent whose connection to the Watergate burglary would later be the first crack in the case, and G. Gordon Liddy, a lawyer and former FBI agent with a reckless attitude toward the law and a fondness for Nazi propaganda, whom Bob Woodward of the *Washington Post* once described as a "possessed, daffy, and very dangerous man." For their first job, the Plumbers broke into the Beverly Hills office of Ellsberg's psychoanalyst, Lewis Fielding, in search of information that might "discredit [Ellsberg] as a nut," as Young put it. The operation was approved by John Ehrlichman—"if done under your assurance that it is not traceable," Ehrlichman scrawled on the memo along with his go-ahead. Two of the burglars who were hired for the Fielding break-in—Bernard Barker and Eugenio Martinez, both Cuban former CIA associates of Hunt—would later be among the five arrested at the Watergate. The burglary, which Martinez described as rather amateurish compared with his past experiences with the CIA, took place on the night of September 9. The burglars made their way inside the building but were disappointed to find nothing of interest beyond Ellsberg's name in Fielding's address book. They oafishly ransacked the office and left pills strewn around the floor among the papers in order to make it look like a drug-seeking burglary. "There was nothing of Ellsberg's there," Martinez would later recall. "There was nothing about psychiatry, not one file of sick people, only bills. It looked more like an import-export office than a psychiatrist's."[31]

The Plumbers' illegal activity soon branched out into broader political intelligence work on behalf of the president and, ultimately, his campaign for reelection in 1972. In addition to the Fielding raid, the Plumbers sought information to smear Nixon's Democratic antagonists, especially the Kennedys, with whom Nixon had a long-standing political rivalry. This included everything from trying to blame the Vietnam quagmire on missteps and corruption by the Kennedy administration (by, among other things, forging diplomatic cables to falsify the historical record) to digging up dirt on Senator Edward Kennedy and the scandal involving the death of a young woman in a car accident at Chappaquiddick Island in Massachusetts. (Despite Chappaquiddick, Nixon still feared that Ted Kennedy would be his strongest Democratic rival in 1972 and was intent on seeing Kennedy further discredited.)[32]

Around the same time, the White House and the Committee to Re-Elect the President devised a range of other plots to investigate, undermine, and sabotage Nixon's political enemies, including (but not limited to) his challengers for the presidency. A group of campaign aides connected to Haldeman through Dwight Chapin, the president's appointment secretary, began to conduct a series of pranks to mess with Democratic campaigns. Chapin, along with White House press secretary Ron Ziegler, had been involved in campus politics as an undergraduate at the University of Southern California in the late 1950s and early 1960s, where they had engaged in dirty electioneering tricks that they called "ratfucking"—stuffing ballot boxes, posting fake campaign flyers, and the like. Scaled up to the national stage, this group pulled stunts like sending large unwanted pizza orders to opposing campaign offices or calling opponents' campaign venues to postpone large events so that the candidate would arrive to find the hall locked and empty. The Nixon campaign also managed to embed a driver as a spy in the presidential campaign of Senator Edmund Muskie, the front-runner for the Democratic nomination through 1971. Nixon's dirty tricksters may also have played a role in forging the so-called Canuck letter, which alleged that Muskie had laughed approvingly when a member of his staff used disparaging language about people of French Canadian ancestry in New England and which indirectly led to Muskie's poor showing in the New Hampshire primary and his ultimate withdrawal from the race.[33]

In response to Nixon's insatiable demands for political intelligence about and skullduggery toward his political enemies, the White House and the Committee to Re-Elect the President ran through a series of schemes with names that seemed like clichés out of mediocre spy movies: Townhouse, Sedan Chair (which came in versions I and II), Sandwedge, and Gemstone. These operations involved a range of illegal activities, from covert and shady campaign funding to more sophomoric dirty tricks (such as stealing the car keys from candidates' motorcades), further infiltration of competitors' campaigns, and the like.[34]

The most advanced of these plots was Operation Gemstone, which Liddy hatched in early 1972 along with Haldeman, Dean, Mitchell, and deputy campaign director Jeb Stuart Magruder. Gemstone had a number of subplots (each with its own suitable moniker: Diamond, Sapphire, Ruby, even Coal, the last of which disparagingly denoted a plot to funnel money to the presidential campaign of African American representative Shirley Chisholm in the hopes of dividing Democrats against themselves). Among Liddy's absurdly grandiose proposals was a plan to kidnap radical leaders and antiwar figures, spirit them across the Mexican border, and hold them outside the country to prevent them from disrupting the Republican National Convention. Another involved hiring prostitutes to lure Democratic delegates from their convention in Miami Beach onto a yacht wired with listening devices. The scheme included plans to bug the campaign headquarters and telephone lines of Muskie and Senator George McGovern.[35]

Mitchell ultimately approved a scaled-down version of Operation Gemstone at the end of March, with a budget of $300,000 to be paid in cash out of a fund at the Committee to Re-Elect the President. Kicking into action, Liddy and Hunt rounded up their band of hapless Cuban operatives and began planning their next moves. ("These are not brilliant guys," FBI associate director Mark Felt—the *Washington Post*'s background source then known only as "Deep Throat"—told Bob Woodward in October 1972.) One of those moves was to break into DNC headquarters at the Watergate and bug the office of DNC chairman Lawrence O'Brien, who was a close associate of the Kennedys. "We want to know whatever's said in his office, just as if it were here," Magruder told Liddy. "Get in there as soon as you can, Gordon; it's important." The team's first entry into the DNC headquarters came in late May. They took some pictures and planted listening devices. When one of these turned out to be faulty, they fatefully returned on June 17.[36]

## DEMOCRACY RESPONDS

Once the second Watergate break-in went awry, with the scandal rapidly unspooling in the press, Nixon and his team covered their tracks. But over the next two years, key democratic institutions responded to the threat of democratic breakdown that became increasingly apparent as the story unfolded. It was the careful and sustained work of people playing their constitutionally prescribed roles in the political system—judges and prosecutors, members of Congress, and journalists—that ultimately followed the trail of breadcrumbs past the president's protective shield, uncovering a sustained pattern of executive attempts to rig the political system in Nixon's favor.

First, dogged investigative work by journalists—most famously at the *Washington Post* but also at the *New York Times* and *Time* magazine, among others—unraveled the intricate web of connections between the Watergate burglary and the administration, uncovering the money trail that linked the burglary to the Committee to Re-Elect the President and ultimately to the White House. Journalists began to report that the Watergate burglary was not an isolated incident but was a small part of a larger pattern of political espionage and illegal clandestine activity. The White House generally responded with vague, sweeping denials that disparaged the stories without specifically contradicting them ("non-denial denials," the *Washington Post's* editor, Ben Bradlee, famously called them).

As the press made inroads toward the center of the story, however, the administration and its surrogates struck back. They denounced the press, and especially the *Post*, as biased and unreliable elites who had it in for Nixon and disdained the values of everyday Americans. "There is," Republican senator Bob Dole said in 1972, "a cultural and social affinity between the McGovernites and the *Post* executives and editors. They belong to the same elite: they can be found living cheek-by-jowl in the same exclusive neighborhoods, and hob-nobbing at the same Georgetown parties."[37]

When it was revealed in 1973 that the Nixon White House kept a written enemies list, journalists figured prominently among its entries. One of the most arresting moments of the Watergate era came on June 27, 1973, when Daniel Schorr, the veteran CBS News correspondent, got hold of the enemies list and immediately went on air to report on it. Only as he read it aloud on live television did he discover that he was number seventeen on the list, which described him as "a real media enemy." To underscore the list's purpose, it was attached to a cover memo by John Dean that outlined "how we can use the available federal machinery to screw our political enemies."[38]

Second, while the press was reporting on Watergate, the Justice Department was simultaneously conducting a criminal investigation, though Nixon and his advisors were largely successful at blocking its progress. From the start, FBI agents quickly uncovered details linking the Watergate break-in to the administration's larger pattern of illegal activity, yet prosecutors chose not to pursue these allegations, focusing their attention narrowly on the Watergate incident itself as a singular act. Acting FBI director L. Patrick Gray, at Ehrlichman's behest, went so far as to destroy some incriminating documents that had been found in Howard Hunt's White House safe.[39]

The so-called Watergate Seven—the five burglars plus their overseers, Hunt and Liddy—were tried in federal court in January 1973. At the trial, Hunt and four of the burglars pled guilty and insisted that they had acted alone or on behalf of the CIA, without instructions from anyone elsewhere in the government or higher up in the administration. Hunt had, in fact, been under considerable pressure from the White House to conceal the administration's culpability and had been pressing the White House for money and clemency in return for silence—essentially blackmailing the president of the United States. Even though the full scope of the cover-up was not known at the time, Hunt's guilty plea at the trial struck observers, including presiding judge John Sirica, as suspicious.

Liddy and the fifth burglar, James McCord, were ultimately sentenced to prison time for burglary, conspiracy, and illegal wiretapping. At the trial, the prosecution tried to tie the burglars' actions to a wider administration conspiracy. Hugh Sloan, the former treasurer of the Committee to Re-Elect the President, testified that he had overseen cash payments to Liddy, but Magruder denied on the witness stand—falsely—that he had given Liddy instructions regarding Watergate. In the end, though the trial shed little light on the bigger picture, Judge Sirica announced his skepticism that "all the pertinent facts that might be made available" had come out. He was soon proved right.

In hopes of obtaining a lighter sentence, McCord sent a letter to Judge Sirica several days before his sentencing in March. He outlined the broader case for the judge: political pressure on the defendants by the White House to keep quiet, perjury by witnesses in the trial, broader government involvement in the Watergate operation beyond just the CIA.

McCord's letter was dynamite; it seemed to substantiate Sirica's suspicions that the trial had not produced a forthright record even of what those who testified knew, and it sent the administration into a panic.

The day after McCord's letter was delivered to Sirica, Dean met with Nixon in the Oval Office and laid out the full scope of the cover-up that the president's aides had been carrying out on his behalf. "We have a cancer—within, close to the presidency, that's growing," Dean told Nixon. "It's growing daily. It's compounding." Dean explained that Hunt's blackmail was ongoing; he was still after money and clemency on behalf of himself and his loyal cadre of operatives. Agreeing that clemency would be a bad idea politically, Nixon asked Dean how much money Hunt's silence would cost. When Dean put the figure at $1 million, Nixon responded, "You could get a million dollars. And you could get it in cash. I, I know where it could be gotten."[40]

Sirica read McCord's letter aloud in court before sentencing the defendants on March 23, and its effects were explosive. The public revelation sent the administration into a frenzy of fear and recrimination as the principals tried simultaneously to inoculate the president and protect themselves. On a single day at the end of April, Nixon fired Haldeman, Ehrlichman, and Dean and accepted Attorney General Richard Kleindienst's resignation.

Nixon nominated Secretary of Defense Elliot Richardson to replace Kleindienst. During his confirmation hearings before the Senate Judiciary Committee, Richardson promised to appoint a special prosecutor because many felt that the Justice Department was not sufficiently independent to investigate thoroughly and fairly. By then, Dean, more responsible than anyone in the White House for orchestrating the cover-up, was cooperating with federal prosecutors.

Shortly after the burglars' trial, the Senate opened a third avenue to investigate Watergate in addition to the press and criminal investigations. The result was the Select Committee on Presidential Campaign Activities, chaired by the rumpled yet shrewd Sam Ervin of North Carolina.[41] The select committee's public hearings were broadcast live on national television starting in May. John Dean, testifying at the end of June under a grant of immunity, implicated the president publicly along with numerous others at the senior levels of the White House and the campaign.

Among the things Dean testified about was the Huston plan. Fearing (correctly) that Nixon would try to make him the fall guy for Watergate, however, Dean turned some of his White House papers, including his copy of the Huston Plan, over to Judge Sirica, who in turn passed them on to the Senate committee. After the plan's existence was publicly revealed during a committee hearing, Nixon made an extraordinary public statement on May 22 acknowledging that the plan had, in fact, been developed—to serve sensitive national security needs, which necessitated secrecy, he said—but had never been implemented.[42] (This, of course, was only a half-truth.)

Although in the end Dean could not produce direct evidence of his most explosive claims, he indirectly led the committee to that evidence when he voiced his suspicions that conversations in the White House were taped. On July 13, members of the committee staff were interviewing Alexander Butterfield, the White House aide who had overseen the installation of the taping system, in preparation for his public testimony the next week. In response to a direct question, he confirmed the existence of the recording system in the Oval Office. He repeated this revelation in open testimony before the committee (and on live television) three days later, and the Watergate investigation was transformed.

Meanwhile, Attorney General Richardson had appointed Archibald Cox, a patrician Harvard law professor and former solicitor general, as the Watergate special prosecutor, yet another line of inquiry into the affair. Cox immediately recognized the significance taped presidential conversations would have for his investigation, and he requested the relevant tapes from the White House. Nixon's lawyers refused. They argued, first, that the president's conversations were shielded from the legal process by executive privilege, the principle that the president and his advisors need to be able to rely on the confidentiality of their internal deliberations so the president can receive honest and unvarnished advice about sensitive matters. Second, the president's lawyers claimed that the tapes contained sensitive national security information that had to remain secret. To Nixon's critics, these claims amounted to presidential overreach. Nixon had already antagonized Congress by impounding (refusing to spend) funds that they had appropriated for programs of which he simply disapproved. On top of the impoundment controversy, Nixon's claim of executive priv-

'DON'T PUT UP ANY RESISTANCE! JUST KEEP IN STEP'

6.1 Executive power overwhelms Congress, 1973

ilege seemed like an abuse of power. One 1973 editorial cartoon from the *Hartford Times* (reproduced above) shows a frightened and diminutive Congress being hustled away from the Capitol Building by three menacing figures representing the veto power, impoundment, and executive privilege—each of whom has Nixon's face.

At Cox's request, Judge Sirica issued a subpoena for the tapes. Nixon appealed the subpoena while looking for a compromise. He proposed to Cox that he would prepare a summary of the tapes and turn the tapes over to Senator John Stennis, a supposedly neutral third party who would verify that the summary was accurate. Stennis was a veteran segregationist Democrat from Mississippi and, like many white southern Democrats, a Nixon ally. He was also notoriously hard of hearing. Cox regarded this proposal as an obvious dodge and also recognized that only the actual tapes themselves could serve as evidence in court. Not surprisingly, Cox refused the "Stennis compromise."

With no apparent alternative to complying with the subpoena, Nixon ordered Richardson to fire Cox on Saturday, October 20. Refusing to do so,

Richardson instead resigned. Nixon turned to Deputy Attorney General William Ruckelshaus, who also refused to fire Cox and resigned. Next up was Solicitor General Robert Bork, now acting attorney general, who complied with Nixon's order and dismissed Cox shortly after 8:00 p.m. The "Saturday Night Massacre," as it became known, was complete, but it proved to be the beginning of Nixon's end.[43]

Nixon hoped that firing Cox would allow him to abolish the special prosecutor's office. If only the Watergate investigation would revert to the Justice Department, he could control it. But to most observers, Democratic and Republican alike, the Saturday Night Massacre looked like a naked abuse of presidential power to manipulate a criminal investigation and dodge the consequences at the expense of the rule of law. In the face of a tremendous backlash from Congress, the press, the legal community, and the public, Nixon was forced to back down.

## SHOWDOWN OVER PRESIDENTIAL POWER

Nixon's public support had dwindled during the public Senate hearings; from a peak of 67 percent around his second inauguration in January 1973, his approval rating declined to 27 percent after the Saturday Night Massacre, and it hovered around 25 percent for the remainder of his presidency. Even among Republicans, Nixon's approval rating had dropped precipitously, from 91 percent in January 1973 to 54 percent in October. Meanwhile, support for his removal was rising, from 19 percent at the beginning of 1973 to 33 percent after the firings.[44]

Three days after the Saturday Night Massacre, Nixon's lawyers told Judge Sirica that they would comply with the court's order to turn over the tapes that Cox had requested. The following week, Acting Attorney General Bork appointed a new special prosecutor, Leon Jaworski, to replace Cox. Jaworski eventually indicted Mitchell, Haldeman, Ehrlichman, and Colson, all of whom would go to prison. (John Dean had already pled guilty and cooperated in the prosecution of his former colleagues.) Jaworski also named Nixon as an "un-indicted co-conspirator," indicating that there was strong evidence for a criminal case against him. (In fact, the grand jury in the case unanimously supported indicting the president, but Jaworski thought an indictment imprudent.)[45]

The Saturday Night Massacre and the first release of the White House tapes also led to the opening of the final line of inquiry into Watergate: impeachment hearings by the House Judiciary Committee. Before Cox's dismissal, impeachment seemed a remote possibility, imagined only at the outside edges of Nixon's opposition. When Thomas P. ("Tip") O'Neill, the new House majority leader, had privately suggested preparing for impeachment in January 1973, his colleagues in the House leadership "wondered whether he was unhinged," as one journalist later recalled. But after the Saturday Night Massacre, what had been a fringe notion moved into the mainstream. Within days, the Democratic leadership of the House met to begin planning impeachment, and the House Judiciary Committee began visibly preparing to open impeachment proceedings.[46] Public hearings on impeachment began in May 1974.

The contents of the White House tapes were pivotal in both the prosecutions and the impeachment proceedings. Backed into a corner by his own statements, Nixon tried to use the rationale of national security to justify both the cover-up and his subsequent determination to withhold the tapes from Congress, the prosecutor, and the courts. As the parallel criminal and congressional processes moved forward and the investigation closed in directly on the president, Nixon increasingly sought to sidestep the legal process and place himself beyond the law's reach. He viewed his own refusal to turn over the tapes as safeguarding future presidents' ability to receive confidential and unvarnished advice about important matters of national security. He had long been obsessed with secrecy in the White House. "How the hell can a president . . . do anything?" he had once ranted over the Pentagon Papers. "How can they make a contingency plan if it's going to be taken out in a trunk and given to a goddamn newspaper?"[47]

And he increasingly came to see his own personal political and legal interests as one and the same with the interests of the presidency. He clung to this view long after he left the presidency, and he remained defiant and unrepentant about his actions. In 1977, he told television interviewer David Frost that in matters of national security, "when the President does it, that means that it is not illegal."[48]

As Jaworski subpoenaed more tapes, Nixon continued to refuse to comply, and by June the key question came before the Supreme Court:

whether the president of the United States was subject to the law, or whether, as Nixon's lawyer James St. Clair argued before Judge Sirica, "he is as powerful a monarch as Louis XIV, only four years at a time, and is not subject to the process of any court in the land."[49]

As Nixon's abuses of power and pattern of deception continued to come to light, the case for impeachment gathered steam. Impeachment had never been particularly popular. Less than a majority of the public supported removing Nixon from office through the end of July, although overall support for removal rose over the course of 1974, reaching as high as 48 percent in June. Democrats and Republicans were divided on impeachment, although not drastically so; in July, 71 percent of Democrats supported impeachment, compared to 31 percent of Republicans, even in the face of mounting evidence against him.[50]

The House Judiciary Committee's push for impeachment initially fell along similarly partisan lines. Most Democrats, who had long mistrusted Nixon, were inclined toward impeachment; Republicans, while privately seething about the damage Nixon was doing to their party, supported him publicly. Pivotal on the committee was a group of southern Democrats whose districts were full of Nixon supporters. Nixon's "southern strategy" had actively aimed at securing the votes of southern whites angry at Lyndon Johnson and his party for their embrace of civil rights and voting rights for African Americans; as president, Nixon's record on civil rights and racial equality was equivocal at best, hostile at worst. Southerners in Congress, though nominally Democrats, repaid Nixon with strong and vocal support.

Through the summer of 1974, the committee built the case for indictment and released nearly four thousand pages of evidence, including transcripts of many of the White House tapes that had already been made available.

During that time, a small group of Republicans and southern Democrats on the committee had wavered on impeachment, caught between their partisan inclinations (Republicans for the president, Democrats against), their constituents' preferences, and the mounting evidence of presidential malfeasance. Because polarization was low and bipartisan cooperation relatively common, neither Republicans nor Democrats felt "locked in" to predetermined partisan positions, even on impeachment.

Representative Walter Flowers, a Democrat from Alabama, embodied the dilemma that many members of Congress confronted. He told journalist Elizabeth Drew in April that he was not inclined to rush to judgment because "in my section of the country, Nixon still enjoys large support." In particular, he said, 85–90 percent of white voters preferred Nixon. But he acknowledged that the evidence was not favorable to the president. The White House's refusal to cooperate with the inquiry was indeed suspicious, he agreed. Did he, Drew asked, "give any credence to the idea that [in withholding the tapes] the President was protecting the principle of confidentiality?" She recorded his response: "'Bull,' he replied. 'Bull.'"[51]

Through the summer, this group met frequently. They sifted through evidence, talked politics, and searched for a way to hold the president accountable short of impeachment. But by late July, the steady drumbeat of damning revelations and the mounting evidence that the president himself had directed the Watergate cover-up ultimately broke the logjam. Tom Railsback, a wavering Republican from Illinois, came to resent his party leadership's position that all were obligated by partisan loyalty to protect a Republican president, and he was irritated by pressure the White House tried to exert on him through business leaders in his district.

On July 23, seven Judiciary Committee members, three southern Democrats and four Republicans, gathered in Railsback's office. Over coffee and Danish, they circled around the subject. The group realized both that they were influential—without their votes, impeachment would fail—and that they would each be safer if they acted together. ("Misery loves company," they told each other.) Ultimately, they agreed unanimously that the president's actions warranted his removal from office.[52]

Once this pivotal group of seven had decided, the die was cast, and over the last week of July the committee adopted three articles of impeachment: for obstruction of justice (covering up the Watergate burglary), abuse of power (deploying the power of the presidency to violate citizens' rights and undermine the rule of law), and defiance of congressional subpoenas. As August began, the House of Representatives prepared to begin debate on impeaching the president of the United States for the first time in more than a century.

Although a majority of House Republicans continued to support Nixon, Democrats were almost entirely united across regions, and a small number of Republicans voted for impeachment as well. Even as it became clear that impeachment by the full House was likely, Nixon and his staff and lawyers were preparing to contest a trial in the Senate, where he believed he had enough support to block the two-thirds majority necessary to convict him and remove him from office.

In the same week in July that the Judiciary Committee recommended impeachment, the Supreme Court unanimously burst Nixon's bubble of privilege and privacy and ordered him to surrender the remaining tapes. The batch of recordings released to the public on August 5 included what became known as the "smoking gun" tape: the Oval Office conversation of June 23, 1972, in which Nixon and Haldeman schemed to use the CIA to conceal the White House's involvement in the burglary.[53]

The evidence was now incontrovertible: the president of the United States had engaged in a criminal conspiracy to obstruct justice in the Oval Office and then went to dramatic lengths to deceive the public about it. Most of Nixon's remaining support among congressional Republicans crumbled, aside from a few stalwarts. One, Republican representative Earl Landgrebe of Indiana, called the impeachment process a "lynch mob." As Nixon was slouching toward his end, Landgrebe famously said, "Don't confuse me with facts: I've got a closed mind. . . . I will stick with my President even if he and I have to be taken out of the building and shot."[54] (For his trouble, Congressman Landgrebe was defeated for reelection that fall.)

On August 7, Republican senators Hugh Scott and Barry Goldwater joined House minority leader John Rhodes in an Oval Office meeting with President Nixon to report on his dwindling support. Perhaps fifty votes for him remained in the House, they estimated, and no more than fifteen in the Senate—far short of what he needed to survive. Among Nixon's last and most ardent congressional supporters were the most conservative, arch-segregationist southern Democrats. "To me," Senator James Eastland of Mississippi told Nixon at a small White House gathering on August 8, "you'll always be a great President."[55]

Nixon resigned the next day.

## WATERGATE AND EXECUTIVE POWER

Watergate revealed the dangers of executive aggrandizement. Unlike Roosevelt, who devoted much attention to building the capacity of the executive branch, Nixon came into an office that had already amassed tremendous power and resources. Nixon's determination to use that power to shield his illegal activities from any legal sanction posed a threat to the rule of law. And the impunity that this shield afforded him to bend the government and the political system to his will threatened Americans' civil liberties and the integrity of national elections.

At a time when three of the four threats were relatively low, an ambitious and determined president still managed to create havoc through his attempt to deploy the powerful executive branch on behalf of his own political interests and obsessions. Low polarization in the 1970s reduced the risk that partisan lines would harden, that opposition would be deemed illegitimate, and that democratic politics would devolve into mortal combat. But even so, he nearly got away with it; most Republicans—both in Congress and among the public—supported him almost until the very end.

Nixon also faced a political establishment dominated by his partisan opponents. Democrats still held majorities in both houses of Congress and federal courts were still full of judges appointed by Democratic presidents. Even in these circumstances, Nixon was able to push presidential power to the limit.

❖

In the end, a variety of actors—members of Congress, judges, journalists, and even executive-branch officials—played their constitutionally prescribed roles in the drama to restrain the president from wielding the tools that he had amassed and to hold him accountable, as democracy is supposed to do.

American democracy survived, but not without ominous portents. Watergate also offered a glimpse into the future. What would happen when a president not only possessed all the tools that came with the office by the late twentieth century, but also governed in a highly polarized setting in which bipartisan cooperation, even on matters of the integrity of democracy, was out of the question? When a single party dominated the government? And in a country riven by deepening economic and racial rifts?

## EPILOGUE

Several months after Nixon left office, the Senate established a select committee to study intelligence abuses. Chaired by Senator Frank Church of Idaho, what would become known as the Church Committee conducted its investigation and held hearings through 1975, issuing an extensive report in April 1976. The committee documented decades of suspect and often illegal covert activity, both foreign (such as assassination plots against foreign leaders) and domestic, including extensive revelations about the FBI's COINTELPRO operations, wiretapping of American citizens, mail-opening, black-bag jobs, and other kinds of surveillance. The committee brought to light Roosevelt's secret wiretapping orders, the FBI's clandestine harassment of Martin Luther King Jr., and the Huston Plan, the last of which was the subject of several days of hearings in September 1975. Huston's dramatic testimony was a high point. "It was my opinion at the time," he told the committee, "that simply the fourth amendment [to the Constitution, prohibiting unreasonable searches and seizures] did not apply to the President" in national security matters. The *New York Times* reported that Huston "surprised the committee members and the capacity crowd in the Old Senate Caucus room when he acknowledged that he no longer believed the Huston plan to be legally and constitutionally justifiable."[56]

The Church Committee's final report outlined in harrowing detail many of the dangers of an extensive executive-branch security apparatus, especially when attached to a powerful presidency and commanded by a politically ambitious president. The committee recommended new rules to rein in covert action by the government and better congressional oversight, including the establishment of permanent House and Senate Intelligence Committees. Although there were certainly disagreements among the committee members and between the committee and the Ford administration (which remained concerned about revealing intelligence secrets), the committee took a studiously bipartisan approach to its work. In presenting the committee's report, Church noted that "this inquiry could have been distracted by partisan argument over allocating the blame for intelligence excesses. Instead, we have unanimously concluded that intelligence problems are far more fundamental. They are not the product of any single administration, party, or man."[57]

But Church himself, appearing on NBC's *Meet the Press* in August 1975, clarified exactly what was at stake. Nixon's resignation after Watergate and his own committee's work had advanced the cause of democratic accountability, for the time being. But he worried that we were not out of the woods:

> If this government ever became a tyranny, if a dictator ever took charge in this country, the technological capacity that the intelligence community has given the government could enable it to impose total tyranny. And there would be no way to fight back, because the most careful effort to combine together in resistance to the government, no matter how privately it was done, is within the reach of the government to know. Such is the capability of this technology.

Why, he then asked, was the investigation important?

> Because I don't want to see this country ever go across the bridge. I know the capacity that is there to make tyranny total in America. And we must see to it that . . . all agencies that possess this technology operate within the law and under proper supervision so that we never cross over that abyss. That's the abyss from which there is no return.[58]

# 7

## At All Costs
### How the Four Threats Endanger Democracy

A presidential election in which one party—which gained fewer electoral votes than the other—threatened to usurp the outcome, and each side warned of violence if it did not prevail. A bloody and destructive civil war fought because one half of the country began to challenge the other half's determination to perpetuate slavery. Provincial governments that disenfranchised millions while national leaders sanctioned it. More than one hundred thousand people rounded up and incarcerated in so-called relocation centers for years because of their national origin. A president running a secret surveillance and political sabotage unit out of the White House. These episodes of democratic backsliding, some of which threatened democratic stability to its core, all happened in the nation renowned as the world's beacon of democracy.

As extreme and abnormal as these episodes might sound, they were not isolated incidents. Rather, they occurred during eras marked by sustained, tumultuous discord, threaded through the nation's history. During these crises, many people feared that the nation's progress toward more complete democracy was at risk. Uncertainty and chaos endured for years, sometimes leaving behind a diminished democracy, with long-lasting damage.

Neither were the democracy-threatening occurrences aberrations; to the contrary, specific tactics and strategies regularly repeated themselves.

Political authorities tried to suppress critical journalists and publishers in the 1790s and 1970s alike. Angry citizens sought vigilante justice in the 1850s, just as their predecessors had in the 1790s. Political operatives engaged in chicanery and even outright fraud to help their party win elections in the 1850s, the 1890s, and the 1970s. Time and again, presidents who lacked support for their policies in other branches of government charged ahead with their plans, from George Washington in pursuit of a treaty with Great Britain that Congress opposed to Franklin D. Roosevelt toying with court-packing when the Supreme Court proved hostile to New Deal legislation.

For those of us who came of age after World War II, this stormy past may sound like that of a foreign country that is ruled by autocrats and lacks established political institutions; we have been accustomed to American democracy growing stronger, more robust, and more inclusive over time, as if by an inexorable logic. But when viewed over the long term, that democracy reveals itself to have been profoundly fragile.

It may seem reassuring that the most turbulent eras occurred in the more distant past. And it is true that although the nation risked secession and civil war in the election of 1800 and succumbed to both after the chaotic 1850s, those dangers have not recurred since. The two periods of upheaval in the twentieth century, moreover, did less to put the system at risk. Although many Americans in the 1930s worried about the rise of a dictator, the nation not only avoided that fate but emerged with some pillars of democracy strengthened. The transgressions of Watergate, as egregious as they were, were nonetheless limited to one branch of national government and were met by resilient courts and bipartisan efforts in Congress to protect the system.

It is tempting to conclude that today we live in a mature democracy that is no longer vulnerable to backsliding. We tend to assume that the Constitution will keep democracy safe, that its checks and balances and its restraints on excessive power will prevent our system from going in reverse.

But that assumption fails to take account of the four threats to democracy, the damage that has occurred when they have been present, and the peril created by their various combinations. Today, all four threats have converged at high levels, as never before. What is it about these threats that makes them so dangerous? Why do they motivate politicians to take off the restraints in ways that harm democracy?

Each of the threats affects political power in destructive ways. Power is an essential part of the normal, healthy practice of democratic politics. Democracy depends on the competition for power through elections, which enable citizens to hold their leaders accountable. Voters use their power to choose people to protect their values and interests; elected officials, in turn, engage in collective action as they use their power to govern responsively; and voters hold them accountable by reelecting them or by voting them out of office.

The problem is that each of the four threats interferes with the normal functioning of democratic politics. A goal takes over that proponents value deeply, more than democracy itself, and in pursuing it—at all costs—they become willing to take measures that endanger democracy. Of course, that is not to say that politicians' hands are tied when they govern in a time when the threats loom large. They can make choices and take action to protect democracy; the question is whether or not they will. The threats, however, create incentives to use power in ways that harm democracy. When the threats merge in various combinations, furthermore, not only is the level of danger compounded, but their interactions with one another make them more combustible, ratcheting up the likelihood of causing harm to democracy.

How did the American constitutional system survive each of these crises? Despite the risks that recurred again and again and the real harm that often took place, ultimately the nation and the Constitution prevailed. Yet, looking across the periods, we find a deeply disturbing pattern: on several occasions, political leaders effectively preserved American democracy by restricting it. They reinforced the "formative rifts," restrictions on who belongs in the political community that descended from the nation's founding, by curtailing the boundaries of membership and warding off challenges to the status of more privileged members. This is not a heroic history, and it does not offer us positive lessons to be replicated in our own time. It does, however, help us to understand the nature of the challenges we face today, and why we must seek a new way forward if we are to protect democracy now.

## HOW THE FOUR THREATS LEAD TO BACKSLIDING

Across American history, each of the four threats that are known to make democracy vulnerable—political polarization, conflict over who belongs in the political community and the status of different groups, rising economic inequality, and executive aggrandizement—has waxed and waned according to its own pattern and trajectory. As a result, different ones have emerged at different times of crisis, sometimes in combination with others. Each of the threats promotes the use of political power in ways that distort the normal functioning of democracy. They embolden leaders to pursue particular goals at all costs, even those detrimental to democracy. While any of the threats can challenge democracy on its own, the merger of two or more can prove formidable indeed. We will now examine what it is about each of these threats that makes them so dangerous for democracy, and what happens when they coalesce.

POLARIZATION

Democracy relies on the presence of ambitious politicians who want to win: to win election, to win policy battles while in office, and to win reelection. Such ambitions prompt them to be responsive to citizens, and in turn enable citizens to hold them accountable. Political parties, furthermore, help make democracy work, by recruiting candidates, simplifying choices for citizens, and coordinating a political agenda. But when partisan loyalty comes to override other goals, it can distort politicians' incentives to be responsive to voters and democracy may suffer. This occurs when polarization becomes the key organizing principle in a political system. Polarization occurs when competition between two opposing sides intensifies to the point where dominating the other side becomes the top priority. Those on each side may adopt the political strategy of acting like devoted members of a team, punishing those who step out of line and cooperate with the opposition. They may devote their energy to distinguishing their team from their opponents and to disparaging the opposition, rather than accomplishing policy-oriented goals, because the first two can be more helpful in winning election.[1] Politics then increasingly takes on the form of mortal combat, with enormous stakes, and each election is portrayed by both sides as an existential crisis. Among ordinary citizens, this polarized politics engenders an "us versus them" mindset, as they adopt increasingly negative views of their opponents.[2]

Polarization has not been a constant in American politics. It emerged quickly in the 1790s and lasted through the election of 1800; it recurred in the 1850s and remained high through the Civil War; and it peaked again in the late nineteenth century. After that, however, it diminished in the early twentieth century and remained low until around the 1980s, when it began growing again; it has continued to intensify to this day, as we will see in Chapter 8.

But why is polarization bad for democracy? It is detrimental because it means, for politicians, that being true to one's political "team" takes priority over representation, over responsiveness to one's constituents, and, ultimately, over democratic accountability. Political skills such as negotiation, compromise, and persuasion fall by the wayside, with destructive effects on policymaking. Polarized sides in a conflict grow increasingly hostile to each other and unwilling to pursue mutual accommodation. They come to view each other as harmful to the future of the polity, and in some instances as a danger to the Constitution, even treasonous. They seek ways to tilt the playing field, to weaken or impede the other side and to advantage their own, to improve their odds of winning.

Polarization may begin over genuine policy differences or divergent views about the role of government in society. As competition grows, however, it tends to take on a life of its own, prompting the two sides to engage in conflict even over matters not related to their policy differences. In other words, power struggles predominate. In some respects, polarization is a two-way street, and both sides in a polarized polity deserve blame for permitting conflicts to germinate and escalate.

Certainly the party in power is in charge. It wields the authority and resources of government, and it can choose to take actions that harm democracy—or not. In the course of political competition, will it use its power to violate the rule of law, to stack the deck against its political opponents, in order to gain a political advantage? If the answer is yes, that party is poised to cause severe damage to democracy. In the 1790s, for example, it was the Federalists who controlled the reins, and therefore it was their actions that had the greatest capacity to harm democracy; the Republicans, in response, aimed to protect it. At the same time, the party that is out of power can also stoke polarization, as the Republicans in that era did through the Kentucky and Virginia Resolutions.

## CONFLICT OVER WHO BELONGS

A robust liberal democracy requires equality and inclusion. Conflicts over who belongs in a political community involve questions about what status should be afforded to those in different groups. Those who value a political order that rests on exclusivity or social hierarchy, whether it is long-standing or from a bygone era, may become alarmed by those who favor more inclusive and egalitarian arrangements, as occurred in the 1850s and the 1890s, and is happening again today. At such moments, the defenders of exclusionary traditions, who worry that the nation's culture is changing, tend to become angry, highly engaged, and politically active to resist such change—all the more so when conflicts relate to "formative rifts."[3]

These conflicts over membership and status can expand or endanger democracy, depending on which side prevails. They are also fundamentally asymmetrical. On one side are those committed to equality. On the other side are those who want to restore old hierarchies that are antithetical to it. The defenders of the old guard may be quite willing to undermine democracy in the quest to restore a social order they prefer. For example, they may consider it justifiable to take civil liberties and civil rights away from particular groups in the process.

Time and again, the forces of white supremacy and racial exclusion have threatened the progress of American democracy. The United States' fundamental formative rift over race was inscribed into the Constitution with its clauses sanctioning the enslavement of African Americans. It undermined the nation's commitment to democratic ideals from the beginning, and it has continued to do so long after the demise of slavery. Conflict over this formative rift was latent during the 1790s, as neither political party fundamentally challenged it then. As the decades proceeded, however, conflict over race became inescapable. By the 1850s, when the two parties took fundamentally different approaches—one advocating the demise of slavery and the other its perpetuation—politics became increasingly inflamed, finally splitting the nation in half and driving it into war.

During Reconstruction, political leaders attempted to eradicate this formative rift and push the country to become a more inclusive democracy. They pursued the ratification of the Thirteenth, Fourteenth, and Fifteenth Amendments, which aimed to make equal rights of citizenship available to Americans regardless of race, and passed civil rights laws to enforce these rights. But recalcitrant courts and often violent resistance slowed the progress of equality and inclusion. By the end of the nineteenth century, as we have seen, democratic progress was reversed and the rift persisted.

The combination of polarization and conflicts over membership is particularly combustible, as the 1850s and the 1890s demonstrate. In the latter period, polarizers stoked conflict over membership in their quest for power because they knew it would reliably produce "us versus them" politics. It provided them with a political strategy that could help unify their supporters by drawing distinctions between themselves and the other side. Southern Democratic leaders in the 1890s were strongly and sincerely motivated by white supremacy. Their top priority, however, was regaining political power and maintaining it, and white supremacy also proved a useful means of pursuing that end. Since the 1890s, politicians have repeatedly used this approach, sparking racist or nativist fervor as a reliable means of promoting participation and gaining support among white voters.

White supremacy appears to be latent, like a stream in the American polity that never quite runs dry. Instead it goes underground, where it remains unseen, ready to flow out in the open again once it is tapped. In the mid-twentieth century, even after formal civil rights had been achieved, ambitious politicians showed that they were willing to utilize this part of the American political playbook yet again, employing white supremacy to gain and activate supporters. The parties divided along racial lines anew over issues, constituencies, and electoral appeals. Republican national campaigns began trading on themes of racial resentment, starting with the nomination of Civil Rights Act opponent Barry Goldwater in 1964 and Nixon's "southern strategy." In time, as we will see in Chapter 8, a generations-old crack between how the two parties deal with conflicts over membership has widened into a chasm.

While polarizers have invoked racism most frequently against African Americans, they have also fueled anger over the membership and status of other groups. Immigrants were a target as early as 1796, for example, when President Adams signed the Alien Acts. Racially based restrictions on immigration have reappeared with considerable regularity, from the Chinese Exclusion Act of 1882 to the Immigration Act of 1924, which severely limited immigration from non-European countries. Certainly Americans can legitimately deliberate through the democratic process about how much immigration they wish to permit at any point in time. If such debates involve conflict over the status of people who have been living in the country for a long time, however, they may shift in a different and more dangerous direction.

Conflicts over who belongs in the political community, particularly when those conflicts relate to formative rifts, have the potential to drive politics down an undemocratic path. This occurs when one side wants to tether membership and status to some characteristic shared by some people but not others, such as race, ethnicity, gender, religion, country of national origin, or sexual orientation. Such demands trample the principles of equality and justice and are fundamentally undemocratic.

## RISING ECONOMIC INEQUALITY

As economic inequality grows, the rich become highly motivated to cement and expand their material gains. If gaining the political power necessary to protect their interests requires some damage to democracy along the way, they will typically be willing to tolerate that.[4]

Certainly it is not new or novel to argue that the rich speak with an outsized voice in politics and wield much clout. Their command of substantial resources, access, and networks gives them extra leverage to influence the political system relative to everyone else. Such dynamics have long been commonplace in the United States, and while they undeniably skew the democratic process, they do not endanger its core features.

Yet when taken to the extreme, rising economic inequality can put democratic stability at risk. The most affluent people and wealthiest corporations are highly motivated to see their interests protected—and ambitious politicians, seeking their support and access to resources, may be highly motivated to do their bidding. In order to gain the power they need for that purpose, they may be game to pursue it at all costs, even if it causes harm to democracy along the way. Here again, politics is characterized by asymmetry, as it is the rich and the politicians who work on their behalf—not both sides in the conflict—who are most willing to compromise democracy.

The combination of polarization, conflicts over membership, and rising economic inequality is particularly dangerous because it permits the rich to pursue their agenda without others taking much notice or concern. Stoking conflicts over membership by fanning the flames of racial antagonism, for example, stimulates widespread political participation among ordinary citizens who want to restore traditional social hierarchies, even if they stand to lose from the policies that the wealthy desire. Uniting voters along these "us versus them" lines of race can prevent society's have-nots from uniting across racial lines against the haves and pursuing their own economic or social agenda.[5] Meanwhile, the rich and their surrogates can go about their business, acting even in plain sight, to accomplish their political and policy goals. In the process, they can tilt the playing field dramatically, achieving policies that advantage them economically and political arrangements that help keep them in power.

The 1890s exemplifies the toxic mix of these first three threats. In 1896, wealthy Americans became politically mobilized to an unprecedented degree to help their candidate, William McKinley, defeat the Democratic populist candidate, William Jennings Bryan, who threatened their interests. Some ordinary Americans did organize on the basis of their class interests, but those efforts faced numerous challenges. At the same time, many industrial workers allied with the Republican candidate, helping to ensure his victory. In the South, affluent people regained power by invoking white supremacy to unify whites of all income groups behind the Democratic Party and disenfranchising African Americans. The economic interests of those who promoted such politics garnered little attention, but ultimately they consolidated power and then dominated the region for the next seventy years.

## EXECUTIVE AGGRANDIZEMENT

Over the past century, Americans have come to look to the national government to deal with problems, and it has frequently risen to the challenge. But this trend can contribute to executive aggrandizement. In a slow-moving political system with the separation of powers and checks and balances, the president is the sole unitary actor, and citizens increasingly expect the president to accomplish things. Presidents, by the same token, aim to be responsive to citizens, or at least to the citizens who support them.

Executive aggrandizement is dangerous for democracy when it prompts presidents to override checks and balances in their quest to exert authority and to get things done, in order to be directly responsive to the people. The 1930s saw the growth of executive power on behalf of the New Deal agenda, but the Roosevelt administration's excesses were mostly constrained by robust resistance from the other branches of government. During Watergate, Nixon did use executive power in ways that circumvented constraints in the service of his own political interests, but the political system ultimately responded effectively and it became clear that his impeachment and removal from office were inevitable.

What distinguished the twentieth-century periods of havoc from those earlier in our history is that executive aggrandizement was the only threat present. Never before in our history, until now, have we experienced executive aggrandizement in combination with any of the other threats, not to mention all three of them, as we do today.

Throughout the twentieth century, presidents gained greater power to act autonomously. The potential grew for a president to behave, quite contrary to the framers' ideals, in a more dictatorial manner. Presidents of both parties expanded the capacity of the office and left new tools behind to await the next inhabitant of 1600 Pennsylvania Avenue. But without the other three threats, the temptation to abuse executive power was weaker and the constraints on doing so were stronger. Still, the danger grew that someday a president could come along who would not respect those limitations, particularly if he governed when any of the other three threats had escalated, thus emboldening him to rule in a more autocratic manner.

The combination of executive aggrandizement with the other three threats presents unprecedented danger to the United States. Already for several decades, as polarization has grown, presidents of both parties have gone to great lengths to deliver to their party faithful.[6] Ultimately an empowered president may seek to further his own political future, and if the political system is divided by polarization and his party controls Congress, it may condone his behavior. If that president at the same time is fighting to restore an older social order and to protect the interests of the wealthy, these incentives may overpower the inclination to respect the constraints of the constitutional system. Today we face this unprecedented confluence.

## DEMOCRACY IN THE BALANCE

An oft-quoted saying typically attributed to Mark Twain goes, "History doesn't repeat itself, but it often rhymes." The history of democracy in the United States is indeed full of rhymes, particularly when it comes to the harm caused in moments of crisis. These crises repeatedly caused damage to the pillars of democracy.

### IMPERILING FREE AND FAIR ELECTIONS

The essential feature of democracy is that government gains its authority and legitimacy from the people. Free and fair elections—the clearest means of conveying the collective voice of the people—therefore constitute a central pillar of a well-functioning representative democracy. Ambitious politicians and parties routinely seek victory in elections by winning the war of ideas and by using campaign strategies that help them to gain enough votes. Generally, such activities amount to fair play. Yet some efforts to achieve victory at the polls unfairly tip the scales, and in the process undermine basic democratic principles; free and fair elections became imperiled repeatedly throughout our history.

Concerns about electoral fairness loomed large before the Civil War and in the 1890s. On the one hand, the United States featured a lively electoral democracy, as political parties thrived and the vote was granted to all white men by the early nineteenth century and all black men after the Civil War. Yet it also provided tempting opportunities for those who sought to manipulate elections.

Even under the best of circumstances, administering free and fair elections is difficult. When tumultuous political battles took place, those challenges were exacerbated, because elections often figured front and center in the conflict. Political parties often made excessive and fraudulent efforts to influence outcomes, at times stuffing ballot boxes and rigging vote counts. In territorial elections in Kansas in 1854 and 1855, proslavery forces from Missouri streamed across the border to vote and to sow chaos on Election Day. Free-state supporters held their own elections and chose members of a rival legislature, and even then proslavery militias engaged in guerrilla tactics.

For years after Reconstruction and right up through the 1898 events in Wilmington, North Carolina, southern Democrats engaged in violence and fear-mongering to intimidate potential voters, and they routinely tampered with ballots and vote counts. By the 1890s, they had also come to adopt new tactics, managing to alter electoral rules in ways that would "legally" disenfranchise millions of African Americans and many poor whites as well. From then until the 1960s, the South ran elections in a manner that befitted an authoritarian regime—and through those practices helped to elect presidents and members of Congress, thus tarnishing national politics as well. The United States failed to live up to the basic distinction associated with democracies, that they champion free and fair elections.

The Voting Rights Act of 1965 dramatically increased the fairness of elections throughout the United States by seeking to ensure ballot access to all citizens. Yet soon after its passage, President Nixon and his aides turned to other means, seeking to discredit their opponents with a range of dirty and illegal tactics.

Electoral malfeasance and unfair electoral rules and procedures undermine the foundation of democracy. Both have a long history in the United States, not just during periods of crisis but in some instances as long-lasting effects of those periods.

## THWARTING THE RULE OF LAW

Any free society is likely to feature a cacophony of citizens and groups with different ideas and interests. These, quite predictably, can lead to differences of opinion and outright disputes. Democratic governance aims to manage these conflicts through the rule of law, procedures agreed on in advance that apply to all citizens. The rule of law also limits the powers of political leaders and defines the scope of power of each branch of government. When the rule of law falters, powerful people—especially those with money or influence—tend to dominate, and they may resort to coercion, intimidation, or violence (threatened or real) to achieve their goals.

Violations of the rule of law proliferated across the periods of political tumult in the United States, as conflicts were settled instead by force, violence, and coercion. On occasion, citizens took the law into their own hands, engaging in vigilante justice, such as the whiskey rebels who assaulted tax collectors in the early 1790s or the proslavery forces in the Kansas territory in the mid-1850s. In some instances, citizens acted because political leaders had mobilized them, as in the case of the paramilitary Red Shirts brigades in North Carolina in the 1898 coup d'état. In other instances, government itself engaged in a show of force, such as when federal troops descended upon the bedraggled veterans protesting for bonus payments during the Great Depression.

Twentieth-century presidents pushed the limits of the rule of law embodied in the constitutional principles of separation of powers. President Franklin D. Roosevelt tested the ambiguity of the tersely written Article II of the Constitution when he established the Executive Office of the President and threatened to add up to six justices to the Supreme Court after it declared several New Deal policies to be unconstitutional. President Richard Nixon tried to circumvent the rule of law when he claimed executive privilege as an excuse not to share tapes requested by a congressional impeachment probe, although ultimately the Supreme Court determined that he was not above the law and had to comply.

Power-seeking politicians in the United States may find it tempting to circumvent the rule of law in order to achieve their goals, but when they do, it defeats the basic principles of democracy upon which the nation was established. This has happened repeatedly in times of crisis.

## FAILING TO RESPECT THE LEGITIMACY OF
## POLITICAL OPPOSITION

Democratic politics requires that people with different points of view be permitted to express their views and compete through the political process to advance their agenda—and that they need to respect the right of others to do the same. If those with political power stack the deck so that dissent and opposition are impossible, democracy ceases. Each period of democratic crisis found those with power trying to vanquish their opponents, changing the rules or shifting resources in ways that would undermine their opportunity to win in the future.

In the 1790s, politicians viewed those who disagreed with them—whether other politicians or ordinary citizens who were critical of government—as treasonous, posing a threat to the Constitution itself. President Washington's reaction to the Democratic-Republican societies', for example, revealed his fear of an active citizenry. As the decade proceeded, tensions escalated, and political battles became all-out efforts to eviscerate the other side.

By the early nineteenth century, formal political parties emerged, and with them the principle that healthy politics entails competition between parties that offer different approaches to government. Some issues, however, remained beyond the scope of the principle of legitimate opposition—most significantly, slavery. The three-fifths compromise and the early party system allowed the proslavery South to pay lip service to the principles of democracy, even while perpetuating this most anti-democratic practice. But the conflict between slavery and democracy was not easily contained, and by the 1850s the country had become overtly and fundamentally divided over it. Once Abraham Lincoln was elected president in 1860, the South engaged in the ultimate expression of failure to recognize the legitimacy of the political opposition—by seceding from the Union.

Southern Democrats in the 1890s wanted to dominate politics in their states, and they did not want to face competition. They aimed to disable the political opposition they faced from Republicans and Populists. The disenfranchisement of African Americans served as an efficient strategy for achieving that goal.

Of course, ambitious politicians and parties want to win, and toward that end they seek to draw attention to their competitors' weaknesses. Some of these actions are legal and amount to fair play. Yet when politicians use their power to shut down or shut out the opposition, they repudiate a basic principle of democracy, transforming the political system into one that resembles authoritarianism. In times of democratic crisis, American politicians with power have repeatedly demonstrated their willingness to undermine the opposition.

## ENDANGERING THE INTEGRITY OF RIGHTS

In each period when American democracy was in distress, the fractious political climate led political leaders to ostracize or suppress some groups or to prohibit free expression of dissent. By defining particular groups as the enemy (such as Republicans in the 1790s) or subordinating their status (such as African Americans in the 1890s), they aimed to consolidate their own supporters or to fracture the opposition. By outlawing certain forms of public engagement, they sought to bolster their own power and to hinder challenges to it. In some instances such efforts amounted primarily to rhetoric, but in others politicians took action that led to a curtailment of voting rights, civil liberties, or civil rights.

The first decade under the new Constitution saw efforts by public officials to curb civil liberties—particularly when the political opposition exercised them to criticize those in power. President George Washington spurned freedom of association when he rebuked the Democratic-Republican societies for their civic organizing and engagement in public affairs. President John Adams, by signing into law the Alien and Sedition Acts, impinged on the civil rights and voting rights of immigrants from particular nations and put restrictions on freedom of the press.

Slavery embodied the most fundamental denial of rights. The defense of slavery, moreover, caused substantial collateral damage to other rights. For decades, proslavery forces sought to restrict forthright debate about slavery by censoring the mail and limiting congressional debate. And the 1850 Fugitive Slave Act both endangered free blacks and effectively enlisted every white American in the business of propping up the slave regime.

In the 1890s, southern Democrats curtailed freedoms of all types. They commenced the Wilmington massacre by destroying the office of the opposition press, the city's black-owned newspaper. Across the region, they eradicated voting rights for African Americans, as well as some whites. Once blacks lost their opportunity to influence the political process, they soon after lost civil liberties and civil rights as well, as Jim Crow laws became firmly entrenched.

During the 1930s, Roosevelt declined to challenge the white supremacy and authoritarianism that prevailed in southern states and he accommodated the South in national legislation as well. After the United States entered World War II—a war against the racist totalitarianism of fascism—his administration went even further, depriving more than a hundred thousand Japanese Americans of their freedom by ordering them into detention camps on the suspicion that they were enemies of the United States.

By the 1970s, freedom of the press faced challenges once again. Among the "enemies" whom the Nixon administration targeted, reporters were prominent. And from the Pentagon Papers to the Watergate investigation, the administration sought to contest the First Amendment protections of speech and the press that are essential to the vitality of democratic politics.

Across American history, when political actors have strived to expand and solidify their power, they have not hesitated to curtail political and civil rights in the process.

## POLITICS AND THREATS

We tend to think that, even with its imperfections, American democracy has generally flourished and has progressed to become more inclusive and robust over time and that the Constitution has kept us moving forward on this democratic path. But, in fact, the Constitution could not prevent serious harm from occurring repeatedly. The United States has not been immune to democratic backsliding. Across the episodes of crisis, all four pillars of democracy endured real damage, and sometimes it lasted for decades. The Constitution is not a machine capable of recalibrating itself, nor is it a homeostatic system that maintains a constant balance among its parts if one gets thrown out of whack. Rather, it is a framework for action, and as these episodes show us, it is a malleable one.

The way political leaders and citizens in any given period behave under the Constitution, as we have seen, depends largely on the presence (or absence) of the four threats. In three of the historical periods, only one threat prevailed. In the 1850s and the 1890s, three were present, and these episodes were accompanied by the most dramatic democratic backsliding that the United States has witnessed in its history.

Yet, just as the Constitution does not operate like a self-regulating system, neither do the four threats by themselves determine what unfolds in politics. They do not operate according to a predictable equation, nor do they foreordain some particular outcome.

Rather, political actors can exert their will and make choices, and it is they—elected officials, organizational leaders, and citizens—who make the crucial difference in whether threats will materialize into full-scale danger and damage. They may or may not choose to engage in action to save democracy.

Sometimes in periods of crisis, powerful leaders themselves showed restraint. In deciding the outcome of the contested election of 1800, for example, the Federalist majority ultimately let the process unfold that led to Jefferson's victory rather than usurping the presidency. At his great moment of triumph at the end of the Civil War, Abraham Lincoln turned away from vindictiveness and the opportunity to assume military power over the vanquished South. "With malice toward none; with charity for all," he said memorably in his second inaugural address, calling for reconciliation rather than retribution between the country's two sections.[7] During the Great Depression, Franklin Roosevelt could have pursued a path closer to that of autocrats in Europe by seizing greater executive power, as many urged him to do. Roosevelt may have stretched the Constitution, but he did not break it.

At other times, political leaders restrained one another in the unfolding drama of democratic fragility. When Roosevelt proposed packing the Supreme Court in order to overcome the Court's hostility to the New Deal, his own fellow partisans reined him in and held him accountable. And during Watergate, a variety of individuals played out their constitutionally prescribed parts: Congress investigated, prosecutors prosecuted, judges judged, reporters reported, and ultimately a renegade president was brought to heel.

When a single group or party gains disproportionate control of the political system and operates in the presence of several threats, the challenge to democracy is likely to be formidable. This will be the case particularly if that dominant party stands on the side of those who wish to reinforce or reestablish traditional social hierarchies and to do the bidding of the affluent. The danger will be accentuated if the dominant party holds the presidency in a time of executive aggrandizement. At such a juncture, the other party must act first and foremost to protect democracy. It can be assisted by parts of the political system not run by the dominant party, including the media, states governed by the opposition party, and civil servants. The United States has not previously encountered the confluence of all four threats at once, but it does now, as we will see in Chapter 8. Before that, however, we need to consider how the political system survived past crises, because understanding that is crucial for thinking about how democracy can be saved today.

## A HISTORY OF SAVING DEMOCRACY BY RESTRICTING IT

An optimist might point out that although each of the pillars of democracy endured harm, still the United States retained its Constitution and its system of government across 230 years. At the national level, the regime itself persevered. The question is, how?

The most sobering observation about the recurring crises of American democracy is that the settlement of these crises has often revolved around a compromise of democratic values that entailed reaffirming or perpetuating racial hierarchy and exclusion. In fact, when challenges to democracy have been overcome, it has not always been through heroic action by virtuous democrats or high-minded political leaders who act with restraint and put partisan concerns aside for the sake of the country. Rather, put simply, Americans have often preserved a version of democracy for themselves by restricting who is included within its promises.

In some periods this happened explicitly, specifically when the crisis itself involved a conflict over race that divided the two major political parties. In the conflictual politics of the late nineteenth century, the parties had been divided over race, with Republicans standing up for the rights African Americans had gained during Reconstruction. In the 1890s, Democrats in the southern states rose up to take voting rights away from more than three million citizens and subsequently subjected them to a brutal regime of segregation backed by law, custom, and violence. As this occurred, national political leaders shamefully turned their backs, then acquiesced, prompting a reconciliation of sorts between the parties. The high degree of political polarization that had separated Democrats and Republicans during the late nineteenth century came to an end. The period of crisis ended, but democracy was left greatly diminished.

In other periods, the political system was preserved through a preexisting accord or institutional arrangement that prevented the two political parties from openly contesting questions about race, and therefore circumscribed the conflict. In other words, the parties suppressed conflict over race, both upholding restrictions on membership in the political community or traditional status hierarchies.

Despite the extreme polarization of the 1790s, for example, both parties suppressed conflict over the enslavement of African Americans. The election of 1800 is often seen as a victory for democracy, as the Federalists, who held power, ultimately allowed the political process to move forward until one person changed his vote, permitting Republican Thomas Jefferson to win, after which control of the presidency changed hands peacefully. Yet this outcome was dictated by the three-fifths compromise, which boosted the power of the white slaveholding South in national politics; without it, the Federalists would have prevailed, a result that may well have produced secession, civil war, and the end of the nation.

Similarly, conflict over race was sidelined during the 1930s, when another version of racial compromise curtailed Roosevelt's response to the crisis. He maintained a tacit understanding with southern Democrats that New Deal policies would leave racial hierarchy intact, excluding African Americans from the protections of social and labor policies. White Americans gained new social rights, but those rights did not apply across the color line. The new national powers claimed by the president did not upend federalism, and only because they were limited in that way were southerners willing to go along with reforms. A different president and a different Democratic Party governing at that time might have transgressed those boundaries—with the possibility of building a multiracial democracy if they prevailed, but alternatively turning the nation's politics in an antidemocratic direction if they failed. Once again, a compromise over race permitted the system to persist, while excluding people of color from the full rights of citizenship.

In two other periods, democracy was furthered by its proponents in the absence of a settlement that rested on racial hierarchy. One of those, the 1850s conflict over slavery, resulted in secession and civil war; slavery was ended, but only at a tragic and bloody cost—"blood drawn with the lash" paid by more blood "drawn with the sword," in Lincoln's arresting metaphor.[8]

Ironically, the resignation of Richard Nixon at the peak of the Watergate scandal in 1974, although it seemed a dark time for democracy, may have been the purest democracy-promoting moment among these episodes. Ultimately, Republicans and Democrats came together in favor of impeachment, and after Nixon resigned, they enacted reforms that sought to prevent a recurrence of the events that had led to the crisis. This peaceful outcome was eased by the fact that by the 1970s, most of the threats had receded; polarization and economic inequality were in relative retreat, and racial conflict, although still omnipresent in American society, had receded as a central organizing conflict of politics. Moreover, by the 1970s, the United States had finally become a democracy across its entire territory: the South had democratized, African Americans had finally been reenfranchised, and voting rights were, for the time being, vigorously protected.

For most of American history, however, democracy has been substantially restricted—by race, gender, national origin, and other markers of difference—that have long taken on political significance. And the threats that have repeatedly challenged American democracy have revealed the fragility of democracy's pillars: free and fair elections, fair competition, the rule of law, and the integrity of rights. These are sobering patterns, ones that modern-day reformers need to heed seriously if they hope to avoid repeating them. In order to move forward into the future, we must save democracy for all Americans, not just some.

Now we will examine the status of the threats in our own time.

# 8

## Dangerous Convergence

From early on, President Donald Trump showed a willingness to put the pillars of democracy at risk, starting with free and fair elections. During the 2016 presidential campaign, he said, "Russia, if you're listening, I hope you're able to find the 30,000 [Hillary Clinton] emails that are missing," essentially inviting a foreign power to conduct espionage against his political adversary. And just weeks after the election, he stoked doubts about the results when he claimed, with no evidence, that he would have won the popular vote (which he lost by nearly three million votes) "if you deduct the millions of people who voted illegally."[1]

Even more striking than Trump's behavior was the apparent lack of anything or anyone who could stop it. Stunned Republican leaders, who spoke disapprovingly of him during the primary, one by one came to support him as he cinched the nomination and then triumphed in the general election. Some public officials tried, in vain, to deter Trump from ignoring democratic principles. Prominent among them was FBI director James Comey, who attempted to nudge him toward upholding the rule of law.

Several weeks before the inauguration, Comey briefed President-elect Trump about the intelligence community's unanimous judgment that Russia had tried to interfere in the election on Trump's behalf. Once in office, Trump invited Comey to the White House for what turned out to be a private dinner, at which the president pressured him, first asking if he wanted to keep his job and then telling him, "I need loyalty." Trump proceeded to tell Comey that he was considering asking the FBI to "investigate"—for the purpose of disproving—salacious rumors regarding his 2013 visit to Moscow; in reply, Comey tried to explain why that would be inappropriate. Yet month after month, Trump made more such requests of Comey, each circumventing the strict parameters imposed by the rule of law. Each time, Comey demurred. Finally, on May 9, Trump fired him.[2] Shortly thereafter, responding to requests from Capitol Hill, Deputy Attorney General Rod Rosenstein appointed Robert Mueller as special counsel to investigate Russian interference in the 2016 election and any links between the Trump campaign and Russia.

Infuriated, Trump directed his anger at Attorney General Jeff Sessions. As a close advisor to Trump's campaign, Sessions had been legally obligated to recuse himself from involvement in the Russia investigation in order to preserve the integrity of the rule of law, which requires that such investigations be free of political influence.[3] Trump was livid at what he perceived as a personal betrayal and stunning lack of loyalty from Sessions, and he fired him.

Trump made no secret of the fact that he viewed both the FBI and the Justice Department not as public entities responsible for carrying out the rule of law but rather as personally answerable to him. He regarded them as a private investigative force and a law firm that could safeguard him through the investigations they conducted or chose not to conduct, and even through the interpretations they reached. At last, in William Barr, Trump found an attorney general who was willing to provide the personal protection he sought.

On March 24, 2019, two days after Mueller submitted his voluminous report to the Justice Department, Barr released a four-page letter framing the findings. The special counsel had refrained from making a judgment on whether the president had obstructed justice, but Barr took it upon himself to do so, concluding that the report failed to make the case. An exuberant Trump tweeted, "No Collusion, No Obstruction, Complete and Total EXONERATION," adding, "KEEP AMERICA GREAT!"[4]

The highly detailed seven-hundred-page report would not become public until weeks later, but when it did, its words contradicted both

Barr's and Trump's interpretations of its findings. According to the report's conclusion, "If we had confidence after a thorough investigation of the facts that the President clearly did not commit obstruction of justice, we would so state. Accordingly, while this report does not conclude that the President committed a crime, it also does not exonerate him." The report documented numerous instances when the president asked people in his administration to derail the Mueller investigation.[5] Yet even after repeatedly and overtly challenging the rule of law, Trump proceeded undeterred.

From the late twentieth century onward, all four threats to democracy escalated and converged, and by the 2010s, they created a perfect storm. Into this political moment stepped a brash businessman-turned-television-personality-turned-politician, with no experience in government. He was ready to ride the storm to political victory, harnessing its fury in his quest for power, with no concern for what might be destroyed in its path. As all four threats reached high velocity and in combination generated even greater momentum, the embattled political system showed a profound lack of capacity to rein in the president. When all four threats crest in tandem, it turns out, a president and his partisan allies who control one or both chambers of Congress can threaten basic principles of American democracy in plain sight and get away with it.

How did the four threats reach this dangerous point? None of them attained its current status merely as a result of natural processes or impersonal social forces beyond human control. To the contrary, political leaders actively nurtured each of them over the past several decades, in the midst of their struggle for political power. They aided and abetted their growth, leading us to where we are now. The convergence of threats, in turn, has catalyzed interactions that imperil democracy.

## BECOMING "US VERSUS THEM": POLARIZATION ASCENDANT

Despite one revelation after another about Trump's actions that endangered democracy, he continued to enjoy steadfast support from his party. Republicans in Congress stood by him, repeatedly declining either to criticize his behavior in public or to participate in congressional oversight of his administration. Republican voters, too, remained faithful, approving of the president at rates that generally surpassed 85 percent, and even 90 percent in early 2020.[6] Polarization today provides a crucial foundation of support for presidents from their own partisans in Congress and from voters. How did it come to this?

Polarization is not a fixed, steady state; rather, it is like a hurricane gathering momentum, intensifying, and sweeping up more and more in its path of danger and destruction.[7] Polarization arises partly from decades of slow-moving changes among ordinary citizens, as they shift their party affiliation. But polarization can also be stimulated by political leaders, deliberately and strategically. Once under way, it can take on a life of its own, as it generates reinforcing dynamics and becomes harder and harder to reverse. Contemporary polarization has developed in these ways, leading us to our present politics.

Certainly long-term trends among voters helped set the stage for today's polarization. New generations of voters in the mid-twentieth century gradually shifted away from the party of their parents and began to re-sort themselves, with liberals increasingly identifying as Democrats and conservatives as Republicans. The Democratic Party's growing support for civil rights and voting rights and the demise of racial segregation in the South coincided with the gradual departure of white southerners from its ranks and their shift into the Republican Party. In fact, white southerners had been leaving the Democratic Party since the late 1930s, as they grew uncomfortable with its embrace of organized labor.[8] By the 1980s the Democrats had shed most of their long-faithful white southern members, leaving behind a party that exhibited more consistent liberal values across the board.

Meanwhile, the Republican Party began to court white southerners. In part, this happened as the party began to emphasize social issues—for example, by signaling hostility to homosexuality as early as the 1950s. Richard Nixon's "southern strategy" hastened the process, as did the emerging alliance between social and economic conservatives. With the rise of the Moral Majority in the 1980s, evangelical Christians and conservative Catholics increasingly identified with the Republican Party, attracted particularly by its opposition to abortion and eventually to its antipathy to gay rights. At the same time, the Republican Party began to embrace a consistent message about small government and low taxes that

8.1  Partisan polarization by party in US House of Representatives, 1969–2019

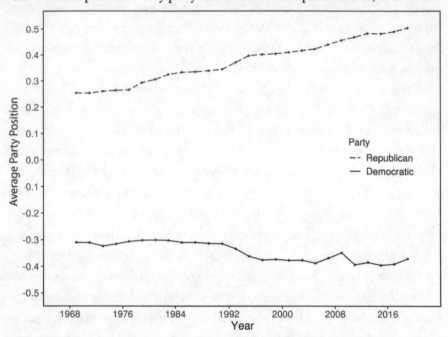

Source: Jeffrey B. Lewis, Keith Poole, Howard Rosenthal, Adam Boche, Aaron Rudkin, and Luke Sonnet, *Voteview: Congressional Roll-Call Votes Database* (2020), https://www.voteview.com/articles/party_polarization.

also resonated with southern white voters as well as many others who felt that the federal government had overreached with its commitments to racial equality and social welfare.[9]

Since that time, the two parties in Congress have grown more distinct from each other. More roll-call votes occur as straight party-line votes, with fewer members acting as swing voters who are willing to vote with the other side. Figure 8.1 shows the change over time, since 1969, in the voting position of the average Democrat in the House compared to the average Republican. Democrats shifted in a slightly more liberal direction in the 1990s, but after that remained fairly constant in their voting patterns. Republicans, meanwhile, moved sharply in a more conservative direction throughout the entire period. The gap between the parties increased dramatically. This occurred in part because moderate Republicans retired or lost their seats and were generally replaced by more conservative Republicans.[10] Relative to the Republicans, the Democratic Party retains "big-tent" characteristics, as it encompasses both progressive members from safe districts and more moderate members from more competitive ones.

But rising polarization in Congress did not happen just in response to voters. Rather, political leaders quite actively promoted it.

## REPUBLICAN LEADERS DRIVE POLARIZATION

Starting in the late 1970s, conservative Republicans in Congress emerged as active agents of polarization. After decades of Democratic dominance of national politics, they increasingly came to feel that everything they believed in was under attack. They strategized to become—at the very least—a more organized and vocal opposition party.

The question was, how? Since the New Deal, the Democratic Party has been composed of a variety of groups, each of which seeks attention from government, and political leaders routinely respond with public policies that address their demands. Throughout the postwar decades, Republican politicians, lacking the power to set the agenda, sought opportunities to influence policymaking by promoting more moderate approaches and finding ways to compromise with Democrats.

But as the Republican Party became both more single-minded in its quest for limited government and low taxes and more determined to win elections, this pattern of mutual accommodation became less appealing. In essence, Republicans faced a conundrum: they could not promise new public programs because those ran counter to their small-government beliefs; neither could they win elections simply by cutting existing programs, because in fact their own constituents relied on them heavily.[11]

It was at this juncture that conservative political leaders rejected the strategy of accommodation and embraced confrontation. Newly elected Republicans in Congress, under the leadership of Newt Gingrich, challenged what they perceived as a leftward drift of their own party under President Nixon and the party's moderate congressional leadership.[12] Gingrich organized the Conservative Opportunity Society, a group that aimed to challenge the House Democratic leadership at every turn. Members used politically motivated amendments and inflated rhetoric, often provoking the Democrats to overreact, and that in turn helped the conservatives to win allies among moderate Republicans. They also grabbed attention by using the public-affairs cable network C-SPAN, created in 1979, to give inflammatory one-minute speeches on issues that were calculated to grab the attention of television viewers.

In those televised speeches, Gingrich and his allies would level outrageous accusations against Democrats—for example, calling them "blind to communism." The lack of a response from the chamber could make it seem, to viewers, that the charges must be true. Yet when Democratic House Speaker Tip O'Neill asked C-SPAN to pan the chamber, it showed that typically the speeches were being delivered to an empty room. O'Neill condemned the strategy as "the lowest thing I've ever seen in my 32 years in Congress." The kerfuffle generated considerable media attention, and a delighted Gingrich announced, "I am now a famous person."[13]

Attracting the media spotlight was crucial to Gingrich's strategy. As he explained to a group of conservative activists, "The number one thing about the media . . . is they love fights. . . . You have to give them confrontations. When you give them confrontations, you get attention; when you get attention, you can educate."[14] Gingrich and his allies criticized the media for its supposed liberal bias, all the while basking in its attention.

Movement conservatives also used confrontational strategies to spur disdain for federal taxes and support for tax cuts. Starting in 1986, Grover Norquist, president of Americans for Tax Reform, succeeded in soliciting pledges not to raise taxes from over 90 percent of House Republicans. In each election since, conservatives pressured candidates to "take the pledge," to state forthrightly that they would oppose any increase in tax rates or government revenues. President George H. W. Bush was chastised for violating that promise, further fanning the fury on the right.[15]

Of course, polarization involves a widening gap between two sides, and certainly while Democrats were in power they did their part, which helped escalate the intensity of conflict.[16] But Republican Party leaders steered the process, with Democrats playing a more responsive role.

Polarization worked: conservative Republicans began to win more elections. In the 1994 election, they triumphed collectively, with the party winning control of the House of Representatives for the first time since 1952. Not only did the Republicans gain fifty-two seats in the chamber, but they filled those seats with Gingrich loyalists. The party embraced the "Contract with America," a list of conservative policy priorities, and achieved some of their goals through legislation such as the Personal Responsibility and Work Opportunity Act, otherwise known as welfare reform. Gingrich embraced obstructionist tactics even when it came to routine matters such as the federal budget (provoking a government shutdown, which has become far more common since then) and the federal debt limit. Once President Bill Clinton's affair with White House intern Monica Lewinsky came to light, House Republicans approved articles of impeachment against the president, the first time the chamber had done so since 1868. House leaders threatened that Republicans who failed to vote in favor of impeachment would face a primary challenge.[17]

Senate Republicans also began to operate in a more concerted fashion, and that chamber became more polarized as well. Senate norms had long dictated deference to colleagues and a spirit of courtesy and bipartisanship, but those dissipated as its business, like that of the House, increasingly centered around partisan struggles. Filibusters proliferated, increasing from fewer than one per two-year Congress in the period from 1955 to 1960 to twenty-eight per Congress between 1993 and 1998.[18] Gridlock ensued, and most bills, lacking the sixty votes necessary to overcome a filibuster, never even came to a vote.[19]

During President George W. Bush's presidency, polarization increased further. The Republican Congress achieved several of its goals, including two sweeping tax cuts and higher defense spending. Yet conservatives grew increasingly disenchanted with their own party, put off by new government spending for expanded Medicare benefits and the No Child Left Behind education law. They aimed to steer the party further to the right.

Already, conservatives' rise had been fueled by their ability to use the media to their advantage, attacking it for biased, liberal reporting, on the one hand, while courting the publicity it provided to their cause, on the other. Soon the media landscape would be transformed in ways that aided them further.

## THE RISE OF CONSERVATIVE MEDIA

Changes in technology ushered in a proliferation of new media sources, and conservatives took advantage of powerful new ways to convey their message, unfettered by mid-twentieth-century journalistic norms of fair reporting.

Of course, partisan media is nothing new in the United States; as we saw, it emerged quickly in the 1790s, and thrived throughout the nineteenth century. The professional, investigative journalism that was commonplace from the 1950s through the 1970s is the exception to the rule. In that era, print and broadcast media won a high degree of trust from a vast majority of the public, including both Republicans and Democrats.[20] The media earned a reputation as a "watchdog" that could hold public officials accountable, as highlighted by 1950s coverage by journalist Edward Murrow of Red-baiting by Senator Joseph McCarthy, scenes of southern resistance to civil rights that played out on national television, and the revelation of the Watergate scandal by *Washington Post* journalists Bob Woodward and Carl Bernstein.

Conservative political leaders tried to stoke distrust of the mainstream media starting as early as Barry Goldwater's 1964 presidential campaign. Over subsequent decades, Republican presidents from Nixon through George H. W. Bush complained of a liberal bias among journalists, despite a lack of evidence.[21]

The floodgates opened to a torrent of new conservative media outlets in 1985 when the Federal Communications Commission stopped enforcing the "fairness doctrine." That rule had required broadcasters who aired programs on controversial issues to provide time for opposing views to be heard. In its absence, conservative outlets proliferated, with talk radio leading the way. By 1990, more than five million listeners per week tuned in to hear Rush Limbaugh's national radio program, and some estimates put the number as high as fifteen million or more.[22]

The advent of cable news and the internet fostered still more sources of partisan news, with conservative choices gaining the largest market share. On television, Fox News became the country's most-watched cable station; by 2019, it crushed the competition, netting an average of 2.4 million viewers during prime time, compared to 1.5 million for MSNBC and 1.0 million for CNN.[23]

The ascent of conservative media has generated an angrier public, undermined trust in government, and stimulated hostility toward those in the other party. The biased presentation of the news on such partisan outlets has been shown to prompt viewers to adopt more negative views of the other party and to trust it less, as well as to become more disapproving of bipartisanship. Fox News and conservative talk radio, in particular, provoke anger and fear among their listeners by portraying politics as a story of heroes and villains, and by using overgeneralizations, sensationalism, and ridicule of opponents to create a sense of melodrama. By cultivating outrage, these outlets foster and maintain an engaged audience.[24]

Not surprisingly, ordinary Americans are becoming more and more socially polarized—divided into separate groups that harbor prejudice and anger toward one another. People's partisan affiliations have assumed the character of social identities, group affiliations based on emotional and social connections rather than ideological agreement—as if they are rooting for a sports team rather than making a carefully considered investment.[25] Such "us versus them" politics reached a fever pitch soon after the election of the country's first black president.

## RISING POLARIZATION FROM THE TEA PARTY ONWARD

During President Barack Obama's first term in office, conservative hostility gave rise to the Tea Party, a mostly grassroots mobilization with roots in long-standing traditions of American conservatism. Members began to hold rallies across the country, waving signs with such slogans as "T.E.A.: Taxed Enough Already" and "Redistribute My Work Ethic!" and wearing Revolutionary War–era costumes. Their organizations proliferated nationwide, drawing members who tended to be older, white, and male. They railed against rising deficits, government spending, and immigration, as well as "handouts" to groups they deemed "undeserving" compared to "hardworking" Americans like themselves. As members of Congress debated the health care bill that became the Affordable Care Act, angry Tea Partiers filled town hall meetings in their districts.[26]

Emboldened by their base, Republicans in Congress refused to cooperate with Democrats on the president's top priorities; they contributed not a single vote to the 2009 economic stimulus bill in the House and only three in the Senate, and none in either chamber supported the Affordable Care Act on final passage in 2010. The Tea Party recruited new candidates to run for office in 2010, many of them challenging moderate Republican incumbents in primary races. A victorious GOP gained sixty-three seats in the House, taking the majority, and new members took a more uncompromising approach than the more moderate members they replaced.[27]

A new generation of House Republican leaders who called themselves the "Young Guns" picked up where Gingrich left off, fighting not only Democrats but even their own fellow partisans. They obstructed key votes on the federal budget and the debt limit by catering to a base that was keenly focused on fiscal conservatism. They pushed the party toward extended brinksmanship, using the need to raise the nation's debt limit to prevent default as a bargaining chip to extract large spending cuts from Democrats and exhibiting an unwillingness to compromise. Ultimately, in 2011, President Obama and congressional Republicans struck a deal to raise the debt limit and try to limit government spending, but not until the nation came perilously close to defaulting on its debt. The close call prompted Standard & Poor's to downgrade the credit rating of the United States for the first time in history.[28]

Senate Republicans also played partisan hardball. Their leader, Mitch McConnell, in outlining the party's top priority in the 2010 midterm election, explained, "The single most important thing we want to achieve is for President Obama to be a one-term president."[29]

## ALL ROADS LEAD TO TRUMP

Although Republican Party leaders themselves did not endorse Trump early on, in fact the work they had done for decades to make the party more competitive paved the way for him. His candidacy marked the natural progression of both contemporary conservatism and polarization more broadly as they had developed from the 1970s onward.

Trump took pages from the playbooks of the up-and-coming party leaders of those decades, from Gingrich through the Young Guns. He outdid them with his confrontational style, eviscerating political foes and sometimes even allies. He excelled at attracting media attention by inciting controversy and making outrageous statements. In equal measure, he castigated the media, slamming negative coverage as "fake news" and journalists as "enemies of the people." For decades, Republicans had normalized the precursors to such behavior; now, with their rank-and-file highly mobilized, they embraced a candidate who took it to a new level.

As polarization has grown, ordinary Americans have come to exhibit

### 8.2 Growing negative partisanship: Partisans' ratings of own party and opposing party on feeling thermometer, 1978–2016

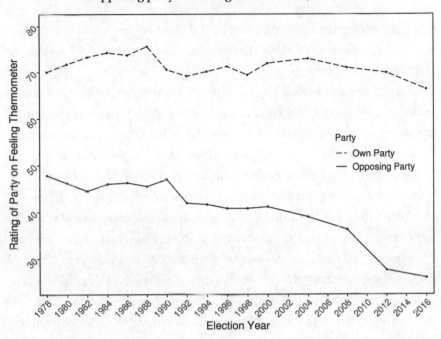

Source: American National Election Studies, Cumulative File, 1948–2016

"negative partisanship," meaning feelings of hostility toward the opposing party that often outweigh their positive feelings toward their own party. People increasingly perceive those in the opposing party as very different from themselves, embracing the "us versus them" mentality. This view drives voting decisions, as the desire to vote against opponents may outweigh enthusiasm for one's own party's candidates.[30]

Negative partisanship drove voting in the 2016 presidential election, as neither candidate received high rankings from their own party, but partisans particularly disliked the opposing party's candidate. Partisan voters have always naturally tended to think better of their own party than the opposing party. But as Figure 8.2 shows, in recent decades voters' positive opinion of the opposing party has declined dramatically, while their positive feelings about their own party have remained stable.

This pattern of mutual antagonism toward the other side reached a high point in the 2016 election. On a "feeling thermometer" of 0 (liked least) to 100 degrees, Republicans on average rated Hillary Clinton at 12 degrees while Democrats rated Trump at 11 degrees. As one evangelical said, explaining his vote for Trump, "As flawed as Trump's character is, it was a lot better than Hillary Clinton's." Ultimately, voters stuck with their parties, as 92 percent of Republicans voted for Trump and 94 percent of Democrats for Clinton.[31]

Trump himself fueled negative partisanship: long after he became president, his persistent attacks on Hillary Clinton remained one of the surest means of unifying his supporters. Even as scandals mounted during the first three years of his administration, Republicans continued to regard him as less disagreeable than any alternative. Republican office-holders, too, despite qualms about Trump, became his solid supporters.

Polarization has been promoted by political leaders, particularly conservatives, for decades. They embraced confrontational strategies, encouraged the rise of partisan media, and fueled a devoted and angry base of voters. Their success gave rise to Trump's presidency. With him in the White House, all Americans must grapple with a president who thrives on creating division and a base that seems unwilling to abandon him. He is a polarizer par excellence.

## FANNING THE FLAMES OF CONFLICT OVER MEMBERSHIP AND STATUS

Trump's candidacy soared as he fanned the flames of conflict over membership and status, shunning "political correctness" and making bold, derogatory remarks about immigrants, women, and people of color. Once in office, he continued this approach, angering his opponents while simultaneously energizing his most ardent supporters. In the first weeks of his presidency, he issued a travel ban against visitors from Muslim-majority countries, an effort that went through numerous iterations before finally meeting with judicial approval. In August 2017, he brushed off the neo-Nazi gathering in Charlottesville, Virginia, and the violence that ensued, stating that "both sides" were at fault.[32] That same month, he pardoned Joe Arpaio, the former Arizona sheriff who had been convicted for his harsh treatment of Latinos, including racial profiling, and who had become known for his campaign against undocumented immigrants. In January 2018, in an Oval Office meeting with senators about protecting immigrants from several African countries, Haiti, and El Salvador, he said, "Why are we having all these people from shithole countries coming here?" Month after month, Trump made such remarks, catering to the sentiments of his electoral base, many of whom delighted in these restrictive and often prejudiced answers to the question of "who belongs."[33]

How did the contemporary United States give rise to such incendiary politics over questions of belonging and status? The question is puzzling, given that a few years earlier it might have seemed that a more inclusive and egalitarian order was taking hold. The election of Barack Obama as the nation's first black president appeared to signal a new era. Shortly after Obama's inauguration, his Supreme Court appointee Sonia Sotomayor became the first Latina to serve on the high court. Although the percentage of women in the lower chamber of the US Congress still lagged behind that of seventy-three nations in the world, the numbers have continued to grow, reaching 24 percent after the 2018 election.[34] Racial and ethnic diversity in Congress also rose to its highest point ever, with 22 percent of members belonging to minority groups.

Yet despite these markers of progress, racial inequality remains deeply entrenched in the United States. African Americans and other racial and ethnic minorities consistently lag behind whites in income, wealth, employment, educational attainment, health, housing, and criminal justice. African Americans, for example, are nearly three times as likely as non-Hispanic whites to be poor, almost six times as likely to be incarcerated, and only half as likely to graduate from college. The average wealth of white households in the United States is ten times as high as that of black households. One recent study showed that the median net worth of a black family in the Boston area is $8.[35] In response to deaths of young black men at the hands of police officers, the Black Lives Matter movement emerged, renewing attention to racial disparities in the criminal justice system. Despite real progress on many fronts, deep racial fault lines continue to permeate the nation.

Meanwhile, the United States has become a more diverse society since the mid-twentieth century, bringing greater attention to questions about who belongs. The nonwhite share of the American population increased due to differences in birthrates and immigration from Latin America and Asia. Non-Hispanic whites declined from 80 percent of the population in 1980 to 60 percent in 2018; the Census Bureau projects that they will be a minority by 2045.[36] Nonwhites, therefore, constitute a growing share of the electorate. These trends provide fodder for politicians who wish to appeal to white voters who hold on to a nostalgic view of white-dominated society.

As in earlier periods, conflict over the boundaries of national community and civic status—particularly when it involves formative rifts—can be easily rekindled when political opportunity presents itself and political actors seize it.[37] In the 1890s, white supremacy provided a powerful means of unifying political support. Now as then, hostility over deep social divisions, when activated in combination with political polarization, provides a toxic and volatile mix.

As the country has become more diverse, the two political parties have increasingly embraced divergent visions of American society with respect to race. The landmark Civil Rights Act of 1964 and Voting Rights Act of 1965 owed their passage to bipartisan coalitions, and neither party proposed scaling back those laws in the ensuing decades. Moreover, the Voting Rights Act was reauthorized, with bipartisan support, under both Presidents Ronald Reagan and George H. W. Bush.[38] But over the last decades of the twentieth century, the parties began to part ways on the extent to which they pursued racial equality or permitted its demise.

At first the shift was more subtle than explicit, since overtly racist or ethnonationalist appeals had become taboo among political leaders. Instead, Republicans used more covert racially coded campaign messages, an approach initiated by Goldwater and Nixon. In 1980, for example, shortly after winning the Republican nomination, Ronald Reagan held his first post-convention campaign appearance at the Neshoba County, Mississippi, State Fair—just a few miles from the county seat, Philadelphia, where three civil rights workers had been slain by the Ku Klux Klan in 1964. In the speech, Reagan celebrated "states' rights," a reference that evoked earlier support for slavery and opposition to civil rights. And in 1988, George H. W. Bush's "Willie Horton" ad used an image of an African American criminal to activate implicit racial bias among white voters.[39] Campaign appeals such as these evoked and sanctioned racism.

Among white Americans, views on race have softened on some measures but have persisted on others. One the one hand, compared to sev-

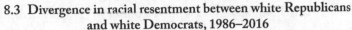

8.3  Divergence in racial resentment between white Republicans
and white Democrats, 1986–2016

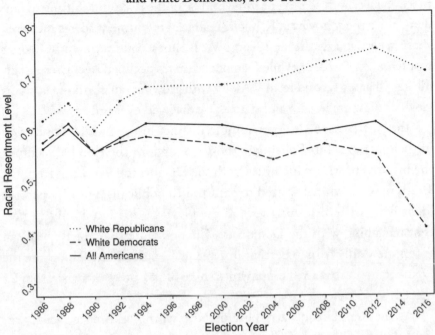

Source: American National Election Studies, Cumulative File, 1948–2016

eral decades ago, whites are now much more likely to support school
integration, oppose job discrimination, and reject the notion of biolog-
ically superior and inferior races.[40] Yet in other respects, racial hostility
among whites overall, though it has vacillated a bit over time, differs little
today from thirty years ago.

We find evidence for this in feelings known collectively as "racial resentment," which blame the persistence of racial inequality on African
Americans themselves, attributable to reasons such as laziness or lack of
a work ethic. Racial resentment indicates that an individual accepts common racial stereotypes about things like the moral superiority of one's own
racial group and the characteristics of other groups. Although the survey
questions used to measure racial resentment focus on whites' attitudes
toward African Americans, people's answers have been shown to correlate
highly with their views toward other racial minorities and immigrants.[41]

Racial resentment has increasingly divided the parties. As Figure 8.3
depicts, in the 1980s, during the presidencies of Ronald Reagan and George

H. W. Bush, white Democrats and white Republicans held very similar attitudes on race, both scoring near the middle of the scale and shifting in tandem. Since then, however, Republicans' racial resentment scores increased
sharply, particularly during George W. Bush's second term and Obama's
first term (2005–2013), while Democrats' scores declined steeply, especially
during Obama's second term.[42] Along with growing polarization, partisans'
views about membership and status have diverged over time as well.

The parties have also grown more distinct in the racial composition
of their membership. Starting in the 1930s and for the next half century,
the majority of whites identified with the Democratic Party, but from the
1980s onward whites shifted toward the Republicans, with 55 percent
identifying with or leaning toward the GOP by 2012 and only 39 percent remaining with the Democrats. The nonwhite share of Republican
voters grew only from 6 percent in 1992 to 12 percent in 2016, while the
Democratic Party saw the nonwhite share of its voters increase from 21
percent to 45 percent.[43]

As the Republican Party became both whiter and more racially re-
sentful than the population generally, its rhetoric surrounding small government and lower taxes took on strong racial overtones. In large part,
Republican voters pushed back against the diversification of American
society, particularly after Obama's election. They took exception to those
they perceived as "freeloaders," who were receiving help from the government and who seemed to be "jumping the queue" to obtain what seemed
like special treatment. The Tea Party movement crystallized for many
Americans the lament that the country they had known—one that was
mostly white, male-dominated, and Christian—was gone.[44]

Donald Trump emerged on the political scene in the midst of the Tea
Party's ascent, peddling the "birther" conspiracy: the false claim that Barack
Obama had not been born in the United States and was therefore not a le-
gitimate president. This notion fused with views popular among Tea Party
adherents. As a radio talk-show host at a Tea Party rally in Coeur d'Alene,
Idaho, charged, "We are seeing a worldview clash in our White House. A
man who is a closet secular-type Muslim, but he's still a Muslim. He's no
Christian. We're seeing a man who's a socialist communist in the White
House, pretending to be an American . . . he wasn't even born here."[45]

Such views might still have seemed to be on the fringes of American politics if not for Trump's emergence as the front-runner for the Republican presidential nomination in 2016. Upon announcing his candidacy, he said, "When Mexico sends its people, they're not sending their best.... They're sending people that have lots of problems, and they're bringing those problems with us. They're bringing drugs. They're bringing crime. They're rapists. And some, I assume, are good people." Soon after, he called for a "total and complete shutdown of Muslims entering the United States."[46] Those who were attracted to him celebrated his dismissal of "political correctness" and his willingness to "tell it like it is." And although Republican elites spoke out against him, Trump continued to gain momentum and won not just the nomination but the presidency itself.

Trump effectively seized a political opportunity that had developed in the Republican Party and that others before him had not touched: he identified the base's already combustible attitudes about race and immigration and threw fuel on the fire. He appealed particularly to voters who felt strongly that American society was becoming too diverse in terms of race and ethnicity. Among Republican primary voters, those who held the least favorable views toward immigration, African Americans, and Muslims were the most likely to support Trump, compared to other, more conventional Republicans.[47]

Unlike Republican officials in recent decades who played the "race card" in more subtle ways, Trump did not veil his intent. And unlike his predecessors, such as George Wallace in 1968 and Pat Buchanan in 1996—unsuccessful candidates who had catered to the same racist and nativist sentiments—Trump won his party's nomination.

The 2016 race also activated voters' views about gender and civic status. Democrat Hillary Clinton earned the distinction of being the first woman in American history to win the presidential nomination of one of the two major parties. In contrast to her first run for the presidency in 2008, Clinton ran an explicitly feminist campaign in 2016. Trump's antipathy to gender equality became apparent not only through the sexist insults he delivered throughout his campaign but also when the *Washington Post* obtained and published a vulgar recording of Trump speaking off-camera with the host of NBC's *Access Hollywood* show and bragging about sexually assaulting women.[48]

In fact, Trump's messaging on gender inequality attracted more voters than Clinton's appeals to equality. The gender gap in voter choice grew in 2016 relative to the two previous elections, primarily because men changed how they voted: Trump won among men by 12 points, compared to just a 1-point advantage they gave John McCain in 2008 and 7 points for Mitt Romney in 2012. (Clinton won by 12 points among women, similar to Obama in the two previous elections.) Sexist attitudes motivated voters in 2016 more than in previous elections, further contributing to Trump's victory.[49]

By some measures, the United States of the early twenty-first century seemed on course to become more egalitarian in terms of race, ethnicity, and gender. Yet conflicts over who belongs and on what terms continued to fester, and they burst into the open once Trump became a candidate. As in the 1890s, party leaders activated racism, which reinforced partisan polarization and mobilized voters. Sexism, unlike in previous recent elections, also came to the fore in shaping vote choice. Trump seized the opportunity to benefit from both. In the process, he demonstrated that formative rifts, far from being eradicated in the United States, still retain the power to anger and energize a sizable part of the electorate that yearns to restore old status hierarchies.

## THE POLITICS OF RISING ECONOMIC INEQUALITY

Unlike the vociferous conflicts over membership and status that surrounded Trump's rise and his presidency, the politics of economic inequality grabs fewer headlines. It is obscured in part by journalists' framing of Trump's victory as driven by working-class whites who were angry about the economy—a claim that, under scrutiny, appears overstated. But it is also no secret that the contemporary Republican Party has long advocated a market-based approach consisting of lower taxes and the removal of regulatory restrictions, changes that most benefit the affluent and large businesses. When Republicans won control of the White House and both chambers of Congress in 2016, they seized the power to pursue these goals. The 2017 tax bill, Trump's major legislative achievement, gave by far the largest rewards to the wealthiest Americans and slashed corporate tax rates. In the day-to-day work of his administration, his cabinet secretaries and political appointees did the bidding of the rich and powerful, pursuing an agenda of deregulation of financial markets, the environment, and health care. The richest Americans, who have easy access to political voice, have benefited a great deal from these policies, and most have expressed no consternation about the fate of democracy on Trump's watch.[50]

Economic inequality has skyrocketed in the United States since the early 1970s. Like polarization and conflict over membership and status, it has also been facilitated by political leaders. Meanwhile, it has generated political inequality, with deleterious effects on the American political system.

In the early twentieth century, the United States featured a pyramid-shaped social structure, with a small wealthy elite on top, a modest-sized middle class, and at the bottom the majority of Americans, a large working class of industrial and agricultural workers. People of low and

### 8.4 Top 1 percent income earners' share of total national income, 1913–2018

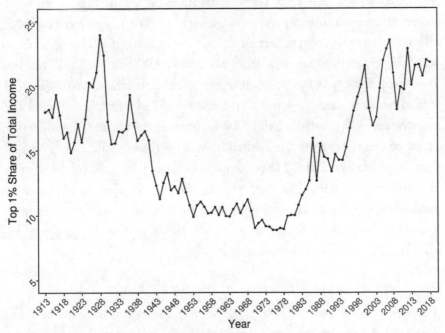

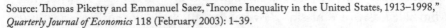

Source: Thomas Piketty and Emmanuel Saez, "Income Inequality in the United States, 1913–1998," *Quarterly Journal of Economics* 118 (February 2003): 1–39.

moderate incomes struggled during the Great Depression. After World War II, economic growth soared and Americans across the income spectrum saw their incomes rise by comparable percentages. The ranks of the middle class swelled, shifting the social structure into a diamond shape. Economic historians refer to the era as "the great compression," signifying how economic inequality diminished.[51]

At first the gains were experienced mostly by white men. Their college degree attainment spiked after the war and led graduates into secure white-collar jobs. White men with less education found plentiful jobs in industry that offered good pay, secure benefits, and the protection of belonging to a labor union. African American men's opportunities remained stymied by segregation and labor market discrimination, and occupational segregation continued to close off options for women. Civil rights laws enacted in the 1960s and feminist achievements of the 1970s lowered these barriers. Progress had barely started, however, before it was halted by new trends that reinforced old racial and gender hierarchies.[52]

This occurred as economic inequality began to widen starting in the mid-1970s. Those at the very top pulled away from everyone else. As Figure 8.4 above shows, the share of income held by the top 1 percent of earners increased from 9 percent in the early 1970s to 22 percent in 2018. These top earners enjoyed stratospheric new heights of affluence, as their average pretax income grew from about $420,000 to $1.3 million; increases for the top 0.1 percent grew even more dramatically, rising by 320 percent, and among the top 0.01 percent by 453 percent. Meanwhile, for Americans in the bottom half of the income distribution, their collective share of the income pie diminished from 20 percent in the early 1980s to just 12 percent in 2014. Making matters worse, jobs held by those with less education became less likely than in the past to offer benefits such as health coverage and retirement savings. The economy was continuing to grow, but the gains were no longer widely distributed, with consequences that transformed American society.[53]

## POLITICAL CHOICES THAT FUELED INEQUALITY

Rising economic inequality resulted not just from choices made by business leaders but also from those made by political leaders. In what might be called sins of omission, lawmakers failed to take sufficient action to mitigate rising economic inequality through public policy. Despite the growth in government social provision over time, relatively little of it assists struggling families in the working-age population or children; most of it goes either to senior citizens or to upper-income households through tax advantages. Benefits in policies that do aim to assist low-income Americans, such as the Earned Income Tax Credit, have not been sufficient to make up for stagnating wages. The rise in college graduation rates has been concentrated among Americans in the top income quartile; the demise of state support for public higher education, in particular, has depressed degree attainment for young people in the bottom 75 percent, among whom improvements have been modest at best.[54]

But sins of commission by lawmakers have fostered inequality as well, as they have promoted the interests of the wealthiest Americans and powerful business interests. From World War I until the 1980s, the top marginal tax rate on the wealthiest taxpayers typically hovered above 70 percent, and it was as high as 94 percent during World War II. Since the Reagan era, by contrast, Republican presidents have signed into law several tax cuts that have lowered the top rate. The 2017 tax bill signed by Trump brought the rate down to 37 percent. Not only have marginal tax rates diminished for the top earners, but lawmakers reduced the capital gains tax as well; its present rate of 23.8 percent permits wealthy people to have their investment income taxed at a much lower rate than earned income. In addition, lawmakers relaxed regulations on business over this long period.[55]

Policymakers' actions and inactions in the service of a tiny sliver of the population beg for an explanation. Whereas their actions to promote polarization and conflict over membership and status engage large constituencies among their partisan supporters, their work to exacerbate inequality aids only a few and is detrimental to the vast majority of Americans. Most Americans, regardless of party, favor policy changes that would reduce inequality by aiding low- and middle-income people. Why would policymakers ignore them and protect the affluent instead?[56]

## THE POLITICALLY ACTIVE RICH

In recent years, the wealthiest Americans and major businesses have devoted considerably greater energy and attention to political action. At first blush, this might appear to be nothing new; those with more education and resources have long tended to engage more in standard political activities than those with less.[57] And businesses have also long been more likely than ordinary Americans to be organized to represent their interests, through groups ranging from the Chamber of Commerce and Business Roundtable to the National Association of Realtors. Yet in recent decades, the affluent have stepped up their game.

The sheer amount of money in politics has proliferated, amplifying the voice of those who have more money to spend. The total amount spent on federal elections has increased in years with presidential elections, from $3.1 billion in 2000 to $6.5 billion in 2016, and in years with only congressional elections from just over $1.6 billion in 1998 to over $5.7 billion in 2018. Campaign contributions, not surprisingly, flow particularly from the most affluent; 20 percent of Americans in the top 10 percent of the income distribution have made campaign contributions, compared to less than 5 percent of those in the bottom half of the income distribution.[58]

When wealthy people become engaged in politics, they often do it quietly, letting their money do the talking. Of the one hundred richest billionaires, 36 percent hosted political fundraisers or bundled their contributions with those of others, and a whopping 92 percent made contributions to political parties or candidates, outside groups, or ballot initiatives, giving an average *annual* contribution of $509,249. These figures do not include so-called dark money, which has been sanctioned by the 2010 *Citizens United v. FEC* Supreme Court decision. Campaign contributions from the wealthy tilt the political playing field toward conservative politics; two-thirds of the billionaires who made political party contributions bestowed them primarily or exclusively on Republicans.[59]

But the affluent have also grown more involved in highly visible politics, particularly through strategic political organizing. A network of organizations funded by the Koch brothers (David, who died in 2019, and Charles), such as Americans for Prosperity, and other groups such as American Crossroads and Heritage Action, raise money from affluent donors and channel it into campaigns and other political networks. They have also invested in organizing, pushing members of Congress to sign a "no climate tax" pledge similar to the "no new taxes" pledge that was initiated by Grover Norquist. At the state level they have advanced efforts to curb unions and have supported other economic policies favored by business organizations. Through such activity, they have pushed the Republican Party to the right.[60]

And it's not just wealthy individuals; the amount that corporations spend on lobbying and the degree of their involvement in politics have also grown dramatically in recent decades. Corporations today are much more likely than a few decades ago to have a full-time governmental relations staff to advocate on their behalf. The amount spent on lobbying by corporations grew from $1.13 billion annually in 1998 to over $2 billion in 2008, 2009, and 2010, though it has tapered off slightly since then. Certainly labor unions and groups that represent the public have lobbyists as well, but corporations outspend them by a ratio of $34 for every $1 they spend, as of 2012.[61]

Labor unions, historically, helped not only to reduce economic inequality, by fighting for higher wages and improved benefits, but also to mitigate political inequality. For decades, they channeled campaign contributions and lobbied on workers' behalf and mobilized their members and supporters for political action. But labor union membership has declined sharply, down from 20.1 percent of all workers in 1983 to 10.5 percent in 2018. As a result, workers have a less powerful voice today than a few decades ago.[62]

Unlike conflict over membership and status, which grabs the attention of many citizens, much of the political mobilization of the rich goes relatively unnoticed by the public. Today, as in the 1890s, wealthy people seek political power so that their fortunes and future earning potential can be protected. As long as the politicians who do their bidding succeed, the wealthy do not mind if they use racism and nativism in the process, whether to consolidate supporters, divert attention, or provide cover. Trump willingly pursued the interests of the richest Americans. Danger to democracy incurred along the way appears to be of little concern to them.

## BIPARTISAN EFFORTS AT EXECUTIVE AGGRANDIZEMENT

Americans have become accustomed to more powerful presidents over the past eighty years. Though most will tell pollsters they prefer limited government and applaud checks and balances, they nonetheless want government to accomplish things, and presidents appear best poised to deliver. Modern-day presidents of both parties have attempted to rise to these expectations by claiming greater power than their predecessors, and Trump has followed suit. When Congress repeatedly and pointedly refused him funding to build his cherished "border wall," for example, he diverted funds allocated for another purpose. He also ordered a drone assassination of the Iranian military leader Qasem Suleimani, violating even the narrow parameters of congressional war powers that other recent presidents respected.[63] In pursuing such actions, Trump is simply taking the next step on a path already cleared by his presidential forebears from both parties.

Revelations of presidential overreach in Vietnam and Watergate led Congress to work to rein in presidential power. In 1973, Congress overrode President Nixon's veto to pass the War Powers Resolution, which attempted to limit the president's authority to commit American troops without congressional authorization. The following year, Congress passed the Congressional Budget and Impoundment Control Act, aiming to bolster its own control over federal spending.

These gambits failed. While they may have slowed the growth of presidential power, they did not manage to restrain future presidents. The tools of presidential power that developed over the twentieth century—delegated authority, the administrative state, the White House staff, and the national security state—not only remain intact but have also continued to grow.[64]

Moreover, the rise of polarization over these decades has inadvertently escalated the rise of executive power. As the parties in Congress have diverged ideologically and engaged in repeated battles of blame and obstruction, making gridlock and stalemate the norm, presidents often struggle to achieve their policy aims. Meanwhile, they face rising expectations from their partisan constituencies, which they are increasingly unable to meet through ordinary legislative channels.[65]

And so presidents continue to push the envelope of unilateral action. They resort to unilateral policymaking approaches, including tools such as executive orders and proclamations, as a work-around. They possess greater power to command American military force on their own than ever before. And they are also increasingly tempted to wield the presidency as a partisan weapon on behalf of their partisan "team."[66] In doing so, they put free and fair elections and the integrity of rights at risk.

Contemporary presidents sit atop a vast and increasingly opaque web of intelligence operations that has unprecedented capacity to investigate, harass, spy on, and disrupt not just suspected enemies but American citizens as well, ostensibly for the purposes of finding and suppressing subversive or otherwise dangerous activity. Even after the cold war with the Soviet Union ended, these powers have persisted and even grown. The USA PATRIOT Act, passed in the wake of 9/11, authorized the executive branch to take unprecedented measures to combat terrorism, including relaxed rules about domestic surveillance and expanded law enforcement access to private information. During the Bush administration's "war on terror," the National Security Agency engaged in extensive warrantless wiretapping of domestic communications. Such activities received justification from the theory of the "unitary executive," which holds that the president should have unfettered power to direct the executive branch. George W. Bush suspended the warrantless wiretapping program after it was revealed by the *New York Times*, but the Bush and Obama administrations continued to defend it in court in order to protect confidential intelligence sources and methods. Documents leaked to the press by Edward Snowden in 2013 revealed even further the extent of lawlessness and lack of oversight that characterized the program.[67]

In domestic policy as well, presidents have used their unilateral authority not just to thwart Congress but to fill vacuums caused by congressional inaction and to placate the demands of their base constituencies. Frustrated by the lack of progress on climate change, for example, President Obama in 2015 developed the Clean Power Plan, an ambitious and sweeping set of administrative regulations—which have the force of law but do not require congressional assent—to limit carbon emissions. Although the plan enraged Republicans, they were powerless to do anything until President Trump took office. His administration promptly set about unraveling the Obama administration's executive actions on environmental policy, including withdrawing the United States from the Paris Climate Accord and starting the administrative process of repealing the Clean Power Plan.

Similarly, only a week into his presidency, Trump unilaterally issued the ban on travel to the United States from several predominantly Muslim countries. Like Obama's Clean Power Plan, Trump's immigration order aroused the ire of Democrats and provoked large demonstrations around the country. But Congress has been mired in a decades-long stalemate on immigration policy, leaving a void that Trump, for whom restricting immigration was a signal issue, was more than happy to fill.

Even more dangerous is the opportunity for presidents, governing in a polarized political climate, to use the tools of the executive branch to undermine the legitimacy of political opponents and to monkey with the electoral system to tilt things in their favor. When polarization is low, presidents have every incentive to seek compromise and consensus and to deploy presidential leadership toward signature policy accomplishments. But when polarization is high, executive power can become a political weapon, and scorched-earth presidential tactics then become the norm.

After making his unsubstantiated claims of widespread voter fraud in the 2016 election, Trump established, by executive order, a presidential commission, chaired by Vice President Mike Pence, to investigate fraudulent voter practices—for which there is next to no evidence. The commission's vice chair was Kansas secretary of state Kris Kobach, who was one of the country's leading perpetrators of fantastical voter-fraud tales. Although the commission was short-lived (the administration disbanded it after nine months), its work suggested that it was a transparently partisan enterprise. Its Democratic members complained that others on the commission did not share documents with them or include them in deliberations. The primary targets of voter fraud allegations and voter suppression attempts, moreover, are likely to be immigrants and minority voters, who lean Democratic. This makes the commission's very existence appear to be an attempt to inflame conflict over the boundaries of membership, disenfranchise Democrats, and tilt the electoral system toward Republicans, all to Trump's direct political benefit.

Similarly, the Trump administration attempted to add a question about citizenship to the 2020 Census. The effort provoked opposition from many experts as well as the Census Bureau's professional staff, who were concerned that asking about citizenship would dampen participation in immigrant communities, particularly those with many Latino residents. Because the Census provides the basis for legislative apportionment, an undercount of these areas, which generally lean Democratic, would have the effect of limiting their representation. After the death of Republican strategist Thomas Hofeller, files found on his computer confirmed that the administration saw the citizenship question as a means to enhance Republican power by tilting the population count in favor of white voters.[68]

Donald Trump arrived in the White House at a moment when both the opportunity and the temptation to use the powers of the presidency as political weapons have reached dramatic heights. Nixon is often regarded as the master of presidential weaponization, but in this respect, Trump has outdone him. Nixon got into hot water when he tried to impound money appropriated by Congress, simply refusing to spend it for the purposes that Congress had intended; Trump went further in ordering the reprogramming of several billion dollars of military funding to begin construction of the border wall. Nixon asserted executive privilege during Watergate but ultimately cooperated with the congressional investigation when the Supreme Court ordered him to do so; Trump has taken Nixon's position to its ultimate extreme and repeatedly instructed his aides (and even former aides) not to cooperate with Congress's demands for information or testimony.

In the presence of all of the other three threats, Trump's assertion of executive power is especially alarming for democracy. It permits him to accomplish his goals even as he pays little or no heed to institutional or political restraints, and it allows him to evade accountability for his actions.

## THE CONFLUENCE OF ALL FOUR THREATS

History has shown that the four threats do not emerge in a predictable, automatic, or mechanistic way. In most instances, while economic, social, or technological changes may initiate their ascent, political action is key in shaping their subsequent development. Political leaders can respond by trying to quell the threats; alternatively, they can encourage their development and use them as a means to increase their power, taking action akin to throwing gasoline on dry brush.

We find ourselves today in a situation not encountered by any previous generation of Americans: all four threats to democracy loom large simultaneously. Each of them is on the rise, and some have never been more formidable. What's more, they have begun to combine with each other in ways that intensify their destructive power.

We did not reach this point merely through the natural evolution of social and economic conditions. Deliberate choices by political leaders have promoted each of the four threats.

Who is to blame for the intensification of these threats? The answer differs in each case. In terms of polarization, both political parties have contributed to it, but Republican leaders have taken the lead and pursued it more purposefully and strategically. This asymmetry likely results from the greater homogeneity of the GOP, whose members share an affinity for conservative values, whereas Democratic leaders must artfully accommodate a broader coalition that ranges from progressive to moderate and embraces greater racial and gender diversity.

When it comes to conflict over membership and status, those who pursue equality defend democratic values. Although numerous Republican leaders championed equal rights in the past, from Abraham Lincoln to Senator Everett Dirksen, today the party has all but relinquished the cause to the Democrats. The Democratic Party, while long internally conflicted over where it stood on such matters, has in the past decade come down more resolutely on the side of equal rights than ever before, and arguably more so than any political party in American history.

Over the past several decades, in the main it is the Republican Party that has pursued policies that most benefit the affluent and big business. Certainly there are exceptions to this; the inclusion of some economic elites into the Democratic Party helps explain why it has in some instances been more accommodating of the finance industry than it was during the New Deal era.[69] Democrats, too, have been reluctant to scale back many tax expenditures, even those that most benefit higher-income people.[70] Nonetheless, the pursuit of lower taxes on the wealthy and corporations and deregulation of industry has occurred primarily under the leadership of Republicans, and party unity has permitted such initiatives to succeed.

Finally, the rise of presidential power has been facilitated by Democratic and Republican presidents alike. Unlike the other three, both parties bear considerable responsibility for its escalation. Note, however, how this threat combines with those just described: a Democratic president is likely to use the tools of the office to further the equality of citizens and to lessen economic inequality, while a Republican is likely to pursue the reverse. Still, given polarization, either may be tempted to use presidential powers to the political advantage of his party.

Now that we are here, is democracy in danger? This convergence has certainly strained the system, but in Chapter 9 we will turn to how democracy's underlying attributes are holding up.

# 9

---

# Putting Democracy First

When President Richard Nixon faced impeachment in 1974, executive aggrandizement buffeted democracy but other threats hovered at a low ebb, making it easier for political leaders ultimately to come together and safeguard rule by the people. When Donald Trump was impeached, however, all four threats had been gaining intensity for decades, preventing checks and balances from functioning effectively. Executive aggrandizement and political polarization provided a toxic mix, particularly due to a radicalized Republican Party, fueled by a base angry over changing terms of membership and status and led by public officials keenly responsive to the demands of the wealthiest Americans. With that party controlling the Senate, it was Trump—not democracy—who gained protection.

The key event that precipitated Trump's impeachment occurred on July 25, 2019, one day after special counsel Robert Mueller testified on Capitol Hill about his findings, when Trump spoke by phone with President Volodymyr Zelenskyy of Ukraine. Zelenskyy, a political novice who had been elected just three months earlier, desperately needed strong American support—ideally both military assistance and an Oval Office meeting—in order to push back against Russian aggression.[1]

Immediately after Zelenskyy made his request for military support, Trump made a request of him in return: "I would like you to do us a favor though because our country has been through a lot and Ukraine knows a lot about it." Trump then referred to a long-debunked conspiracy theory suggesting that Ukraine, not Russia, had interfered in the 2016 US election, hacking the Democratic National Committee and Hillary Clinton's campaign. "The server, they say Ukraine has it," Trump said. "I would like to have the Attorney General call you or your people and I would like you to get to the bottom of it."[2]

Then Trump made a second request. "The other thing, there's a lot of talk about Biden's son, that Biden stopped the prosecution and a lot of people want to find out about that so whatever you can do with the Attorney General would be great." On both counts, Zelenskyy responded affirmatively, commenting, "I just want to assure you once again that you have nobody but friends around us."[3] Trump appeared to be offering US support for Ukraine only if Zelenskyy would do political favors for him, both to clear suspicions that Russia aided Trump in the 2016 election and to gather dirt that might harm the leading contender to be his 2020 rival, former vice president Joe Biden, whose son Hunter had served on the board of a politically connected Ukrainian energy company.

Two months later, in mid-September, the call became public knowledge, exposed by an anonymous whistleblower. The whistleblower's complaint claimed that "the President of the United States is using the power of his office to solicit interference from a foreign country in the 2020 U.S. election." Over the coming weeks and months, more evidence came to light indicating that Trump was undermining the rule of law by putting himself above it; endangering free and fair elections by requesting that another country interfere in US elections on his behalf; and attempting to tarnish the legitimacy of the opposition by implying that it and not he was involved in a corrupt deal with a foreign power.[4]

The revelations united the House Democratic majority behind an impeachment inquiry. Speaker Nancy Pelosi announced it, stating, "The president must be held accountable. No one is above the law."[5] Experts on Ukraine—civil servants and military officials—testified before Congress, providing extensive details that corroborated the whistleblower's report and indicating that Trump had also withheld aid from Ukraine. Yet Congress's ability to check the executive was stymied as the Trump administration refused to comply with subpoenas from the House, forbidding officials from testifying and refusing to share documents.

Although the House followed the constitutionally mandated process for investigating and punishing presidential misconduct, Trump and congressional Republican leaders railed against Democrats in the language of politics as mortal combat, deriding the inquiry as a "scam" and a "witch hunt." On October 1, Trump tweeted that "what is taking place is not an impeachment, it is a COUP, intended to take away the power of the People, their VOTE, their Freedoms." His supporters in the conservative media adopted the coup narrative, and his reelection campaign quickly produced a TV ad featuring the claim. Some of the president's supporters began to warn of civil war if impeachment proceeded, and armed white supremacist militia groups responded with threats of violent resistance.[6]

In December, House leaders announced two articles of impeachment against Trump: abuse of power and obstruction of justice. The Judiciary Committee approved the articles, but unlike in 1974, when six committee Republicans joined all the Democrats in approval, in this polarized era the vote fell strictly along party lines. The full chamber proceeded to pass the two articles on December 18, with not a single Republican voting in favor. Trump became only the third president in history, following Andrew Johnson and Bill Clinton, to receive the enduring indignity of impeachment.

Then action turned to the Senate, where a trial began in mid-January 2020. Unlike all previous impeachments of presidents and judges throughout American history, for which numerous witnesses were summoned to testify in every single case, Republican senators (all except Mitt Romney and Susan Collins) voted against calling a single one. The trial wrapped up quickly and Trump was acquitted along party lines, with Romney providing the one dissenting Republican vote. Several Republicans acknowledged that Trump's behavior had been inappropriate, with some even implying that it was impeachable, but they insisted that removal was not warranted. Said Senator Lamar Alexander, referring to the divided nation, "It would pour gasoline on cultural fires that are burning out there." Indeed, among the public, only 9 percent of Republicans supported removal, compared to 84 percent of Democrats.[7]

With the trial completed, a president remained in office who had used the powers of the presidency for his own political gain while flouting democratic principles. His behavior had been clearly condoned by his own party. In the face of virulent threats to democracy, checks and balances failed to restrain egregious abuses of power. Now the president ruled, unshackled.

The Constitution has never preserved democracy all by itself, and it is not poised to do so today. The potential for contemporary democratic backsliding is substantial given that all four threats to democracy have escalated, converged, and grown more combustible through their interaction with one another. Real harm to democracy is already occurring, as we will show.

The threats, moreover, have taken on a life of their own. They predated Trump and they are on course to persist well beyond his departure from public life. The nation seems to be in for years of careening, volatile partisan conflict, and more democratic backsliding. The question for Americans must be how to make the preservation and restoration of democracy our first priority, so that future generations can take part in "government of, by, and for the people."

## DANGER TO THE PILLARS OF DEMOCRACY

Decades of the ascendance of the four threats gave rise to the candidacy of Donald Trump, a political neophyte seemingly ignorant of and uninterested in public policy and the process of governance. Trump played the four threats like a master puppeteer. He is polarization personified, utterly dismissive of opponents and vicious toward all antagonists. He has repeatedly stoked racial antagonism and nativism. Despite the populist atmospherics of his rallies, his approach to governing has been plutocratic, not redistributive, effectively delivering robust benefits to the wealthy and business interests. And more than any president since Nixon, Trump views the presidency as his personal domain, and he has wielded its weapons to promote his personal interests—political and financial—at the expense of democratic accountability.

Early in Trump's presidency, some believed his unorthodox behavior would be of little consequence to democracy. They reasoned that he lacked the discipline required to pursue policy change. His stumbles on several of his own initiatives, such as the voter fraud commission and separations of immigrant children from their parents at the border, seemed to bear out this view.[8] Yet as time has gone on, it has become increasingly clear that Trump's presidency is denigrating institutions that are crucial to democracy and normalizing behavior more typically associated with corrupt and authoritarian regimes. The sheer torrent of daily developments in this era can make it difficult to keep track of what has transpired, never mind its impact on democracy.

A well-functioning democracy thrives on the existence of competitive elections, the capacity of elected officials to engage in collective decision-making that is responsive to citizens, and the opportunity for citizens to hold those elected officials accountable. When any of its central pillars are harmed, these dynamics fail to function properly. The four threats, by channeling power in perverse directions, can degrade them. Here we provide a brief inventory of how the pillars of democracy have fared during the Trump administration to date.

*Free and fair elections* are the foundational feature of a democracy, permitting citizens to have a voice and collectively to choose their public officials and to vote them out of office if they see fit. Without such elections, citizens' voices are easily ignored, and representation and accountability fail to function effectively. Throughout his time in the White House, Trump has launched a frontal attack on elections and the public's confidence in them. This began with his unsubstantiated 2016 claims that the electoral system was "rigged" and his warnings that he would not accept the results if they went against him. In 2017, he launched his accusations of voter fraud in the 2016 election. When states were counting votes in close elections in the 2018 midterms, Trump made false charges about their procedures, claiming that ballots were "infected" in Florida and that "electoral corruption" had taken place in Arizona.[9]

But it has not been only through his words that Trump has threatened American elections. He has also done so by promoting the entanglement of corrupt foreign influence in elections, starting with his failure to discourage it in the 2016 election. Numerous Trump campaign associates have been indicted, and some convicted, in connection with improper dealings with Russian government contacts during that campaign. And as his interactions with Ukraine's president indicate, Trump has actively courted a foreign government with the aim of rigging the 2020 elections. Such actions threaten to tip the scales, making elections an unfair contest and thereby diminishing their effectiveness as a means to convey the choice of the electorate.

Congress also has abandoned the duty to protect free and fair elections. Granted, it did enact punitive sanctions on Russia because of its role in the 2016 elections, and the strong bipartisan support for the measure forced Trump to sign it, against his wishes, or face a veto override. Also, numerous congressional investigations looked into Russian interference in that election, the role of social media, and related issues. Yet this elected body of members who have all sworn an oath to uphold the Constitution has yet to enact legislation protecting this most essential component of democracy. For much of 2019, Senate majority leader Mitch McConnell blocked consideration of election security measures passed by the House; he relented only after a *Washington Post* columnist called him a "Russian asset," earning him the nickname "Moscow Mitch."[10] Yet the chamber has yet to approve any measures.

The attacks on elections combined with the failure to protect them put this most crucial pillar of democracy in danger. The concern is not that Trump or any American president will cancel elections, nor that votes will not be counted. Rather, in our fractious political climate, the possibility grows that some communities—particularly those marginalized in society—will have their access to the ballot curtailed. In addition, the public may increasingly lose confidence in elections, particularly if leaders themselves stoke fears of electoral fraud and malfeasance. The spreading of unfounded rumors may make voters less willing to participate in elections or to accept their results. A recent poll found that only 53 percent of registered voters said that the 2020 election will be open and fair—which may heighten skepticism about the validity of the results and the willingness of a sizable share of the public to accept them. If over the course of time elections cease to be free, fair, and trusted, the country may gradually transition into competitive authoritarianism, a regime that preserves some outward appearances of democracy but eviscerates its substance.

The *rule of law* is crucial to democracy for making it a "government of laws, not of men," in which power flows not from an individual or a small group but rather from the people generally. Although all modern presidents have expanded executive powers, presidents before Trump exhibited a greater respect for the rule of law and for the limits it placed on their own power. Previous presidents have stretched the law and even violated it in pursuit of policy goals and political advantage. But few have so resolutely flouted the line between presidential power and personal gain. Trump, by contrast, remains oblivious to the very idea that there is a difference between them, and he proceeds undeterred, violating this boundary at will time and time again.

This pattern began during the transition, when Trump refused to separate himself from his businesses before taking office. He has failed to abide by the two emoluments clauses of the Constitution, which prohibit the president from receiving either any compensation from a foreign government or leader without the consent of Congress, or any compensation from domestic sources beyond his salary. Trump-branded hotels in Washington and around the world have reaped substantial benefits by becoming destinations for people and organizations seeking to curry favor with the president. Unlike other modern presidents, he has been unwilling to put his private affairs aside to prevent considerations of personal gain from influencing his conduct in office.

Also deviating from past practice, Trump has been unwilling to make his tax returns public, shielding information about his private affairs. To defend this refusal, he has proffered the claim that as president, he is immune from any investigation into his personal conduct, an argument that goes beyond executive privilege and which a federal judge called "repugnant to the nation's governmental structure and constitutional values."[11]

If future presidents follow Trump's lead, the United States will lose one of the hallmarks that have distinguished it from many other countries in the world: the absence of outright corruption in national politics. If we continue to permit presidents to use their political power to make deals that enrich them personally, helping their companies and investments, the notion of "government for the people" will become a remote ideal.

Trump's presidency has also weakened the role and authority of the other branches of government, particularly Congress. This occurred, for example, when he claimed emergency powers to use funds appropriated for other purposes to commence the border wall project, and when he overrode congressional war powers in ordering the assassination of an Iranian leader. Also, while the legislative branch since the 1930s has been delegating to the executive much of its constitutional authority over setting tariffs and regulating commerce with foreign nations, Trump seized an unprecedented degree of such authority by taking advantage of a provision that permits a president to impose import restrictions if they are justified by national security.[12]

The White House has also undercut Congress's capacity to engage in oversight of the executive branch, effectively undermining a crucial means of ensuring accountability. It has done this by refusing to comply with numerous congressional subpoenas and other legal demands on all manner of topics. (Congress has gone to court over these refusals, but the judiciary has failed to respond expeditiously enough to make a difference.) Also, as the formal impeachment inquiry got under way, the administration stonewalled all congressional requests, whether for documents or in-person testimony.[13] President Nixon's similar refusal formed the basis of one of the articles of impeachment that the House Judiciary Committee recommended against him in July 1974. In 2019, the House replicated this effort, charging Trump with obstruction of Congress in one of its articles of impeachment, but the Senate acquitted the president nonetheless.

All these violations of the rule of law threaten democracy in fundamental ways. Unless public officials insist that faithful adherence to the rule of law be reinstated and adopt safeguards to protect it, presidents will become increasingly powerful while Congress, the branch designed to be closest to the people and to represent the diversity of interests that make up the country, will become weaker. Authoritarian rule may seem incomprehensible in the American context, but damage to the rule of law is facilitating transformations of the political system that veer in that direction.

Maintaining democracy also requires respecting the *legitimacy of the political opposition*: its right to exist, compete in elections, and exercise the political authority it gains when it wins those elections. It means recognizing that political opponents are simply other citizens with different points of view about public policies and the role of government, not enemies. In 2008, when presidential candidate John McCain was running against Barack Obama, he demonstrated his respect for this principle. A woman at a campaign event said to him, "I can't trust Obama. I read about him, and he's an Arab." McCain quickly shook his head, took the microphone, and replied, "No ma'am. He's a decent family man, a citizen that I just happen to have disagreements with on fundamental issues, and that's what this campaign is all about."[14]

Trump, by contrast, delights in portraying his antagonists as unworthy and illegitimate, a tactic enabled by the rise of the four threats. His "birtherism" claims tapped into and inflamed racial resentment. His embrace of "lock her up" chants at his rallies, directed at Hillary Clinton, and his threats to prosecute her repudiated the notion that competition between candidates and the existence of an organized opposition party are essential to making democracy real and meaningful, by giving voters a choice. Once Representative Adam Schiff, chair of the House Intelligence Committee, became the lead impeachment manager, Trump issued what appeared to be a veiled threat in a tweet: "Shifty Adam Schiff is a CORRUPT POLITICIAN, and probably a very sick man. He has not paid the price, yet, for what he has done to our Country!"[15]

By portraying the opposition as the enemy, political actors damage the possibilities for partisans to work together effectively, through negotiation and compromise, on behalf of the public good, exacerbating dysfunction that has already been evident in Congress for more than a decade now. As the "us versus them" approach escalates, party loyalty overpowers differences of ideas about how to govern as the legitimate basis for political competition.[16] Collective decision-making becomes more and more difficult. Taken to the extreme, if a party in power stacks the deck against the other, it may succeed in advantaging itself permanently, undermining democracy. In addition, a politics that demonizes the opposition may, at least in the minds of some supporters, justify violence against them.

The *integrity of rights* can be injured even by speech that fails to show respect for it. Trump has challenged the freedom of the press by threatening to revoke the licenses of various news outlets. He has not followed through, yet his frequent attacks on the mainstream media, which he calls a "disgrace, . . . false, horrible," "fake news," and "enemies of the people," may further undermine confidence in it, with invidious effects. In a conversation with Trump after he won the 2016 election, Lesley Stahl of CBS News asked him why he continued to bash the press, and he answered, "You know why I do it? I do it to discredit you all and demean you all so that when you write negative stories about me no one will believe you."[17] Partisan media outlets have frequently fanned the flames of polarization in American politics. At other times, however, sound, fact-based journalism has played an important role in uncovering abuses of power. Undermining such media outlets can prove harmful to democratic accountability.

When it comes to civil rights, Trump's frequent verbal assaults on immigrants and African Americans may themselves sanction bias against them and even instigate violence. These appeals to a restrictive vision of the American political community have been part of the American political vocabulary from before the beginning of the republic, though politicians have invoked them more in some historical periods than in others. But they fall on especially fertile ground now, as the parties are increasingly sharply divided between two conceptions of who truly constitutes "we the people," one multiracial and inclusive and the other inclined toward an exclusionary vision of white dominance. Such speech, common since Trump became a presidential candidate, may have helped to provoke the rise in hate crimes in recent years, targeted against people particularly because of their race or ethnicity, religion, or sexual orientation.[18]

Besides Trump's vitriolic speech toward marginalized groups, his administration has also taken action, through several policy and administrative changes, to scale back rights for vulnerable communities. The travel ban on visitors from Muslim-majority countries, after several earlier versions were rejected in the courts, was upheld by the Supreme Court in June 2018, and expanded to more countries in January 2020. At Trump's request, Immigration and Customs Enforcement agents have more aggressively pursued undocumented immigrants for deportation, including established community members who have lived in the United States for years. The administration adopted a new rule permitting fast-track deportations, conducted without a fair legal process, for immigrants who could not prove they had lived continuously in the country for at least two years.[19]

Our examination of historical episodes has shown that when democracy is under threat in the United States, marginalized groups are typically the first to bear the brunt. Their membership or status in the political community has sometimes been endangered by the national government. In other instances it permitted states to take charge, leaving them free to exclude many from specific policies or protections. In either case, the integrity of rights was compromised and the polity fragmented.

The four pillars of democracy are indeed under attack today. Americans may wish to assume that the nation will survive this onslaught with rule by the people intact. It may be tempting to think that we have weathered severe threats before and that the Constitution protected us. But that would be a misreading of history, which instead reveals that democracy is indeed fragile, and that surviving threats to it is by no means guaranteed. The unprecedented convergence of all four threats today, moreover, requires that we consider very seriously how to protect and preserve democracy.

## LEARNING FROM THE PAST

American democracy has always been a work in progress, and it has often been vulnerable to deterioration. Today, we live in a time of intense stress on democracy. Yet the United States is not doomed to proceed toward authoritarianism. We can strengthen American democracy by learning from times of crisis in the past. Our historical inquiry has conveyed much about what threatens democracy, but it also tells us what kind of society is more conducive to a healthy and robust democracy.

Democracy works better in a society that is less polarized, and where public officials and citizens share a common sense of belonging and purpose. Distinctions between parties on issues help to promote democracy, but high levels of partisan polarization can lead to escalating conflict that may be deeply harmful. Real violence and bloodshed can ensue when democracy breaks down. The spiraling polarization of the 1790s threatened to lead the country into civil war; the conflicts of the 1850s actually did so. Democracy works best when politics is conducted as an ongoing means of resolving disagreements and achieving consensus or compromise around public problems, not as an all-out high-stakes battle in which the aim is to eliminate opponents and vanquish foes.

In a healthy democracy, those involved in politics can take the long view that over the course of time their side may win some elections and policy battles and lose others. They must commit themselves to abiding by the rules and values that make this ongoing competition possible, not least by respecting the legitimacy of their political opponents. Fair procedures need to ensure the right to compete by both sides, the necessity that those who lose elections must concede, and the privilege of winners to exercise the power they gain to govern.

Democracy also functions better when society is less tribal, when it is more inclusive of members across racial, ethnic, gender, and other differences, and when social divisions are not mapped onto political cleavages. It works better in a society that is more equal in economic terms, where resources and opportunity are more widely shared. The 1890s featured the poisonous fusion of high levels of conflict over membership and status, polarization, and economic inequality. Repeatedly, in fact, American democracy has been threatened when political forces committed to maintaining racial exclusion and hierarchy gained the upper hand.

Democracy thrives in a society where many voices can speak, power is dispersed across political institutions rather than concentrated, and those in authority can be held accountable for their actions. The crises of the twentieth century saw lower levels of threat on the other three dimensions, but executive power grew over time, making possible the Watergate scandal. Presidential power needs to be constrained and presidents held accountable in order to prevent them from abusing the office to entrench their own personal or political interests.

These are extraordinarily difficult things to achieve and maintain, however, not least because progress on one front has often been accompanied by retreat on others. Time and again in the history of American democracy, we have confronted democratic crises by compromising one or more of our most important democratic values. In order to assuage economic vulnerability in the Great Depression, for example, we accepted the expansion of executive power, with dangerous consequences down the road.

In particular, American democratic crises have frequently been resolved in ways that conformed to or even deepened profound racial inequality in American society. In order to reduce polarization or soften conflict over economic inequality, political leaders sought to diminish the distance between white Americans in the service of democratic values, with disastrous consequences for African Americans. Threats were managed or mitigated by reinforcing the racial hierarchy of American society. The settlement of 1800 was built on the foundation of the three-fifths compromise, which disproportionately empowered the slaveholding South. White leaders in the 1890s unified southern whites across lines of economic conflict by agreeing to disempower and subjugate African Americans, returning the South to authoritarianism. And in order to keep domestic peace and address economic crisis, Franklin Roosevelt turned a blind eye to racial subjugation and kicked the can of multiracial democracy down the road for a generation. These settlements to past crises will no longer suffice today; we need to find a new way forward, one that embraces the core American value that all are created equal.

Nor is it enough to simply call for political actors to strive to lessen these threats. Democratic politics by definition involves a contest for power. The very structure of American democratic institutions depends on ambitious politicians to keep each other in check and requires active citizens to hold leaders accountable. We cannot always expect leaders to act with self-restraint or adhere to norms of behavior that hold them back in the face of opportunities for political advantage. The problem is that the combination of threats amplifies the opportunities for willful politicians and citizens to make choices in the quest for political victory that have the effect of degrading democracy.

But the United States does not have to operate this way. In addition to showing us how politics can go wrong and lead to democratic deterioration, history also offers a guide to the kind of choices that we and our leaders can make to restore democracy's promise. To do that, we need to put democracy first and take action to protect its central pillars.

## PUTTING DEMOCRACY FIRST

Many forms of Government have been tried, and will be tried in this world of sin and woe. No one pretends that democracy is perfect or all-wise. Indeed it has been said that democracy is the worst form of Government except for all those other forms that have been tried from time to time.

— Winston Churchill, November 11, 1947

It's easy to be cynical about democracy. Some will say that focusing on backsliding misses the bigger point that American democracy was far from perfect even in recent decades, never mind prior to the 1960s. We do not dispute that, but we think that the state of democracy in recent decades—imperfect though it has been—nonetheless continued some of the best-established traditions of the United States, such as the rule of law, and represented a vast improvement on earlier periods with respect to free and fair elections and the integrity of rights. Those crucial features are now endangered. We consider that to be of grave concern, and reason for Americans to come together to protect democracy.

Others will point to the need for deep structural reforms to keep democracy functioning. Equal representation of states in the Senate, for example, is the modern-day version of the three-fifths rule, giving extra representation to residents of sparsely populated states while diminishing the power of people who live in more densely populated places. The Electoral College makes possible a perverse and undemocratic result in which the candidate for president who receives the most votes does not win; in fact, this has happened in two out of the last five presidential elections.[20] These and other features of the Constitution certainly do make American politics less democratic because they render elections less fair and discourage accountability to the majority of citizens. Many have made cogent calls for them to be changed. But such changes are unlikely to happen. Amending the Constitution is difficult under the best of circumstances, and probably next to impossible in today's polarized climate. Moreover, those in power are the beneficiaries of current constitutional arrangements, so they have little incentive to change them. As beneficial as some of these reforms might be for American democracy, we need to look elsewhere in the short term to restore democracy's promise.

Still others may wonder why we should bother to put our energies toward saving democracy at all, when so many issues call out for urgent action. The truth is that democracy is the only way that masses of people can have a voice and a chance to influence what government does. It is the only hope for those who wish to pursue policy goals that benefit the public good. If democracy deteriorates, only the most affluent individuals, powerful industries, and best-organized groups will triumph. The vast majority of Americans will see their priorities jettisoned again and again. And society's most powerless groups, particularly racial and ethnic minorities and immigrants, will suffer grievous harm. Liberal democracy is crucial, furthermore, to ensuring that individuals' liberties and rights are protected.

In fact, most Americans do value democracy. A 2018 national survey conducted by the Pew Research Center found that vast majorities of Americans considered fifteen different democratic values as "very important." For example, 84 percent considered it very important for the rights and freedoms of all people to be respected, 83 percent believe elected officials should face serious consequences for misconduct, 82 percent think that everyone should have an equal opportunity to succeed, and 76 percent think there should be a balance of power between the branches of government. Yet when asked how well the United States is doing in these respects, most Americans were deeply skeptical. For the four questions just mentioned, at the very most only 20 percent ranked the country as doing very well, and that was on the question of everyone having an opportunity to succeed; on the other three dimensions, as few as 11 percent offered this same appraisal. On most of the fifteen values, in fact, a large gap existed between the priority Americans put on those values and their assessments of how well democracy is actually functioning in each respect.[21]

The most striking aspect of the survey, however, was that despite the high degree of polarization in the country, Democrats and Republicans barely diverged in their assessments of the importance of each of the democratic values. In other words, the value of preserving democracy may be one thing we can all agree on. As we seek to move forward, shared democratic values may be our best hope of finding the way.

In fact, it is precisely these shared democratic values that enable people to live in the same political community and to have divergent views about public policy. It permits them to pursue those goals through the political process, rather than through outright power or violence. In the 1930s, a national conversation about the merits of democracy took place around the country. Under the leadership of John W. Studebaker, first as superintendent of schools in Des Moines, Iowa, and then as federal education commissioner, the Federal Forum Project sponsored local gatherings where citizens would gather to listen to guest speakers, debate democracy's virtues and defects, and discuss the challenges facing their communities and the nation.[22] Communities across the country could aim to foster such discussions once again, facilitated by moderators, in which citizens come together to affirm what they share in democracy, and to ponder a way forward despite our differences on policy issues and in partisan preferences.

Both the fate of the threats to democracy and whether remedies will emerge depend on the choices made by political leaders and citizens. American history has been full of such choices, and in some instances people have chosen a destructive path—as in the 1890s, when African Americans' rights were sacrificed—while in others they found a productive way forward, such as by enacting the bipartisan post-Watergate reforms.

Generally, when people think about politics, they evaluate candidates, policy proposals, or reform plans in one of three ways. The first is ideological. Like any heterogenous group of people, Americans have divergent views about the role of government in society generally and what kinds of things the government should (and should not) do to address what they perceive as social problems. Accordingly, when they look at a proposed course of action, they ask themselves, Do I agree? Does this proposal advance ideas or approaches that I prefer? Or does it go against my beliefs?

A second lens that people might use to view politics is material. Everything that government does has costs and benefits, winners and losers. And so citizens and leaders often ask themselves, What's in it for me? Does this proposal benefit me? Does it confer advantages on a group to which I belong? Or does it impose costs on me in order to benefit someone else?

Third, an increasingly prominent filter for assessing politics is partisan. Since the beginning of the republic, Americans have divided themselves into groups that evolved into parties, political teams that contend with each other for power. Increasingly, leaders' and citizens' attachments to those teams are passionate. And so people consider, Does this proposal benefit my party? Will my team win?

These are all valuable and important political perspectives. Politics is an arena for the struggle over ideas and visions of what makes a better society. It is a contest over resources. And it is undoubtedly a team sport. Without these kinds of competition, democracy would cease to exist.

But to this list, we add a fourth criterion, and we argue that it must be given pride of place as the first priority: the impact on democracy itself. Any proposal or political choice needs to be evaluated in terms of whether it will diminish democracy or strengthen it. Will it affect one of the pillars of democracy, and if so, does it reinforce or weaken it? By the same token, how might it influence the threats to democracy? These questions are vital. We cannot take it for granted that democratic politics will endure if we do not pay careful attention to the democracy-enhancing (or democracy-eroding) consequences of the things we do in politics.

Democracy needs to be the top priority, and democratic processes should set the standard for public life. The most important thing we can do is to insist on strong protection for free and fair elections, the rule of law, the legitimacy of competition, and the integrity of rights. These pillars are the rules of the game that permit all of us, whether liberals, conservatives, moderates, or independents, to be able to continue to participate and engage in politics, regardless of which party wins office. They are essential to the health and vigor of democracy. They are under stress today, and that makes the United States subject to backsliding for years to come. Yet their decay should concern all Americans and we should be willing to come together to prevent it. While as a society we might not agree broadly on policies that can reduce the four threats (though we might agree more than meets the eye), protecting the pillars of democracy is a task akin to picking the low-hanging fruit, and we should make it our top priority.

In our contemporary context, one party has led the way in exacerbating several of the four threats, in ways that are harmful to democracy. Today's Republican Party has abandoned its willingness to protect the pillars of democracy, despite its legacy of having done so in earlier periods. It is currently on track to engage in increasingly repressive behavior as it seeks to maintain and expand its power. It will sanction punishment of its political enemies, efforts to limit voting by those who favor Democrats, and even dismissal of election results that do not favor it. Faced with rising support for authoritarianism, opposition parties elsewhere have embraced the role of becoming the champion of democracy. The Democratic Party today is faced with that obligation: its primary goal must be defending democracy itself and insisting on the strengthening of its pillars. It must assume this role for the service of the nation and its future.

As we seek the way forward, the settlements of the past—which reinforced or restored racial hierarchy and imposed limits on the political community—will not do. The Declaration of Independence's insistence that all are "created equal" has always been an aspirational value, and by fits and starts over time the United States has moved closer to realizing it, but it has also succumbed to severe backsliding. Today, more Americans than ever embrace egalitarian values; in fact, much of the conflict the nation faces pertains to the divide between those who embrace such values and those who oppose them. The political challenge is how to move forward democratically while negotiating and deliberating over who belongs in the political community and on what terms. Our future will not be democratic if a settlement is forged that leaves one group or another cordoned off from full membership and equal status as citizens.

Early generations of Americans made immense personal sacrifices for the sake of democracy. During World War II, Americans defeated Nazism and fascism through military service overseas and substantial efforts on the home front. During the 1950s and 1960s, Americans marched for civil rights, took part in lunch counter sits-ins, and volunteered for Freedom Summer. The time has come once again for Americans to defend democracy, joining in a long legacy.

In the most troubled time in our history for democracy, when the nation split into two sections that fought a brutal war against each other, President Abraham Lincoln called on Americans to take part in the "unfinished work" of democracy. Speaking at Gettysburg, Pennsylvania, on November 19, 1863, four months after fifty-one thousand people had been killed, suffered injuries, or gone missing there in the bloodiest battle in our history, he said, "It is for us the living, rather, to be dedicated here to the *unfinished work* which they who fought here have thus far so nobly advanced . . . that this nation, under God, shall have a new birth of freedom—and that government of the people, by the people, for the people, shall not perish from the earth."

A year and a half later, in his second inaugural address, Lincoln reiterated the call: "With malice toward none; with charity for all; with firmness in the right, as God gives us to see the right, let us strive on to *finish the work we are in*." With the spirit of magnanimity and shared citizenship that Lincoln invoked, let us carry on the work to strengthen and revitalize democracy.

# Acknowledgments

Each of us, at our respective universities, has spent the past many years teaching the bread-and-butter undergraduate course, "Introduction to American Government and Politics." In fact, each of us also taught it early in our careers, when we were just out of graduate school and Bill Clinton was president. We then both returned to teaching it years later, during the presidency of Barack Obama, only to discover that it was like teaching a different course, about a transformed nation. The "textbook" version of American politics that we absorbed in graduate school depicted American political institutions like the gears of a clock that fit together neatly and ran smoothly, promoting moderation, compromise, and incrementalism. Even in the mid-1990s, this account of American politics already seemed a bit strained, as if there was some grit in the gears, but it still served as an adequate guide that we could present, with some modifications, to our students. By the 2010s, however, the clockworks seemed to be coming apart altogether. Rising polarization and growing political dysfunction were disrupting the machine's smooth operation and now needed to figure front and center in our efforts to explain American politics to ourselves, let alone to our students. We found ourselves running to keep up.

Then along came the 2016 election. Suddenly, even topics in American politics that had seemed long settled—such as freedom of the press or confidence in the integrity of elections—were thrown into question by the ascendancy of an unorthodox candidate, Donald Trump. The very framing of our lectures seemed inadequate, as if we were missing the big picture.

It was at that juncture that Suzanne found herself in conversations with colleagues at Cornell, political scientists who study the rise and decline of democracy in nations around the world. In a discussion in the mailroom one day, one of them shrugged, "Democracies don't last forever. They come and they go. We've had a good run in the United States." Another nodded sagely, "This is all very familiar to us. We've seen it before." He proceeded to list autocratic leaders around the world who, in recent decades, had ascended to power in nations that previously qualified as democracies. As the conversations continued, it became apparent that these scholars of politics in other countries were in many ways better equipped to think about what the United States was undergoing and the possibilities that might ensue than those of us who specialize in American politics.

We were also both engaged in riveting conversations with our good friend Rick Valelly, a brilliant scholar of American politics who teaches at Swarthmore College. Like us, Rick studies American political development, meaning that he thinks about politics historically and with an emphasis on the role of political institutions. While both of us had previously examined twentieth-century developments from the New Deal to the present, Rick's expertise went much further back, to the demise of Reconstruction and black disenfranchisement later in the nineteenth century. Rick not only possesses a granular knowledge of these periods of American history, but he is also an extraordinarily broad thinker and voracious reader, with a deep understanding of what democracy requires if it is to be sustainable. Together with Rick, we groped for better ways to understand how American politics was unfolding and where it might lead.

In combination, these conversations led several of us, in 2017, to convene what we call the American Democracy Collaborative. The group's premise is that in order to understand contemporary political developments in the United States, we need to think more broadly than has been the norm, learning from scholars who study democracy in other nations, scholars who think about American politics historically, and a wide array of experts on specific American political institutions and aspects of political behavior. The ADC comprises two of the Cornell comparativists, the exceptionally smart and insightful scholars Tom Pepinsky and Ken Roberts, as well as Rick Valelly and ourselves. Together, the five of us have organized several conferences, yielding a rich and productive series of conversations that gave rise to a joint article, "The Trump Presidency and American Democracy: A Historical and Comparative Analysis," published in *Perspectives on Politics* in 2019. The ideas for this book grew directly out of this collaboration, and we could not have written it otherwise. In addition, we thank Rick for being our guide to understanding the nineteenth century, offering indispensable advice about literature and interpretation as we began and as we completed chapters later on. Ken opened our eyes to so much, particularly about political parties, polarization, populism, and the possibilities for democratic deterioration, and he offered excellent advice on the manuscript. Tom generously read the entire manuscript and gave us incredibly useful feedback on each chapter. We are so appreciative of this intellectually dynamic and fruitful collaboration.

We are tremendously thankful to all of the individuals who presented their ideas at our American Democracy Collaborative workshops, offering perspectives that have spurred and refined our thinking. In particular, we are grateful to: David Bateman, Richard Bensel, Jamelle Bouie, Valerie Bunce, Christian Caryl, Eliot Cohen, John DiIulio, E. J. Dionne, Lee Drutman, Sergio Garcia-Rios, Dan Gillion, Matt Glassman, Paul Glastris, Alex Hertel-Fernandez, Larry Jacobs, Kimberley Johnson, Hahrie Han, Nathan Kalmoe, Tom Keck, Desmond King, Robert Kuttner, Didi Kuo, Doug Kriner, Matthew Lacombe, Frances Lee, Matt Levendusky, Adam Levine, Steve Levitsky, Michele Margolis, Lilliana Mason, Jennifer McCoy, Jamila Michener, Rob Mickey, Sid Milkis, Norman Ornstein, Chris Parker, Paul Pierson, Dave Robertson, Phil Rocco, Jennifer Rubin, Kori Schake, Eric Schickler, Danny Schlozman, Theda Skocpol, Rogers Smith, Murat Somer, Sid Tarrow, Sabrina Tavernise, Nic van de Walle, Keith Whittington, and Christina Wolbrecht. A few individuals played particularly instrumental roles in helping these events come to be, not least: Gretchen Ritter, Daniel Stid, and Kim Weeden, as well as

Jerrica Brown, Clara Elpi, and Dave Nelson. Cornell University has been magnanimous in funding the American Democracy Collaborative conferences through the John L. Senior Chair, the Center for the Study of Inequality, and the Einaudi Center. Our conferences have also benefited from the generosity of the Hewlett Foundation, Atlantic Philanthropies, and the New America Foundation.

We are also thankful to participants at other conferences and department seminars where we presented papers that contributed to this book project, including "Political Institutions and Challenges to Democracy: America in Comparative Perspective," a 2019 conference at Columbia University hosted by the Social Science Research Council (SSRC); the 2019 annual meeting of the American Political Science Association (APSA); and a department seminar of the Government Department at Harvard University. At the SSRC conference, Kate Krimmel gave us extraordinarily trenchant suggestions that prompted us to rethink and reorganize our analytical tasks quite fundamentally, and to add a full historical episode to the book. Rick Valelly and Theda Skocpol each offered fabulous comments at APSA.

We have been remarkably fortunate to have received feedback on the project from several additional scholars. Roger Sharp served as our Sherpa as we embarked on a journey into the 1790s; he provided invaluable insight through his marvelous scholarship, conversations as we tested our ideas, and later on, reading and commenting on our chapters. Deondra Rose played an indispensable role by bringing the 1898 Wilmington massacre to our attention and sharing invaluable materials about it. Danny Scholzman and Mary Summers each read chapters, and Jeff Stonecash kindly read the entire manuscript, and each of them provided us with terrific suggestions. Linda Kerber, Frances Lee, Eileen McDonagh, Adam Sheingate, Steve Teles, and Vesla Weaver took time to hear out our ideas and offer sage advice. Steve Levitsky, whose scholarship with Daniel Ziblatt has so strongly influenced our own, generously read the entire manuscript and offered us tremendously valuable advice that dramatically shaped our revisions.

Several talented research assistants have helped us to learn about the myriad topics encompassed by a book that attempts to understand five periods in American history in addition to our contemporary era. These include, at Cornell, Richard Barton, Trevor Brown, and Colin Cepuran; at Johns Hopkins, Maye Henning; and at the Radcliffe Institute, Audrey Hanson and Ian Lutz. Stephen Roblin did a superb job of preparing the graphs for Chapter 8.

Suzanne is deeply appreciative of her department at Cornell, the wonderful colleagues who provided the intellectual ferment that helped stimulate the book project and the support that permitted her to write it, as well as an enriching fellowship from the Radcliffe Institute of Advanced Study, which made the book's completion possible. Likewise, Rob is grateful for the collegiality and support of his colleagues in political science and across the social sciences at Johns Hopkins and for two groups of Hopkins undergraduates—the students in his 2019 seminar on "The Future of American Democracy" and the students in the Program on Social Policy—on whom he inflicted many of the working ideas for the book, to which they responded with patience and penetrating insight.

Our agent Lisa Adams of the Garamond Agency has watched over us and offered moral support and professional guidance every step of the way, from writing a proposal onward. Brandon Proia read the entire manuscript and provided extremely useful coaching on writing historical narrative. At St. Martin's Press, our editor Tim Bartlett posed challenging questions on every chapter, pushing us to overhaul the book when we revised it, improving it greatly in the process. We are appreciative of the entire team at St. Martin's, including Alice Pfeifer, Alan Bradshaw, Callum Plews, Rebecca Lang, and Sara Beth Haring.

Our spouses, Wayne Grove and Lauren Osborne, have quite literally lived with this project for these past few years, engaging in numerous conversations with us as we studied each period of history, and putting up with our demanding writing schedules and intense deadlines. For their love and support we are, as ever, truly thankful.

We have written this book because we love what the United States, at its best, aspires to be and because we dearly wish for younger and future generations to be able to know and love that as well. We invite them to participate in a long American tradition of revitalizing our political fabric. In that spirit, this book is dedicated to our children, Ben, Martha, and Aaron Lieberman, and Sophie and Julia Mettler-Grove.

# Notes

## Introduction: Democracy Under Siege

1 Stanley Elkins and Eric McKitrick, *The Age of Federalism: The Early American Republic, 1788–1800* (New York: Oxford University Press, 1993), 591, quotation on 694. The Republican Party of the 1790s was formed as an opposition party, in reaction to the Federalists. Within a decade, it became known as the Democratic-Republican Party, and by the 1830s was transformed into the Democratic Party. The contemporary Republican Party, by contrast, was founded in the 1850s.

2 Andrew W. Robertson, "'Look on This Picture . . . And on This!' Nationalism, Localism, and Partisan Images of Otherness in the United States, 1787–1820," *American Historical Review* 106 (October 2001): 1273–74; David Waldstreicher, *In the Midst of Perpetual Fetes: The Making of American Nationalism, 1776–1820* (Chapel Hill: University of North Carolina Press, 1997), 129, 205–6 (quotation on 206), 219–20.

3 Elkins and McKitrick, *Age of Federalism*, 592; Robertson, "Look on This Picture," 1275.

4 This argument is made by Raúl L. Madrid and Kurt Weyland, "Conclusion: Why US Democracy Will Survive Trump," in *When Democracy Trumps Populism: European and Latin American Lessons for the United States*, edited by Kurt Weyland and Raúl L. Madrid (Cambridge: Cambridge University Press, 2019), 154–86.

## Chapter 1: Threats to Democracy

1 Some insist that the Constitution's framers did not actually intend to create a democracy and that the nation is more aptly termed a "republic" at its inception, but we think this is a distinction without a difference. The characteristics of democracy that we describe apply to representative government as well as direct democracy. Robert A. Dahl, "Democracy," *Encyclopedia Britannica*, https://www.britannica.com/topic/democracy, February 8, 2019; Alexis de Tocqueville, *Democracy in America*, trans. Arthur Goldhammer (New York: Library of America, 2004); Gordon S. Wood, *The Radicalism of the American Revolution* (New York: Alfred A. Knopf, 1991).

2 David A. Bateman, *Disenfranchising Democracy: Constructing the Electorate in the United States, the United Kingdom, and France* (Cambridge: Cambridge University Press, 2018).

3 Desmond King, Robert C. Lieberman, Gretchen Ritter, and Laurence Whitehead, eds.,

*Democratization in America: A Comparative-Historical Analysis* (Baltimore: Johns Hopkins University Press, 2009); Robert Mickey, *Paths Out of Dixie: The Democratization of Authoritarian Enclaves in America's Deep South, 1944–1972* (Princeton, NJ: Princeton University Press, 2015); Robert C. Lieberman, *Shifting the Color Line: Race and the American Welfare State* (Cambridge, MA: Harvard University Press, 1998); Suzanne Mettler, *Dividing Citizens: Gender and Federalism in New Deal Public Policy* (Ithaca, NY: Cornell University Press, 1998).

4   Nancy Bermeo, "On Democratic Backsliding," *Journal of Democracy* 27 (January 2016): 5–19.

5   Philippe C. Schmitter and Terry Lynn Karl, "What Democracy Is . . . and Is Not," *Journal of Democracy* 2 (Summer 1991): 76–80; Robert A. Dahl, *Democracy and Its Critics* (New Haven, CT: Yale University Press, 1991).

6   Some theorists of democracy, such as the economist Joseph Schumpeter, define democracy simply as a political system in which the people choose their rulers through competitive elections. But many authoritarian regimes hold elections as well, so elections by themselves are not sufficient to classify a regime as a democracy. Joseph A. Schumpeter, *Capitalism, Socialism, and Democracy* (New York: Harper & Brothers, 1942), 269. Also see Adam Przeworski, "Minimalist Conception of Democracy: A Defense," in *Democracy's Value*, edited by Ian Shapiro and Casiano Hacker-Cordón (Cambridge: Cambridge University Press, 1999), 23–55.

7   Barry R. Weingast, "The Political Foundations of Democracy and the Rule of Law," *American Political Science Review* 91 (June 1997): 262.

8   Adam Przeworski, *Democracy and the Market: Political and Economic Reforms in Eastern Europe and Latin America* (Cambridge: Cambridge University Press, 1991), 10–14.

9   Charles Tilly, *Democracy* (Cambridge: Cambridge University Press, 2007), chap. 1; Judith Shklar, *American Citizenship: The Quest for Inclusion* (Cambridge, MA: Harvard University Press, 1991); Dahl, *Democracy and Its Critics*.

10   Steven Levitsky and Lucan Way, "The Rise of Competitive Authoritarianism," *Journal of Democracy* 13 (April 2002): 51–65.

11   Carol Morello, "Freedom House Downgrades U.S. on Its Freedom Index, Rebukes Trump," *Washington Post*, February 4, 2019; "Declining Trust in Government Is Denting Democracy," *The Economist*, January 25, 2017.

12   Steven Levitsky and Daniel Ziblatt, *How Democracies Die* (New York: Crown, 2018); Timothy Snyder, *The Road to Unfreedom* (New York: Tim Duggan Books, 2018); Madeleine Albright, *Fascism: A Warning* (New York: HarperCollins, 2018).

13   On the particularities of US institutions, see Alfred Stepan and Juan Linz, "Comparative Perspectives on Inequality and the Quality of Democracy in the United States," *Perspectives on Politics* 9 (December 2011): 841–56.

14   Lynn Vavreck, "A Measure of Identity: Are You Wedded to Your Party?" *New York Times*, January 31, 2017.

15   Kenneth M. Roberts, "Parties, Populism, and Democratic Decay: A Comparative Perspective on Political Polarization in the United States," in *When Democracy Trumps Populism: European and Latin American Lessons for the United States*, edited by Kurt Weyland and Raúl L. Madrid (Cambridge: Cambridge University Press, 2019), 132–53.

16   Murat Somer and Jennifer McCoy, "Transformations Through Polarizations and Global Threats to Democracy," *Annals of the American Academy of Political and Social Science* 681 (January 2019): 13; Jennifer McCoy, Tahmina Rahman, and Murat Somer, "Polarization and the Global Crisis of Democracy: Common Patterns, Dynamics, and Pernicious Consequences for Democratic Politics," *American Behavioral Scientist* 62 (January 2018): 16–42.

17   Thomas E. Mann and Norman J. Ornstein, *It's Even Worse Than It Looks: How the American Constitutional System Collided with the New Politics of Extremism* (New York: Basic Books, 2012), 31–33, quotation on 33, cited in Matt Grossman and David A. Hopkins,

*Asymmetric Politics: Ideological Republicans and Group Interest Democrats* (Oxford: Oxford University Press, 2016), 286.

18  Barbara Sinclair, *Party Wars: Polarization and the Politics of National Policymaking* (Norman: University of Oklahoma Press, 2006), 114–15.

19  Frances E. Lee, *Insecure Majorities: Congress and the Perpetual Campaign* (Chicago: University of Chicago Press, 2016); Frances E. Lee, *Beyond Ideology: Politics, Principles, and Partisanship in the U.S. Senate* (Chicago: University of Chicago Press, 2009); Sarah Binder, "Polarized We Govern?" Center for Effective Public Management, Brookings Institution, May 2014, https://www.brookings.edu/wp-content/uploads/2016/06/BrookingsCEPM_Polarized_figReplacedTextRevTableRev.pdf; Suzanne Mettler, "The Policyscape and the Challenges of Contemporary Politics to Policy Maintenance," *Perspectives on Politics* 14 (June 2016): 369–90.

20  Theda Skocpol and Vanessa Williamson, *The Tea Party and the Remaking of Republican Conservatism* (Oxford: Oxford University Press, 2012), 170–71.

21  Jennifer McCoy and Murat Somer, "Toward a Theory of Pernicious Polarization and How It Harms Democracies: Comparative Evidence and Possible Remedies," *Annals of the American Academy of Political and Social Science* 681 (January 2019): 257; Paul Pierson and Eric Schickler, "Madison's Constitution Under Stress: A Developmental Analysis of Political Polarization," *Annual Review of Political Science* 23 (2020), https://doi.org/10.1146/annurev-polisci-050718-033629.

22  Alan Abramowitz, "The Rise of Negative Partisanship and the Nationalization of U.S. Elections in the 21st Century," *Electoral Studies* 41 (March 2016): 12–22; Lilliana Mason, *Uncivil Agreement: How Politics Became Our Identity* (Chicago: University of Chicago Press, 2018).

23  McCoy, Rahman, and Somer, "Polarization and the Global Crisis of Democracy," 16, 26–27, 33–34.

24  Dankwart Rustow, "Transitions to Democracy: Toward a Dynamic Model," *Comparative Politics* 2 (April 1970): 337–63; Somer and McCoy, "Transformations," 15.

25  Somer and McCoy, "Transformations," 15.

26  For an introduction to this topic, see Gretchen Ritter, *The Constitution as Social Design: Gender and Civic Membership in the American Constitutional Order* (Stanford, CA: Stanford University Press, 2006); Linda Kerber, *No Constitutional Right to Be Ladies: Women and the Obligations of Citizenship* (New York: Hill and Wang, 1998); Eileen McDonagh, *The Motherless State: Women's Political Leadership and American Democracy* (Chicago: University of Chicago Press, 2009); Christina Wolbrecht, *The Politics of Women's Rights: Parties, Positions, and Change* (Princeton, NJ: Princeton University Press, 2000), 26.

27  Rogers M. Smith, *Civic Ideals: Conflicting Visions of Citizenship in US History* (New Haven, CT: Yale University Press, 1997).

28  Donald R. Kinder and Cindy D. Kam, *Us Against Them: Ethnocentric Foundations of American Opinion* (Chicago: University of Chicago Press, 2010), 30; Nicholas Valentino, Carly Wayne, and Marzia Oceno, "Mobilizing Sexism: The Interaction of Emotion and Gender Attitudes in the 2016 Presidential Election." *Public Opinion Quarterly* 82, no. S1 (2018): 213–35; Davin L. Phoenix, *The Anger Gap: How Race Shapes Emotion in Politics* (Cambridge: Cambridge University Press, 2019).

29  W. E. B. Du Bois, *Black Reconstruction: An Essay Toward a History of the Part Which Black Folk Played in the Attempt to Reconstruct Democracy in America, 1860–1880* (New York: Harcourt, Brace, 1935); Eric Foner, *Reconstruction: America's Unfinished Revolution, 1863–1877* (New York: Harper & Row, 1988); Richard M. Valelly, *The Two Reconstructions: The Struggle for Black Enfranchisement* (Chicago: University of Chicago Press, 2004).

30  Frances E. Lee, "Populism and the American Party System: Opportunities and Constraints," *Perspectives on Politics* (forthcoming), https://doi.org/10.1017/S1537592719002664; Alan I. Abramowitz, *The Great Alignment: Race, Party Trans-*

*formation, and the Rise of Donald Trump* (New Haven, CT: Yale University Press, 2018), 130–31.

31  Adam Przeworski, Michael Alvarez, José Antonio Cheibub, and Fernando Limongi, "What Makes Democracies Endure?" *Journal of Democracy* 7 (January 1996): 43.

32  Carles Boix, *Democracy and Redistribution* (Cambridge: Cambridge University Press, 2003); Daron Acemoglu and James A. Robinson, *Economic Origins of Dictatorship and Democracy* (Cambridge: Cambridge University Press, 2006); for a contrasting view, see Ben W. Ansell and David J. Samuels, *Inequality and Democracy* (Cambridge: Cambridge University Press, 2014).

33  Claudia Goldin and Robert A. Margo, "The Great Compression: The Wage Structure in the United States at Mid-Century," *Quarterly Journal of Economics* 107 (February 1992): 1–34; Thomas Piketty, *Capital in the Twenty-First Century,* trans. Arthur Goldhammer (Cambridge, MA: Harvard University Press, 2014); Jacob S. Hacker and Paul Pierson, *Winner-Take-All Politics: How Washington Made the Rich Richer— and Turned Its Back on the Middle Class* (New York: Simon and Schuster, 2010).

34  See Larry Bartels, *Unequal Democracy: The Political Economy of the New Gilded Age* (Princeton, NJ: Princeton University Press, 2008); Lawrence R. Jacobs and Theda Skocpol, eds., *Inequality and American Democracy: What We Know and What We Need to Learn* (New York: Russell Sage Foundation, 2005); Benjamin I. Page, Jason Seawright, and Matthew J. Lacombe, *Billionaires and Stealth Politics* (Chicago: University of Chicago Press, 2019); Lee Drutman, *The Business of America Is Lobbying: How Corporations Became Politicized and Politics Became More Corporate* (Oxford: Oxford University Press, 2015); Theda Skocpol and Alexander Hertel-Fernandez, "The Koch Network and Republican Party Extremism," *Perspectives on Politics* 14 (September 2016): 681–99; Alexander Hertel-Fernandez, *State Capture: How Conservative Activists, Big Businesses, and Wealthy Donors Reshaped the American States—and the Nation* (Oxford: Oxford University Press, 2019).

35  Bermeo, "On Democratic Backsliding," 10.

36  Juan J. Linz, "The Perils of Presidentialism," *Journal of Democracy* 1 (Winter 1990): 51–69.

37  Arthur M. Schlesinger Jr., *The Imperial Presidency* (Boston: Houghton Mifflin, 1973).

38  Desmond King and Rogers M. Smith, "White Protectionism in America," *Perspectives on Politics* (forthcoming).

39  McCoy, Rahman, and Somer, "Polarization and the Global Crisis of Democracy," 17.

## Chapter 2: Polarization Wreaks Havoc in the 1790s

1  James Roger Sharp, *American Politics in the Early Republic: The New Nation in Crisis* (New Haven, CT: Yale University Press, 1993), quotation on 227.

2  Sharp, *American Politics*, 226–28.

3  Sharp, *American Politics*, 247.

4  Sharp, *American Politics*, 250–66.

5  Richard Hofstadter, *The Idea of a Party System: The Rise of Legitimate Opposition in the United States, 1780–1840* (Berkeley: University of California Press, 1970); Sharp, *American Politics*, 66.

6  Sharp, *American Politics*, 141, 158, 166, 187, 196, 204; Hofstadter, *Idea*, chap. 1; Jeffrey S. Selinger, *Embracing Dissent: Political Violence and Party Development in the United States* (Philadelphia: University of Pennsylvania Press, 2016), chap. 1.

7  Peter H. Lindert and Jeffrey G. Williamson, *Unequal Gains: American Growth and Inequality Since 1700* (Princeton, NJ: Princeton University Press, 2016), 36–42.

8  The data are from the 1800 United States Census. See https://www.census.gov /population/www/censusdata/files/table–2.pdf; https://www.census.gov/history/pdf /histstats-colonial–1970.pdf, 30.

9  James Madison, "A Candid State of Parties," *National Gazette*, December 22, 1792,

Founders Online, National Archives, https://founders.archives.gov/documents/Madison/01-14-02-0334.

10 *Gazette of the United States*, September 29, 1792.

11 Stanley Elkins and Eric McKitrick, *The Age of Federalism: The Early American Republic, 1788–1800* (New York: Oxford University Press, 1993), 115–16; Sharp, *American Politics*, 34–38.

12 Sharp, *American Politics*, 40.

13 Elkins and McKitrick, *Age of Federalism*, 284; Jeffrey L. Pasley, *"The Tyranny of Printers": Newspaper Politics in the Early American Republic* (Charlottesville: University Press of Virginia, 2001), 64.

14 Theresa M. Welford, "Philip Freneau," *Oxford Encyclopedia of American Literature*, edited by Jary Parini and Phillip W. Leininger (Oxford University Press, 2005) (online); Elkins and McKitrick, *Age of Federalism*, 285.

15 Sharp, *American Politics*, 44.

16 Elkins and McKitrick, *Age of Federalism*, 285, 291.

17 Sharp, *American Politics*, 31, 36, 42.

18 Thomas P. Slaughter, *The Whiskey Rebellion: Frontier Epilogue to the American Revolution* (New York: Oxford University Press, 1986), 113, 115.

19 Quotations in Sharp, *American Politics*, 94; Slaughter, *Whiskey Rebellion*, 111–12.

20 Elkins and McKitrick, *Age of Federalism*, 463; Sharp, *American Politics*, 96.

21 Elkins and McKitrick, *Age of Federalism*, 463–67.

22 Sharp, *American Politics*, 95–96, quotation on 96.

23 Sharp, *American Politics*, 96, puts the number at 15,000. Slaughter, *Whiskey Rebellion*, 212, puts it at 12,950; see also 212–15.

24 Elkins and McKitrick, *Age of Federalism*, 480–82; Slaughter, *Whiskey Rebellion*, 218–21; Carrie Hagen, "The First Presidential Pardon Pitted Alexander Hamilton Against George Washington," *Smithsonian Magazine*, August 29, 2017.

25 Sharp, *American Politics*, 96.

26 The Democratic-Republican societies had no formal affiliation to either of the emerging political parties, though their views more closely resembled those of the Republicans.

27 Sharp, *American Politics*, 87.

28 Philip Foner, *The Democratic-Republican Societies, 1790–1800: A Documentary Sourcebook of Constitutions, Declarations, Addresses, Resolutions, and Toasts* (Westport, CT: Greenwood Press, 1976), quotations on 3, 3–4.

29 Eugene Perry Link, *Democratic-Republican Societies, 1790–1800* (New York: Columbia University Press, 1942), 14–16, chap. 4; Sharp, *American Politics*, 85–86; Foner, *Democratic-Republican Societies*, quotation on 5.

30 Foner, *Democratic-Republican Societies*, 11; Michelle Orihel, "Political Fever: The Democratic Societies and the Crisis of Republican Governance in 1790s America," Ph.D. dissertation, Syracuse University, 2010; Sharp, *American Politics*, 87; quotation in John L. Brooke, "Ancient Lodges and Self-Created Societies: Voluntary Association and the Public Sphere in the Early Republic," in *Launching the "Extended Republic": The Federalist Era*, edited by Ronald Hoffman and Peter J. Albert (Charlottesville: University of Virginia Press, 1996), 316.

31 Link, *Democratic-Republican Societies*, 164; Foner, *Democratic-Republican Societies*, 10, 12, 14, 26; Seth Cotlar, "Democratic Republican Societies," in *The Bloomsbury Encyclopedia of the American Enlightenment*, edited by Mark G. Spencer (New York: Bloomsbury Academic, 2015), online.

32 Sharp, *American Politics*, 69–71, 74–75, quotation on 77; Matthew Schoenbachler, "Republicanism in the Age of Democratic Revolution: The Democratic Republican Societies of the 1790s," *Journal of the Early Republic* 18 (Spring 1998): 246.

33 Quotation in Sharp, *American Politics*, 78.

34 Sharp, *American Politics*, 78–81.

35 Foner, *Democratic-Republican Societies*, 24, 25, quotation on 23.

36 Quotation in Jeffrey S. Selinger, "Rethinking the Development of Legitimate Party Opposition in the United States, 1793–1828," *Political Science Quarterly* 127, no. 2 (Summer 2012): 276; quotation in Sharp, *American Politics*, 100.

37 Foner, *Democratic-Republican Societies*, 31; Sharp, *American Politics*, 100–103, quotation on 103.

38 Sharp, *American Politics*, 87, 103; Foner, *Democratic-Republican Societies*, 32.

39 Sharp, *American Politics*, 113–14.

40 Sharp, *American Politics*, 126.

41 Sharp, *American Politics*, 123, including quotation.

42 Sharp, *American Politics*, 129–30.

43 Andrew W. Robertson, "'Look on This Picture . . . And on This!'" Nationalism, Localism, and Partisan Images of Otherness in the United States, 1787–1820," *American Historical Review* 106, no. 4 (2001): 1267; Sharp, *American Politics*, 175.

44 Sharp, *American Politics*, 176.

45 Elkins and McKitrick, *Age of Federalism*, 590; Sharp, *American Politics*, 177.

46 Sharp, *American Politics*, 177, including quotations.

47 Sharp, *American Politics*, 178–79.

48 Sharp, *American Politics*, 194–95.

49 Sharp, *American Politics*, 195, 196.

50 Carol Berkin, *A Sovereign People: The Crises of the 1790s and the Birth of American Nationalism* (New York: Basic Books, 2017), 233. One year later, Kentucky enacted a new version of this resolution, this time including the nullification language (p. 236).

51 Elkins and McKitrick, *Age of Federalism*, 696–97; Paul Douglas Newman, "John Fries," American National Biography, https://www-anb-org.ezp-prod1.hul.harvard.edu/view /10.1093/anb/9780198606697.001.0001/anb-9780198606697-e-0200133; Sharp, *American Politics*, 209.

52 Quotations in Sharp, *American Politics*, 210.

53 Elkins and McKitrick, *Age of Federalism*, 698.

54 Elkins and McKitrick, *Age of Federalism*, 699; Sharp, *American Politics*, 201.

55 James Morton Smith, "Sedition in the Old Dominion: James T. Callender and the Prospect Before Us," *Journal of Southern History* 20 (May 1954): 157–82; Sharp, *American Politics*, 218.

56 Elkins and McKitrick, *Age of Federalism*, 704–5; Sharp, *American Politics*, 218–19.

57 Robert E. Ross, "Federalism and the Electoral College: The Development of the General Ticket Method for Selecting Presidential Electors," *Publius* 46, no. 2 (2016): 147–69; Sharp, *American Politics*, 233–34.

58 Sharp, *American Politics*, 240.

59 Douglas R. Egerton, "Gabriel's Conspiracy and the Election of 1800," *Journal of Southern History* 56, no. 2 (May 1990): 191–96, 202, 207. An alternate interpretation appears in Michael L. Nicholls, "'Holy Insurrection': Spinning the News of Gabriel's Conspiracy," *Journal of Southern History* 78, no. 1 (February 2012): 37–68.

60 Linda K. Kerber, *Federalists in Dissent: Imagery and Ideology in Jeffersonian America* (Ithaca, NY: Cornell University Press, 1970), 23–66.

61 Sharp, *American Politics*, 250–52, 266.

62 Sharp, *American Politics*, 268–70.

63 Sharp, *American Politics*, 259.

64 Sharp, *American Politics*, 167; quotation from James Roger Sharp, *The Deadlocked Election of 1800: Jefferson, Burr, and the Union in the Balance* (Lawrence: University Press of Kansas, 2010), 152.

65 Sharp, *Deadlocked Election*, 153, including quotations.

66 Sharp, *Deadlocked Election*, 160–62, 271. Also, later it came out that Bayard had received

a letter from Hamilton endorsing Jefferson, though it is not known whether that was persuasive. Elkins and McKitrick, *Age of Federalism*, 749; Sharp, *American Politics*, 271.

67 Sharp, *American Politics*, 274.

68 Sean Wilentz, *The Rise of American Democracy: Jefferson to Lincoln* (New York: W. W. Norton, 2005), 94, 96, 97, 114; John Yoo, "Jefferson and Executive Power," *Boston University Law Review* 88 (2008): 421; Garry Wills, *"Negro President": Jefferson and the Slave Power* (Boston: Houghton Mifflin, 2003), 96.

69 Lindert and Williamson, *Unequal Gains*, 36–42.

70 US Bureau of the Census, *Historical Statistics of the United States, Colonial Times to 1970* (Washington, DC: US Government Printing Office, 1975), Series A172–209, 22–38; William W. Freehling, *The Road to Disunion, Vol. 1, Secessionists at Bay, 1776–1854* (New York: Oxford University Press, 1990), 147.

71 Quotation in Leonard L. Richards, *The Slave Power: The Free North and Southern Domination, 1780–1860* (Baton Rouge: Louisiana State University Press, 2000), 33.

72 Richards, *Slave Power*, 9.

## Chapter 3: Democratic Disintegration in the 1850s

1 *Congressional Globe*, 34th Cong., 1st Sess., Appendix, 529–30 (1856).

2 *Herald of Freedom* (Lawrence, KS), January 19, 1856, 3.

3 Nicole Etcheson, *Bleeding Kansas: Contested Liberty in the Civil War Era* (Lawrence: University Press of Kansas, 2004), 89–90.

4 Etcheson, *Bleeding Kansas*, 91.

5 Peter H. Lindert and Jeffrey G. Williamson, *Unequal Gains: American Growth and Inequality Since 1700* (Princeton, NJ: Princeton University Press, 2016), 114–19, 136–39; Gavin Wright, *Slavery and American Economic Development* (Baton Rouge: Louisiana State University Press, 2006).

6 Martha S. Jones, *Birthright Citizens: A History of Race and Rights in Antebellum America* (Cambridge: Cambridge University Press, 2018); Eric Foner, *Free Soil, Free Labor, Free Men: The Ideology of the Republican Party Before the Civil War* (New York: Oxford University Press, 1970); see David A. Bateman, "Partisan Polarization on Black Suffrage, 1785–1868," *Perspectives on Politics* (forthcoming), https://doi.org/10.1017/S1537592719001087.

7 Don E. Fehrenbacher, *The South and Three Sectional Crises* (Baton Rouge: Louisiana State University Press, 1980), 17; William W. Freehling, *The Road to Disunion: Secessionists at Bay, 1776–1854* (Oxford: Oxford University Press, 1990), 559.

8 David M. Potter, *The Impending Crisis, 1848–1861* (New York: Harper & Row, 1976), 452–54; Carl Lawrence Paulus, *The Slaveholding Crisis: Fear of Insurrection and the Coming of the Civil War* (Baton Rouge: Louisiana State University Press, 2017); Jones, *Birthright Citizens*; Manisha Sinha, *The Slave's Cause: A History of Abolition* (New Haven, CT: Yale University Press, 2017).

9 Daniel Walker Howe, *What Hath God Wrought: The Transformation of America, 1815–1848* (Oxford: Oxford University Press, 2007), 430–31; Edwin G. Burrows and Mike Wallace, *Gotham: A History of New York City to 1898* (Oxford: Oxford University Press, 1999), 573–75.

10 Jon Grinspan, *The Virgin Vote: How Young Americans Made Democracy Social, Politics Personal, and Voting Popular in the Nineteenth Century* (Chapel Hill: University of North Carolina Press, 2016), 4, 7, 12; Howe, *What Hath God Wrought*, 496–97.

11 William W. Freehling, "The Divided South, Democracy's Limitations, and the Causes of the Peculiarly North American Civil War," in *Why the Civil War Came*, edited by Gabor S. Boritt (New York: Oxford University Press, 1996), 173.

12 Michael F. Holt, *The Political Crisis of the 1850s* (New York: Wiley, 1978), 11–13.

13 William Gienapp, "The Crisis of American Democracy: The Political System and the

Coming of the Civil War," in *Why the Civil War Came,* edited by Gabor S. Boritt (New York: Oxford University Press, 1996), 82; Fehrenbacher, *South and Three Sectional Crises,* 45; William Lee Miller, *Arguing About Slavery: The Great Battle in the United States Congress* (New York: Alfred A. Knopf, 1996), 13.

14  Freehling, *Secessionists at Bay,* 290–92.

15  Freehling, *Secessionists at Bay,* 342–52; Freehling, "Divided South," 153; Foner, *Free Soil, Free Labor, Free Men,* 100–101.

16  *Congressional Globe,* 29th Cong., 1st Sess. 1214 (1846); Potter, *Impending Crisis,* 20–21.

17  *Congressional Globe,* 29th Cong., 1st Sess. 1217–18 (1846); Potter, *Impending Crisis,* 21–22.

18  *Congressional Globe,* 30th Cong., 1st Sess. 391 (1848); Abraham Lincoln, "Speech at Peoria, Illinois," October 16, 1854, in *The Collected Works of Abraham Lincoln,* edited by Roy P. Basler (New Brunswick, NJ: Rutgers University Press, 1953), 2:252.

19  Freehling, *Secessionists at Bay,* 516.

20  *Congressional Globe,* 31st Cong., 1st Sess. 452 (1850).

21  *Congressional Globe,* 31st Cong., 1st Sess. 453–35 (1850).

22  Abraham Lincoln, "Speech at Peoria, Illinois," 2:254–56.

23  Potter, *Impending Crisis,* 113–14; Freehling, *Secessionists at Bay,* 509–10, 520; Gienapp, "Crisis of American Democracy," 82; David Brion Davis, *The Slave Power Conspiracy and the Paranoid Style* (Baton Rouge: Louisiana State University Press, 1969).

24  *The Liberator* 20, no. 42 (October 18, 1850): 166; Benjamin Quarles, "Douglass and the Compromise of 1850," *Negro History Bulletin* 14, no. 1 (1950): 20–21; Frederick Douglass, "What to the Slave Is the Fourth of July," July 5, 1852, available at the Frederick Douglass Project, University of Rochester, https://rbscp.lib.rochester.edu/2945; David W. Blight, *Frederick Douglass: Prophet of Freedom* (New York: Simon and Schuster, 2018), 231–36.

25  Freehling, *Secessionists at Bay,* 519.

26  Potter, *Impending Crisis,* 130–32; Eric Foner, *Gateway to Freedom: The Hidden History of the Underground Railroad* (New York: W. W. Norton, 2015), 119–50; Jones, *Birthright Citizens,* 130.

27  Foner, *Gateway to Freedom,* 126–30.

28  Spencer R. Crew, "'When the Victims of Oppression Stand Up Manfully for Themselves': The Fugitive Slave Law of 1850 and the Role of African Americans in Obstructing Its Enforcement," in *Congress and the Crisis of the 1850s,* edited by Paul Finkelman and Donald R. Glennon (Athens: Ohio University Press, 2012); Daniel J. Sharfstein, "When the Slave-Catcher Came to Town," *Humanities* 32 (September/October 2011): 28–52.

29  Potter, *Impending Crisis,* 146–52; Paul Frymer, *Building an American Empire: The Era of Territorial and Political Expansion* (Princeton, NJ: Princeton University Press, 2017), 143–47.

30  "Appeal of the Independent Democrats in Congress to the People of the United States," 1854.

31  Potter, *Impending Crisis,* 162–65.

32  Foner, *Free Soil, Free Labor, Free Men,* 94.

33  Potter, *Impending Crisis,* 159–62.

34  Etcheson, *Bleeding Kansas,* 35–39; Potter, *Impending Crisis,* 199–200.

35  Etcheson, *Bleeding Kansas,* 33–34, 47; Freehling, *Secessionists at Bay,* 545–49.

36  Etcheson, *Bleeding Kansas,* 55–56, 59; Potter, *Impending Crisis,* 201.

37  Etcheson, *Bleeding Kansas,* 58.

38  Etcheson, *Bleeding Kansas,* 57–59; Potter, *Impending Crisis,* 201.

39  Etcheson, *Bleeding Kansas,* 61–64; Potter, *Impending Crisis,* 204.

40  Etcheson, *Bleeding Kansas,* 66–68, 73–74.

41  *Report of the Special Committee Appointed to Investigate the Troubles in Kansas,* House of

Representatives, 34th Cong., 1st Sess., Report No. 200 (Washington: Cornelius Wendell, 1856), 652–57; Etcheson, *Bleeding Kansas*, 60.

42  *Report of the Special Committee*, 62–64, 67.

43  *Report of the Special Committee*, 68–109.

44  *Congressional Globe*, 34th Cong., 1st Sess. 1856–73 (1856); Etcheson, *Bleeding Kansas*, 128–29.

45  "Governor Reeder's Escape from Kansas," *Transactions of the Kansas State Historical Society*, vol. 3 (Topeka: Kansas Publishing House, 1886), 205–23.

46  Etcheson, *Bleeding Kansas*, 81–86, 100–102; Tony R. Mullis, *Peacekeeping on the Plains: Army Operations in Bleeding Kansas* (Columbia: University of Missouri Press, 2004), 157–60, 166–68.

47  David Herbert Donald, *Charles Sumner and the Coming of the Civil War* (New York: Alfred A. Knopf, 1967); Brooks D. Simpson, "'Hit Him Again': The Caning of Charles Sumner," in *Congress and the Crisis of the 1850s*, edited by Paul Finkelman and Donald R. Glennon (Athens: Ohio University Press, 2012), 206–7.

48  Joanne B. Freeman, *The Field of Blood: Violence in Congress and the Road to Civil War* (New York: Farrar, Straus and Giroux, 2018), 281; William E. Gienapp, "The Crime Against Sumner: The Caning of Charles Sumner and the Rise of the Republican Party," *Civil War History* 25, no. 3 (1979): 219–20.

49  *Congressional Globe*, 34th Cong., 1st Sess., Appendix, 530 (1856).

50  Freeman, *Field of Blood*, 219–21; Gienapp, "Crime Against Sumner," 220; Potter, *Impending Crisis*, 210–11; Donald, *Charles Sumner and the Coming of the Civil War*, 312–47.

51  Freeman, *Field of Blood*, 223–25; Gienapp, "Crime Against Sumner," 220–21; Williamjames Hull Hoffer, *The Caning of Charles Sumner: Honor, Idealism, and the Origins of the Civil War* (Baltimore: Johns Hopkins University Press, 2010), 72–95; Potter, *Impending Crisis*, 220–21; James M. McPherson, *Battle Cry of Freedom: The Civil War Era* (New York: Oxford University Press, 1988), 150–51.

52  Potter, *Impending Crisis*, 208; Etcheson, *Bleeding Kansas*, 104–5.

53  Etcheson, *Bleeding Kansas*, 108–11.

54  Etcheson, *Bleeding Kansas*, 113–19, 131–35, 202–8; Mullis, *Peacekeeping on the Plains*, 220–33.

55  Kenneth M. Stampp, *America in 1857: A Nation on the Brink* (New York: Oxford University Press, 1990), 167–68, 272; Etcheson, *Bleeding Kansas*, 145–47; Mark W. Summers, *The Plundering Generation: Corruption and the Crisis of the Union, 1849–1861* (New York: Oxford University Press, 1987), 248–51.

56  Potter, *Impending Crisis*, 307–10; Etcheson, *Bleeding Kansas*, 156–57; Stampp, *America in 1857*, 319–21.

57  Potter, *Impending Crisis*, 312–14; Stampp, *America in 1857*, 301–7, 310–12; *Congressional Globe*, 35th Cong., 1st Sess. 14–18 (1857); Gienapp, "Crisis of American Democracy," 113; John Niven, *The Coming of the Civil War, 1837–1861* (Arlington Heights, IL: Harlan Davidson, 1990), 107–8.

58  William E. Gienapp, "The Republican Party and the Slave Power," in *New Perspectives on Race and Slavery in America: Essays in Honor of Kenneth M. Stampp*, edited by Robert H. Abzug and Stephen E. Maizlish (Lexington: University Press of Kentucky, 1986).

59  Stampp, *America in 1857*, 326–29; Potter, *Impending Crisis*, 322–25; Etcheson, *Bleeding Kansas*, 179–84.

60  Dale E. Watts, "How Bloody Was Bleeding Kansas? Political Killings in Kansas Territory, 1854–1861," *Kansas History* 18, no. 2 (1995): 116–29; Potter, *Impending Crisis*, 360–73; Paulus, *The Slaveholding Crisis*, 221–22; McPherson, *Battle Cry of Freedom*, 206–13.

61  William W. Freehling, *The Road to Disunion: Secessionists Triumphant, 1854–1861* (Oxford: Oxford University Press, 2007), 143.

62  Potter, *Impending Crisis*, 439.

63  Potter, *Impending Crisis*, 477–78.

64  Freehling, *Secessionists Triumphant*, 503.

65  Michael J. Kline, *The Baltimore Plot: The First Conspiracy to Assassinate Abraham Lincoln* (Yardley, PA: Westholme, 2013), 230–39.

66  Daniel Stashower, *The Hour of Peril: The Secret Plot to Murder Lincoln Before the Civil War* (New York: Minotaur Books, 2013), 273.

67  Stashower, *Hour of Peril*, 281–83, 287–90; Kline, *Baltimore Plot*, 283–88; David Herbert Donald, *Lincoln* (New York: Simon and Schuster, 1995), 277–79.

## Chapter 4: Backsliding in the 1890s

1  H. Leon Prather Sr., *We Have Taken a City: Wilmington Racial Massacre and Coup of 1898* (Cranbury, NJ: Associated University Presses, 1984), 22–23; Timothy B. Tyson, "The Ghosts of 1898: Wilmington's Race Riot and the Rise of White Supremacy," *News and Observer*, November 17, 2006, 4; 1898 Wilmington Race Riot Commission, "1898 Wilmington Race Riot Report," LeRae Umfleet, principal researcher, North Carolina Department of Cultural Resources, May 31, 2006, http://digital.ncdcr.gov /cdm/compoundobject/collection/p249901coll22/id/5842/rec/16; Tyson, "Ghosts of 1898," 4.

2  1898 Wilmington Race Riot Commission, "Report," 60.

3  1898 Wilmington Race Riot Commission, "Report," chaps. 3, 4.

4  1898 Wilmington Race Riot Commission, "Report," 156; Tyson, "Ghosts of 1898," 4, 11.

5  1898 Wilmington Race Riot Commission , "Report," 111–18, 152–56; Tyson, "Ghosts of 1898," 1, 4, 11.

6  1898 Wilmington Race Riot Commission, "Report," 194; Richard M. Valelly, *The Two Reconstructions: The Struggle for Black Disenfranchisement* (Chicago: University of Chicago Press, 2004), 132.

7  Richard Franklin Bensel, *The Political Economy of American Industrialization, 1877–1900* (Cambridge: Cambridge University Press, 2000), xvii; Michael McDonald, United States Elections Project, http://www.electproject.org/national–1789-present.

8  Frances E. Lee, "Patronage, Logrolls, and 'Polarization': Congressional Parties of the Gilded Age, 1876–1896," *Studies in American Political Development* 30 (October 2016): 118–19; Peter J. Lindert and Jefferey G. Williamson, *Unequal Gains: American Growth and Inequality Since 1700* (Princeton, NJ: Princeton University Press, 2016), 173.

9  Robert Mickey, *Paths Out of Dixie: The Democratization of Authoritarian Enclaves in America's Deep South, 1944–1972* (Princeton, NJ: Princeton University Press, 2015).

10  Valelly, *Two Reconstructions*, 2. Some might question why Nazi Germany is not mentioned; the point is that it came to be considered an authoritarian regime, whereas the United States continued to be regarded as a democracy after disenfranchisement.

11  Eric Foner, *Freedom's Lawmakers: A Directory of Black Officeholders During Reconstruction* (New York: Oxford University Press, 1993), xi; Valelly, *Two Reconstructions*, 31–34.

12  Valelly, *Two Reconstructions*, 33, 40, 41.

13  Foner, *Freedom's Lawmakers*, xiv–xvii.

14  Valelly, *Two Reconstructions*, 52.

15  Valelly, *Two Reconstructions*, 69–70; J. Morgan Kousser, *The Shaping of Southern Politics: Suffrage Restriction and the Establishment of the One-Party South, 1880–1910* (New Haven, CT: Yale University Press, 1974), 16, 17, 26.

16  Kousser, *Shaping of Southern Politics*, 12 (authors' calculations of data in table 1.1), 27, 28.

17  Valelly, *Two Reconstructions*, 246; Richard M. Valelly, "Partisan Entrepreneurship and Policy Windows: George Frisbie Hoar and the 1890 Federal Elections Bill," in *Formative Acts: American Politics in the Making*, edited by Stephen Skowronek and Matthew Glassman (Philadelphia: University of Pennsylvania Press, 2007), 142, quotation at 126.

18  Richard White, *The Republic for Which It Stands: The United States During Reconstruction and the Gilded Age, 1865–1896* (New York: Oxford University Press, 2017), 628.

19 Quotations in Valelly, "Partisan Entrepreneurship," 129, 136.

20 Quotation in White, *Republic*, 629; quotations in C. Vann Woodward, *Origins of the New South, 1877–1913* (Baton Rouge: Louisiana State University Press, 1971), 254.

21 White, *Republic*, 630–35; Valelly, "Partisan Entrepreneurship," 127.

22 Valelly, *Two Reconstructions*, 146–48.

23 Valelly, *Two Reconstructions*, 131, including quotation.

24 Quoted in Valelly, "Partisan Entrepreneurship," 147.

25 Karen Orren, *Belated Feudalism: Labor, the Law, and Liberal Development in the United States* (Cambridge: Cambridge University Press, 1991); Suzanne Mettler, *Dividing Citizens: Gender and Federalism in New Deal Public Policy* (Ithaca, NY: Cornell University Press, 1998), 31.

26 David Brian Robertson, *Capital, Labor, and State: The Battle for American Labor Markets from the Civil War to the New Deal* (Lanham, MD: Rowman and Littlefield, 2000), 38; White, *Republic*, 346–54, 518–22.

27 White, *Republic*, 666–67.

28 David O. Whitten, "The Depression of 1893," EconomicHistory.net, https://eh.net /encyclopedia/the-depression-of–1893; White, *Republic*, 783–88.

29 Elizabeth Sanders, *Roots of Reform: Farmers, Workers, and the American State 1877–1917* (Chicago: University of Chicago Press, 1999), 101–8, 111.

30 Monica Prasad, *The Land of Too Much: American Abundance and the Paradox of Poverty* (Cambridge, MA: Harvard University Press, 2012), 65–66.

31 Gretchen Ritter, *Goldbugs and Greenbacks: The Antimonopoly Tradition and the Politics of Finance in America, 1865–1896* (New York: Cambridge University Press, 1997), 24, 47–49; Sanders, *Roots of Reform*, 109–11; James L. Sundquist, *Dynamics of the Party System: Alignment and Realignment of Political Parties in the United States* (Washington, DC: Brookings Institution, 1983), 112–13.

32 Sanders, *Roots of Reform*, 117–28.

33 Richard Valelly, "The Populist Scare of the 1890s—and the Aftermath That Changed American Populism," unpublished paper, 2017, 5–7. Also see Sanders, *Roots of Reform*, 128–31. Charles Postel stresses the limits of the biracial alliance in *Equality: An American Dilemma, 1866–1896* (New York: Farrar, Straus and Giroux, 2019), 303–8.

34 Sanders, *Roots of Reform*, 128–31; quotations appear on 131.

35 Valelly, "Populist Scare."

36 Data compiled by authors, from "Atlas of US Presidential Elections," https:// uselectionatlas.org; Woodward, *Origins*, 244, 262.

37 Kousser, *Shaping of Southern Politics*, 186; 1898 Wilmington Race Riot Commission, "Report," 39.

38 Michael J. Dubin, *Party Affiliations in the State Legislatures: A Year by Year Summary, 1796–2006* (Jefferson, NC: McFarland, 2007).

39 Tyson, "Ghosts of 1898," 5; Sanders, *Roots of Reform*, 134–36; "Fusion Politics," North Carolina History Project, https://northcarolinahistory.org/encyclopedia/fusion -politics.

40 Valelly, *Two Reconstructions*, 130.

41 Timothy B. Smith, *James Z. George: Mississippi's Great Commoner* (Oxford: University Press of Mississippi, 2014), chaps. 7, 10; "James Z. George," *Mississippi Encyclopedia*, https://mississippiencyclopedia.org/entries/james-z-george.

42 Kousser, *Shaping of Southern Politics*, 139–42.

43 Kousser, *Shaping of Southern Politics*, 32; V. O. Key Jr., *Southern Politics in State and Nation* (New York: Alfred A. Knopf, 1949), 537–38, including quotation.

44 Kousser, *Shaping of Southern Politics*, 144; Edward L. Ayers, *The Promise of the New South: Life After Reconstruction* (New York: Oxford University Press, 1992), 149.

45 Authors' calculation of data presented in Kousser, *Shaping of Southern Politics*, 41, table 1.5; also 42–43.

46 Sanders, *Roots of Reform*, 139; Pollock v. Farmers' Loan and Trust Co. (1895).

47 Sundquist, *Dynamics*, 154–55.

48 Sanders, *Roots of Reform*, 140; Seth Masket, "More Spending on Presidential Elections and the Peculiar Case of 1896," Enik Rising (blog), March 2, 2012, http://enikrising .blogspot.com/2012/03/more-spending-on-presidential-elections.html; Herbert Croly, *Marcus Alonzo Hanna, His Life and Work* (New York: Macmillan, 1912); Sundquist, *Dynamics*, 156–57.

49 Bensel, *Political Economy of American Industrialization*, 285; Robertson, *Capital, Labor, and State*, chap. 3.

50 Sundquist, *Dynamics*, 157–58; Valelly, *Two Reconstructions*, 138.

51 Quotations in 1898 Wilmington Race Riot Commission, "Report," 59.

52 Tyson, "Ghosts of 1898," 6; quotations in 1898 Wilmington Race Riot Commission, "Report," 58.

53 Quotations in 1898 Wilmington Race Riot Commission, "Report," 60, 61, 65.

54 Prather, *We Have Taken a City*, 96; quotations in 1898 Wilmington Race Riot Commission, "Report," 66n30.

55 Quotations in 1898 Wilmington Race Riot Commission, "Report," 60.

56 Prather, *We Have Taken a City*, 49; quotations in 1898 Wilmington Race Riot Commission, "Report," 84.

57 Quotations in 1898 Wilmington Race Riot Commission, "Report," 79, 80.

58 Quotations in 1898 Wilmington Race Riot Commission, "Report," 81.

59 Glenda Elizabeth Gilmore, *Gender and Jim Crow: Women and the Politics of White Supremacy in North Carolina, 1896–1920* (Chapel Hill: University of North Carolina Press, 1996), 105–8; 1898 Wilmington Race Riot Commission, "Report," 97–98.

60 1898 Wilmington Race Riot Commission, "Report," 112, 115.

61 Tyson, "Ghosts of 1898," 10.

62 1898 Wilmington Race Riot Commission, "Report," chap. 5; Tyson, "Ghosts of 1898," 11.

63 Williams v. Mississippi, 170 U.S. 213 (1898); Plessy v. Ferguson, 163 U.S. 537 (1896).

64 Quotation in Woodward, *Origins*, 327.

65 Quotations in Michael Perman, *Struggle for Mastery: Disfranchisement in the South, 1888–1908* (Chapel Hill: University of North Carolina Press, 2001), 163.

66 Kousser, *Shaping of Southern Politics*, 190–91.

67 Kousser, *Shaping of Southern Politics*, 193.

68 Kousser, *Shaping of Southern Politics*, 195.

69 Woodward, *Origins*, chap. 12.

70 William Taft, "Inaugural Address," March 4, 1909, Miller Center, University of Virginia, https://millercenter.org/the-presidency/presidential-speeches/march–4–1909 -inaugural-address.

71 Mickey, *Paths Out of Dixie*; Kousser, *Shaping of Southern Politics*, 224 (including Burnham quotation), 236.

72 Kousser, *Shaping of Southern Politics*, 224.

73 Kousser, *Shaping of Southern Politics*, 228.

74 Kousser, *Shaping of Southern Politics*, 228–29.

75 Valelly, *Two Reconstructions*, 144, including quotation.

76 C. Vann Woodward, *The Strange Career of Jim Crow*, 3rd ed. (New York: Oxford University Press, 1974), chap. 3; Valelly, *Two Reconstructions*, 146.

77 Desmond King, *Separate and Unequal: Black Americans and the US Federal Government* (Oxford: Oxford University Press, 2005); Valelly, *Two Reconstructions*, 146–48.

78 Kent Redding, *Making Race, Making Power: North Carolina's Road to Disfranchisement* (Urbana: University of Illinois Press, 2003). See also Kousser, *Shaping of Southern Politics*, and Valelly, *Two Reconstructions*.

79 Bensel, *Political Economy of American Industrialization, 1877–1900*.

80 Lee, "Patronage, Logrolls, and 'Polarization,'" 116–27; Bensel, *Political Economy of American Industrialization, 1877–1900*, 285.

81 Key, *Southern Politics*; quotation in Tyson, "Ghosts of 1898," 8.

## Chapter 5: Executive Aggrandizement in the 1930s

1 Paul Dickson and Thomas B. Allen, *The Bonus Army: An American Epic* (New York: Walker, 2005), 29.

2 Dickson and Allen, *Bonus Army*, 65–72, 78–80; Roger Daniels, *The Bonus March: An Episode of the Great Depression* (Westport, CT: Greenwood Press, 1971), 81.

3 Dickson and Allen, *Bonus Army*, 73–78.

4 Daniels, *Bonus March*, 91–101; Dickson and Allen, *Bonus Army*, 107–8.

5 Dickson and Allen, *Bonus Army*, 117–20.

6 Daniels, *Bonus March*, 121; Dickson and Allen, *Bonus Army*, 31–39, 127–30.

7 Daniels, *Bonus March*, 102, 157–58; Dickson and Allen, *Bonus Army*, 74–76.

8 Dickson and Allen, *Bonus Army*, 179–81; David M. Kennedy, *Freedom from Fear: The American People in Depression and War, 1929–1945* (New York: Oxford University Press, 1999), 92.

9 Daniels, *Bonus March*, 173–74; Dickson and Allen, *Bonus Army*, 181–83.

10 Arthur M. Schlesinger Jr., *The Age of Roosevelt, Vol. 1, The Crisis of the Old Order, 1919–1933* (Boston: Houghton Mifflin, 1956).

11 David A. Bateman, Ira Katznelson, and John S. Lapinski, *Southern Nation: Congress and White Supremacy After Reconstruction* (Princeton, NJ: Princeton University Press, 2018).

12 Megan Ming Francis, *Civil Rights and the Making of the Modern American State* (Cambridge: Cambridge University Press, 2014).

13 US Bureau of the Census, *Historical Statistics of the United States, Colonial Times to 1970* (Washington, DC: US Government Printing Office, 1975), Series D85–86, p. 135; Series F 31, p. 226.

14 Ira Katznelson, *Fear Itself: The New Deal and the Origins of Our Time* (New York: Liveright, 2013).

15 Katznelson, *Fear Itself*, 51–70; Alan Brinkley, *The Publisher: Henry Luce and His American Century* (New York: Alfred A. Knopf, 2010), 131–34; Michael Rosenthal, *Nicholas Miraculous: The Amazing Career of the Redoubtable Nicholas Murray Butler* (New York: Farrar, Straus and Giroux, 2006), 381; Ronald Steel, *Walter Lippmann and the American Century* (Boston: Little, Brown, 1980), 299.

16 Kennedy, *Freedom from Fear*, 236.

17 Franklin D. Roosevelt, "Inaugural Address," March 4, 1933, in *The Public Papers and Addresses of Franklin D. Roosevelt*, edited by Samuel I. Rosenman (New York: Random House, 1938), 2:11.

18 James Madison, *Federalist* #51.

19 Franklin D. Roosevelt, "The President Calls the Congress into Extraordinary Session. Proclamation No. 2038," March 5, 1933, in *Public Papers and Addresses*, 2:17; Franklin D. Roosevelt, "The President Proclaims a Bank Holiday. Gold and Silver Exports and Foreign Exchange Transactions Prohibited. Proclamation No. 2039," March 6, 1933, in *Public Papers and Addresses*, 2:24–29.

20 Arthur M. Schlesinger Jr., *The Age of Roosevelt, Vol. 2, The Coming of the New Deal* (Boston: Houghton Mifflin, 1959), 7–8; Jonathan Alter, *The Defining Moment: FDR's Hundred Days and the Triumph of Hope* (New York: Simon and Schuster, 2006), 228–31, 250–52; Anthony J. Badger, *FDR: The First Hundred Days* (New York: Hill and Wang, 2008), 25–26, 35–41.

21 Arthur Krock, "Roosevelt Gets Powers of Dictator," *New York Times*, March 11, 1933.

22 Steel, *Lippmann*, 299–300; Alter, *Defining Moment*, 4.

23 Quoted in Barry D. Karl, "Executive Reorganization and Presidential Power," *Supreme Court Review*, 1977, 23.

24  Roosevelt, "Inaugural Address," 12, 15–16.
25  Kennedy, *Freedom from Fear*, 249–57; Badger, *FDR*, 54–63, 85–88; Lewis Meriam, *Relief and Social Security* (Washington, DC: Brookings Institution, 1946), 403.
26  Franklin D. Roosevelt, "Presidential Statement upon Signing the Social Security Act," August 14, 1935, in *Public Papers and Addresses*, 4:324; Kennedy, *Freedom from Fear*, 257–73, 290–91, 344–46, 368–70.
27  Suzanne Mettler, *Dividing Citizens: Gender and Federalism in the New Deal* (Ithaca, NY: Cornell University Press, 1998); Robert C. Lieberman, *Shifting the Color Line: Race and the American Welfare State* (Cambridge, MA: Harvard University Press, 1998); Linda Faye Williams, *The Constraint of Race: Legacies of White Skin Privilege in America* (University Park: Pennsylvania State University Press, 2003); Ira Katznelson, *When Affirmative Action Was White: An Untold History of Racial Inequality in Twentieth-Century America* (New York: W. W. Norton, 2005).
28  Kenneth T. Jackson, *Crabgrass Frontier: The Suburbanization of the United States* (Oxford: Oxford University Press, 1985); Richard Rothstein, *The Color of Law: A Forgotten History of How Our Government Segregated America* (New York: Liveright, 2017); Chloe N. Thurston, *At the Boundaries of Homeownership: Credit, Discrimination, and the American State* (Cambridge: Cambridge University Press, 2018).
29  Kennedy, *Freedom from Fear*, 153, 177–89, 202–14, 365–68; Badger, *FDR*, 122–34.
30  Roosevelt, "Inaugural Address," 14–15.
31  Roosevelt, "Inaugural Address," 15.
32  Clinton Rossiter, *Constitutional Dictatorship: Crisis Government in the Modern Democracies* (Princeton, NJ: Princeton University Press, 1948).
33  Douglas A. Irwin, *Peddling Protectionism: Smoot-Hawley and the Great Depression* (Princeton, NJ: Princeton University Press, 2011), 33, 71.
34  Douglas Irwin, *Clashing over Commerce: A History of US Trade Policy* (Chicago: University of Chicago Press, 2017), 386; Kennedy, *Fear Itself*, 50.
35  Steel, *Lippmann*, 288.
36  Irwin, *Clashing over Commerce*, 423–33; Ian F. Fergusson, "Trade Promotion Authority (TPA) and the Role of Congress in Trade Policy," Congressional Research Service, 2015, https://crsreports.congress.gov/product/pdf/RL/RL33743, pp. 3, 20.
37  *78 Congressional Record* 5613 (1934); Karen E. Schnietz, "The Institutional Foundation of U.S. Trade Policy: Revisiting Explanations for the 1934 Reciprocal Trade Agreements Act," *Journal of Policy History* 12, no. 4 (2000): 417.
38  Theodore J. Lowi, *The End of Liberalism: The Second Republic of the United States*, 2nd ed. (New York: W. W. Norton, 1979), 92–107, quotation on 106.
39  Joanna L. Grisinger, *The Unwieldy American State: Administrative Politics Since the New Deal* (Cambridge: Cambridge University Press, 2012), 2.
40  *Historical Statistics of the United States*, Series Y308–317, p. 1102; Series Y339–342, p. 1105.
41  Matthew J. Dickinson, *Bitter Harvest: FDR, Presidential Power and the Growth of the Presidential Branch* (Cambridge: Cambridge University Press, 1996), 63–71.
42  Karl, "Executive Reorganization."
43  Dickinson, *Bitter Harvest*, 92–94.
44  *Report of the President's Committee on Administrative Management* (Washington, DC: US Government Printing Office, 1937), 5; Alan Brinkley, *The End of Reform: New Deal Liberalism in Recession and War* (New York: Alfred A. Knopf, 1995), 21–22.
45  A.L.A. Schechter Poultry Corp. v. United States, 295 U.S. 495 (1935), 537–38.
46  William E. Leuchtenburg, "The Origins of Franklin D. Roosevelt's 'Court-Packing' Plan," *Supreme Court Review* (1966): 390–92.
47  Steven Levitsky and Daniel Ziblatt, *How Democracies Die* (New York: Crown, 2018), 80, 130–31; Kennedy, *Freedom from Fear*, 325–37; Kevin J. McMahon, *Reconsidering Roosevelt on Race: How the Presidency Paved the Road to* Brown (Chicago: University of Chicago Press, 2004), 73–86; West Coast Hotel v. Parrish, 300 U.S. 379 (1937).

48  Franklin D. Roosevelt, "The President Presents a Plan for the Reorganization of the Judicial Branch of the Government," February 5, 1937, in *Public Papers and Addresses*, 6:51; McMahon, *Reconsidering Roosevelt on Race*, 77; Brinkley, *End of Reform*, 22; Harold L. Ickes, *The Secret Diary of Harold L. Ickes* (New York: Simon and Schuster, 1954), 2:325–26; Frank Freidel, *Franklin D. Roosevelt: A Rendezvous with Destiny* (Boston: Little, Brown, 1990), 277.

49  Richard Polenberg, *Reorganizing Roosevelt's Government: The Controversy over Executive Reorganization, 1936–1939* (Cambridge, MA: Harvard University Press, 1966), 152–54; Lauren D. Lyman, "Senate Acts Today on Reorganization; Protests Pour In," *New York Times*, March 28, 1938; "Father Coughlin Urges Group Protest," *New York Times*, April 4, 1938.

50  Theodore J. Lowi, *The Personal President: Power Invested, Promise Unfulfilled* (Ithaca, NY: Cornell University Press, 1985).

51  Betty Houchin Winfield, *FDR and the News Media* (Urbana: University of Illinois Press, 1990).

52  Jean Edward Smith, *FDR* (New York: Random House, 2007), 238; Frances Perkins, *The Roosevelt I Knew* (New York: Viking, 1946), 72.

53  Amos Kiewe, *FDR's First Fireside Chat: Public Confidence and the Banking Crisis* (College Station: Texas A&M University Press, 2007), 101–2; Robert S. McElvaine, ed., *Down and Out in the Great Depression: Letters from the Forgotten Man* (Chapel Hill: University of North Carolina Press, 1983); Kennedy, *Freedom from Fear*, 137.

54  Sean Wilentz, *The Rise of American Democracy: Jefferson to Lincoln* (New York: W. W. Norton, 2005), 581–84; William W. Freehling, *The Road to Disunion: Secessionists at Bay, 1776–1854* (New York: Oxford University Press, 1990), 456–58; *Ex parte* Milligan, 71 U.S. 2 (1866).

55  Curt Gentry, *J. Edgar Hoover: The Man and the Secrets* (New York: W. W. Norton, 1991), 75–102; Beverly Gage, *The Day Wall Street Exploded: A Story of America in Its First Age of Terror* (Oxford: Oxford University Press, 2009), 233–41.

56  Athan Theoharis, *The FBI and American Democracy: A Brief Critical History* (Lawrence: University Press of Kansas, 2004), 31–32; Richard Gid Powers, *Broken: The Troubled Past and Uncertain Future of the FBI* (New York: Free Press, 2004), 127–28.

57  Olmstead v. United States, 277 U.S. 438 (1928).

58  Richard E. Morgan, *Domestic Intelligence: Monitoring Dissent in America* (Austin: University of Texas Press, 1980), 89; Olmstead v. United States, 485; Samuel Dash, "Morality in American Politics: Is It Possible?" *Brandeis Law Journal* 39, no. 4 (2001): 773–74.

59  Neal Katyal and Richard Caplan, "The Surprisingly Stronger Case for the Legality of the NSA Surveillance Program: The FDR Precedent," *Stanford Law Review* 60 (April 2010): 1037–39.

60  United States v. Nardone, 302 U.S. 379 (1937); United States v. Nardone, 308 U.S. 338 (1939), 341.

61  Katyal and Caplan, "Surprisingly Stronger Case," 1047–48; "Justice Department Bans Wire Tapping; Jackson Acts on Hoover Recommendation," *New York Times*, March 18, 1940.

62  Katyal and Caplan, "Surprisingly Stronger Case," 1049–50.

63  Quoted in Katyal and Caplan, "Surprisingly Stronger Case," 1050.

64  Franklin D. Roosevelt, "Memorandum for the Attorney General," May 21, 1940, in Katyal and Caplan, "Surprisingly Stronger Case," 1076–77.

65  Athan Theoharis, *Spying on Americans: Political Surveillance from Hoover to the Huston Plan* (Philadelphia: Temple University Press, 1978), 98–100; Tim Weiner, *Enemies: A History of the FBI* (New York: Random House, 2012), 88.

66  Franklin D. Roosevelt, "The President Establishes the Committee on Fair Employment Practices and Reaffirms the Policy of Full Participation in the Defense Program by All

Persons, Regardless of Race, Creed, Color, or National Origin. Executive Order No. 8802," June 25, 1941, in *Public Papers and Addresses*, 10:233–35; Franklin D. Roosevelt, "A New Committee on Fair Employment Practice Is Established. Executive Order No. 9346," May 27, 1943, in *Public Papers and Addresses*, 12:228–30; Anthony S. Chen, *The Fifth Freedom: Jobs, Politics, and Civil Rights in the United States, 1941–1972* (Princeton, NJ: Princeton University Press, 2009), 35–46; Steven White, *World War II and American Racial Politics: Public Opinion, the Presidency, and Civil Rights Advocacy* (Cambridge: Cambridge University Press, 2019), 119–26.

67  Franklin D. Roosevelt, "Executive Order 9066—Authorizing the Secretary of War to Prescribe Military Areas," American Presidency Project, https://www.presidency .ucsb.edu/documents/executive-order-9066-authorizing-the-secretary-war-prescribe -military-areas; Kennedy, *Freedom from Fear*, 746–60; Smith, *FDR*, 549–53; Korematsu v. United States, 323 U.S. 214 (1944); Trump v. Hawaii, 138 S. Ct. 2392 (2018).

## Chapter 6: The Weaponized Presidency in the 1970s

1  US Bureau of the Census, *Historical Statistics of the United States, Colonial Times to 1970* (Washington, DC: US Government Printing Office, 1975), Series Y308–317, p. 1102; Series Y339–342, p. 1105.

2  Robert Mickey, Steven Levitsky, and Lucan Way, "Is America Still Safe for Democracy? Why the United States Is in Danger of Backsliding," *Foreign Affairs* 96 (May/June 2017): 20–29.

3  Athan Theoharis, *The FBI and American Democracy: A Brief Critical History* (Philadelphia: Temple University Press, 1978), 120–22; Curt Gentry, *J. Edgar Hoover: The Man and the Secrets* (New York: W. W. Norton, 1991), 442–45; David Garrow, *The FBI and Martin Luther King, Jr.: From "Solo" to Memphis* (New York: W. W. Norton, 1981), 125–26; Taylor Branch, *Pillar of Fire: America in the King Years, 1963–65* (New York: Simon and Schuster, 1998), 528–29, 556–57; Beverly Gage, "I Have a [Redacted]," *New York Times Magazine*, November 16, 2014.

4  "Toward a More Responsible Two-Party System: A Report of the Committee on Political Parties, American Political Science Association," *American Political Science Review* 44 supp. (1950); Frances E. Lee, *Insecure Majorities: Congress and the Perpetual Campaign* (Chicago: University of Chicago Press, 2016).

5  Robert Mickey, *Paths Out of Dixie: The Democratization of Authoritarian Enclaves in America's Deep South, 1944–1972* (Princeton, NJ: Princeton University Press, 2015).

6  Vesla Weaver, "Frontlash: Race and the Development of Punitive Crime Policy," *Studies in American Political Development* 21 (Fall 2007): 230–65; Dan Baum, "Legalize It All," *Harper's Magazine* 332 (April 2016): 22.

7  Rick Perlstein, *Nixonland: The Rise of a President and the Fracturing of America* (New York: Scribner, 2008), 277–81; John A. Farrell, *Richard Nixon: The Life* (New York: Doubleday, 2017), 369; Scott Laderman, "How Richard Nixon Captured White Rage—and Laid the Groundwork for Donald Trump," *Washington Post*, November 3, 2019.

8  Tim Weiner, *Enemies: A History of the FBI* (New York: Random House, 2012), 265–70; Gentry, *J. Edgar Hoover*, 586–88; David Wise, *The American Police State: The Government Against the People* (New York: Random House, 1976), 149; Brian Hochman, "Eavesdropping in the Age of *The Eavesdroppers*; or, The Bug in the Martini Olive," Post45, February 3, 2016, http://post45.research.yale.edu/2016/02/eavesdropping-in-the-age -of-the-eavesdroppers-or-the-bug-in-the-martini-olive/#identifier_71_6796; Berger v. New York, 388 U.S. 41 (1967); Katz v. United States, 389 U.S. 347 (1967).

9  Athan Theoharis, *Spying on Americans: Political Surveillance from Hoover to the Huston Plan* (Philadelphia: Temple University Press, 1978), 17, 19; Beverly Gage, "Deep Throat, Watergate, and the Bureaucratic Politics of the FBI," *Journal of Policy History* 24, no. 2 (2012): 166–67.

10  Theoharis, *Spying on Americans*, 16; Gage, "Deep Throat," 169.

11  Tom Charles Huston Interview Transcription, April 30, 2008, Richard Nixon Presiden-
    tial Library, https://www.nixonlibrary.gov/sites/default/files/virtuallibrary/documents
    /histories/huston–2008-04–30.pdf, p. 16.

12  Wise, *American Police State*, 18; William C. Sullivan with Bill Brown, *The Bureau: My
    Thirty Years in Hoover's FBI* (New York: W. W. Norton, 1979), 14–15; Gage, "Deep
    Throat," 167; "William Sullivan, Ex-F.B.I. Aide, 65, Is Killed in a Hunting Accident,"
    *New York Times*, November 19, 1977.

13  Rick Perlstein, *Before the Storm: Barry Goldwater and the Unmaking of the American Con-
    sensus* (New York: Hill and Wang, 2001), 104–10, 254, 372, 389; Alvin S. Felzenberg, *A
    Man and His Presidents: The Political Odyssey of William F. Buckley Jr.* (New Haven, CT:
    Yale University Press, 2017), 92–93, 134; Perlstein, *Nixonland*, 129–30, 462; Christo-
    pher Lydon, "Conservative Architect of Security Plan Tom Charles Huston," *New York
    Times*, May 24, 1973; Huston interview, April 30, 2008; Theoharis, *Spying on Americans*,
    16; Richard Gid Powers, *Broken: The Troubled Past and Uncertain Future of the FBI* (New
    York: Free Press, 2004), 284; Stanley I. Kutler, *The Wars of Watergate: The Last Crisis of
    Richard Nixon* (New York: Alfred A. Knopf, 1990), 105–7; David Burnham, *A Law unto
    Itself: Power, Politics, and the IRS* (New York: Random House, 1989), 249–54, 278.

14  Theoharis, *Spying on Americans*, 17, 20–21.

15  Gage, "Deep Throat."

16  Wise, *American Police State*, 270; Theoharis, *Spying on Americans*, 23; Weiner, *Enemies*,
    290.

17  Theoharis, *Spying on Americans*, 23–24; Wise, *American Police State*, 270–71.

18  Theoharis, *Spying on Americans*, 25–26.

19  Theoharis, *Spying on Americans*, 26.

20  "Special Report, Interagency Committee on Intelligence (Ad Hoc)," in *Hearings Be-
    fore the Select Committee to Study Governmental Operations with Respect to Intelligence
    Activities, United States Senate*, vol. 2, 1975, 168 (hereafter cited as Church Committee
    Hearings).

21  Huston interview, April 30, 2008, 22–23.

22  Theoharis, *Spying on Americans*, 31; Tom Charles Houston, Memorandum to H. R.
    Haldeman, July 1970, Church Committee Hearings, vol. 2, pp. 189–97; H. R. Halde-
    man, Memorandum to Tom Charles Huston, July 14, 1970, Church Committee Hear-
    ings, vol. 2, p. 198; Tom Charles Huston, Memorandum to Richard Helms, July 23,
    1970, Church Committee Hearings, vol. 2, pp. 199–202.

23  Fred Emery, *Watergate: The Corruption and Fall of Richard Nixon* (London: Jonathan
    Cape, 1994), 10.

24  Huston Interview, April 30, 2008, 26; Theoharis, *Spying on Americans*, 35; Gage, "Deep
    Throat," 171.

25  Neil Sheehan, "Vietnam Archive: Pentagon Study Traces 3 Decades of Growing U.S.
    Involvement," *New York Times*, June 13, 1971.

26  Douglas Brinkley and Luke Nichter, eds., *The Nixon Tapes, 1971–1972* (Boston:
    Houghton Mifflin Harcourt, 2014), 171–72.

27  New York Times Co. v. United States, 403 U.S. 713 (1971); Barry Sussman, *The Great
    Cover-Up: Nixon and the Scandal of Watergate* (New York: Thomas Y. Crowell, 1974),
    212–20; Daniel Ellsberg, *Secrets: A Memoir of Vietnam and the Pentagon Papers* (New
    York: Viking, 2002), 406–8.

28  H. R. Haldeman with Joseph DiMona, *The Ends of Power* (New York: Times Books,
    1978), 5.

29  Farrell, *Richard Nixon*, 425–26; Carl Bernstein and Bob Woodward, *All the President's
    Men* (New York: Simon and Schuster, 1974), 324–25; Kutler, *Wars of Watergate*, 107.

30  "The Plumbers," *New York Times*, July 22, 1973.

31  Farrell, *Richard Nixon*, 465; Bob Woodward, "Gordon Liddy Spills His Guts," *Wash-
    ington Post*, May 18, 1980; Kutler, *Wars of Watergate*, 114; Emery, *Watergate*, 61; Eugenio

Martinez, "Mission Impossible: The Watergate Bunglers," *Harper's* 249, no. 1493 (October 1974): 52–53.

32  Emery, *Watergate*, 33, 52–53, 70–73, 106; Bernstein and Woodward, *All the President's Men*, 253–54.

33  Bernstein and Woodward, *All the President's Men*, 115–27; Emery, *Watergate*, 95–96, 127–29, 136–42; Kutler, *Wars of Watergate*, 199; Perlstein, *Nixonland*, 628–29.

34  Daniel J. Galvin, *Presidential Party Building: Dwight D. Eisenhower to George W. Bush* (Princeton, NJ: Princeton University Press, 2010), 84–89; Kutler, *Wars of Watergate*, 199; Emery, *Watergate*, 96–97.

35  Emery, *Watergate*, 88–91; Carl Bernstein and Bob Woodward, "Forty Years Later, the Two Reporters Who Uncovered the Scandal Say Nixon's Crimes Were Worse Than They Knew," *Washington Post*, June 10, 2012; Farrell, *Richard Nixon*, 466–71.

36  Bernstein and Woodward, *All the President's Men*, 131; Emery, *Watergate*, 5–6, 101–18.

37  Bernstein and Woodward, *All the President's Men*, 168–69, 181–82; Kutler, *Wars of Watergate*, 161–62.

38  John Dean, Memorandum, "Dealing with Our Political Enemies," August 16, 1971, in *Hearings Before the Select Committee on Presidential Campaign Activities of the United States Senate*, Book 4, 1973, p. 1689.

39  Bernstein and Woodward, *All the President's Men*, 305–7.

40  Tape of March 21, 1973, https://www.nixonlibrary.gov/sites/default/files/forresearchers /find/tapes/watergate/trial/exhibit_12.pdf.

41  Kutler, *Wars of Watergate*, 227–35; Sussman, *Great Cover-Up*, 59–60; Bernstein and Woodward, *All the President's Men*, 247.

42  Marjorie Hunter, "C.I.A. Memo Said to Quote Haldeman on Nixon 'Wish' to Halt F.B.I. Fund Study," *New York Times*, May 22, 1973; Seymour M. Hersh, "A Broad Program," *New York Times*, May 24, 1973; Richard M. Nixon, "Statements About the Watergate Investigations," May 22, 1973, American Presidency Project, https://www .presidency.ucsb.edu/documents/statements-about-the-watergate-investigations; Elizabeth Drew, *Washington Journal: The Events of 1973–1974* (New York: Random House, 1975), 16–17; Bob Woodward and Carl Bernstein, *The Final Days*, (New York: Simon and Schuster, 1976), 38–41.

43  Drew, *Washington Journal*, 51–52.

44  The survey data are from Gallup polls in 1973 and 1974. Gallup Presidential Job Approval Center, https://news.gallup.com/interactives/185273/presidential-job-approval -center.aspx; Andrew Kohut, "How the Watergate Crisis Eroded Public Support for Richard Nixon," Pew Research Center, August 8, 2014, https://www.pewresearch.org /fact-tank/2019/09/25/how-the-watergate-crisis-eroded-public-support-for-richard -nixon.

45  Kutler, *Wars of Watergate*, 462–65.

46  Emery, *Watergate*, 225; Jimmy Breslin, *How the Good Guys Finally Won: Notes from an Impeachment Summer* (New York: Viking, 1975), 12–13; Stephen Stathis and David C. Huckabee, "Congressional Resolutions on Presidential Impeachment: A Historical Overview," Congressional Research Service, Report 98-763 GOV, updated September 16, 1998.

47  Farrell, *Richard Nixon*, 422.

48  Kutler, *Wars of Watergate*; James M. Naughton, "Nixon Says a President Can Order Illegal Actions Against Dissidents," *New York Times*, May 19, 1977.

49  Tim Weiner, *One Man Against the World: The Tragedy of Richard Nixon* (New York: Henry Holt, 2015), 94; Samuel Dash, "Morality in American Politics: Is It Possible?" *Brandeis Law Journal* 39, no. 4 (2001): 781.

50  Kohut, "Watergate Crisis"; Justin McCarthy, "Congress Approval, Support for Impeaching Trump Both Up," Gallup, October 16, 2019, https://news.gallup.com/poll /267491/congress-approval-support-impeaching-trump.aspx.

51 Drew, *Washington Journal*, 203–6, 233–36.

52 Drew, *Washington Journal*, 329–30; Woodward and Bernstein, *Final Days*, 256–57.

53 United States v. Nixon, 418 U.S. 683 (1974); Kutler, *Wars of Watergate*, 218–20, 534–40; Woodward and Bernstein, *Final Days*, 34–35, 266–72, 413–17; Drew, *Washington Journal*, 389–94.

54 Les Gapay, "Rep. Landgrebe Says He Has Closed Mind; Do Voters Approve?" *Wall Street Journal*, October 9, 1974; Emery, *Watergate*, 471–72.

55 James M. Naughton, "Nixon Slide from Power: Backers Gave Final Push," *New York Times*, August 12, 1974; Kutler, *Wars of Watergate*, 539–40; Emery, *Watergate*, 473–74; Woodward and Bernstein, *Final Days*, 441.

56 Church Committee Hearings, vol. 2, 1975, p. 20; "Senator Says Nixon's Ban on Illegal Acts Was Defied," *New York Times*, September 24, 1975.

57 *Final Report of the Select Committee to Study Governmental Operations with Respect to Intelligence Activities*, United States Senate, Book 2, 1976, p. iii.

58 Senator Frank Church on NBC's *Meet the Press*, August 17, 1975.

## Chapter 7: At All Costs

1 Frances E. Lee, *Beyond Ideology: Politics, Principles, and Partisanship in the U.S. Senate* (Chicago: University of Chicago Press, 2016).

2 Jennifer McCoy, Tahmina Rahman, and Murat Somer, "Polarization and the Global Crisis of Democracy: Common Patterns, Dynamics, and Pernicious Consequences for Democratic Politics," *American Behavioral Science* 62 (January 2018): 16–42.

3 Desmond King and Rogers M. Smith, *Still a House Divided: Race and Politics in Obama's America* (Princeton, NJ: Princeton University Press, 2011); Nicholas Valentino, Carly Wayne, and Marzia Oceno, "Mobilizing Sexism: The Interaction of Emotion and Gender Attitudes in the 2016 Presidential Election," *Public Opinion Quarterly* 82, no. S1 (2018): 213–35; Davin L. Phoenix, *The Anger Gap: How Race Shapes Emotion in Politics* (Cambridge: Cambridge University Press, 2019).

4 Carles Boix, *Democracy and Redistribution* (Cambridge: Cambridge University Press, 2003); Daron Acemoglu and James A. Robinson, *Economic Origins of Dictatorship and Democracy* (Cambridge: Cambridge University Press, 2006).

5 V. O. Key Jr., *Southern Politics in State and Nation* (New York: Alfred A. Knopf, 1949).

6 Desmond King and Sidney Milkis, "Polarization, the American State, and Executive-Centered Partisanship," in *Democratic Resilience: Can the United States Withstand Rising Polarization?* edited by Robert C. Lieberman, Suzanne Mettler, and Kenneth M. Roberts (forthcoming).

7 Abraham Lincoln, "Second Inaugural Address," March 4, 1865, in *The Collected Works of Abraham Lincoln*, edited by Roy P. Basler (New Brunswick, NJ: Rutgers University Press, 1953), 8:333.

8 Lincoln, "Second Inaugural Address," 333.

## Chapter 8: Dangerous Convergence

1 Ashley Parker and David E. Sanger, "Donald Trump Calls on Russia to Find Hillary Clinton's Missing Emails," *New York Times*, July 27, 2016; Michael D. Shear and Maggie Haberman, "Trump Claims, with No Evidence, That 'Millions of People' Voted Illegally," *New York Times*, November 27, 2016.

2 James B. Comey, "Statement for the Record, Senate Select Committee on Intelligence," June 8, 2017, pp. 3–7, https://www.intelligence.senate.gov/sites/default/files/documents/os-jcomey-060817.pdf.

3 Helen Klein Murillo, "Does Sessions Have to Recuse Himself on Russia Investigations?" *Lawfare*, February 20, 2017, https://www.lawfareblog.com/does-sessions-have-recuse-himself-russia-investigations.

4 Washington Post, *The Mueller Report* (New York: Scribner, 2019), appendix 10, p. 727;

John Kunzel, "Fact-Checking Donald Trump's Claim of No Collusion, No Obstruction from Mueller Report," *Politifact*, March 24, 2019, https://www.politifact.com/truth-o meter/article/2019/mar/24/donald-trump-claims-complete-and-total-exoneration.

5  *Mueller Report*, 444; Benjamin Wittes, "Notes on the Mueller Report," *Lawfare*, April 19, 2019 [parts E, F], https://www.lawfareblog.com/notes-mueller-report-reading -diary#Factual%20Results%20of%20the%20Obstruction%20Investigation.

6  Gallup, "Presidential Approval Ratings, Donald Trump," https://news.gallup.com/poll /203198/presidential-approval-ratings-donald-trump.aspx.

7  Paul Pierson and Eric Schickler, "Madison's Constitution Under Stress: A Developmental Analysis of Political Polarization," *Annual Review of Political Science* 23 (2020), https://doi.org/10.1146/annurev-polisci-050718-033629.

8  Eric Schickler, *Racial Realignment: The Transformation of American Liberalism, 1932– 1965* (Princeton, NJ: Princeton University Press, 2016).

9  Richard M. Valelly, "Uncle Sam's Closet: Gay and Lesbian Enfranchisement and the American State," unpublished manuscript; Sam Rosenfeld, *The Polarizers: Postwar Architects of Our Partisan Era* (Chicago: University of Chicago Press, 2018), 5, 214–15; Thomas Byrne Edsall with Mary D. Edsall, *Chain Reaction: The Impact of Race, Rights, and Taxes on American Politics* (New York: W. W. Norton, 1991).

10  For more on the history of these trends, see Nolan McCarty, Keith T. Poole, and Howard Rosenthal, *Polarized America: The Dance of Ideology and Unequal Riches* (Cambridge, MA: MIT Press, 2006).

11  Matt Grossman and David A. Hopkins, *Asymmetric Politics: Ideological Republicans and Group Interest Democrats* (Oxford: Oxford University Press, 2016); Suzanne Mettler, *The Government-Citizen Disconnect* (New York: Russell Sage Foundation, 2018).

12  Grossman and Hopkins, *Asymmetric Politics*, 283.

13  Thomas E. Mann and Norman J. Ornstein, *It's Even Worse Than It Looks: How the American Constitutional System Collided with the New Politics of Extremism* (New York: Basic Books, 2012), 36; 130 *Congressional Record* 13037, 13039 (1984).

14  Quoted in Mann and Ornstein, *It's Even Worse Than It Looks*, 36.

15  Julian E. Zelizer, "Seizing Power: Conservatives and Congress Since the 1970s," in *The Transformation of American Politics: Activist Government and the Rise of Conservatism*, edited by Paul Pierson and Theda Skocpol (Princeton, NJ: Princeton University Press, 2007), 16, 122–23; Isaac William Martin, *The Permanent Tax Revolt: How the Property Tax Transformed American Politics* (Stanford, CA: Stanford University Press, 2008).

16  Barbara Sinclair, *Party Wars: Polarization and the Politics of National Policymaking* (Norman: University of Oklahoma Press, 2006).

17  Grossman and Hopkins, *Asymmetric Politics*, 293.

18  Sinclair, *Party Wars*, 190–91.

19  Grossman and Hopkins, *Asymmetric Politics*, 289–91.

20  Jonathan M. Ladd, *Why Americans Hate the Media and How It Matters* (Princeton, NJ: Princeton University Press, 2012), 1.

21  Ladd, *Why Americans Hate the Media*, 78; Grossman and Hopkins, *Asymmetric Politics*, 138–39.

22  Lewis Grossberger, "The Rush Hours," *New York Times Magazine*, December 16, 1990; "Top Talk Audiences," *Talkers*, http://www.talkers.com/top-talk-audiences, accessed January 28, 2020.

23  Mark Joyella, "Fox News Crushes Cable News Competition with 71st Consecutive Quarterly Win," *Forbes*, October 1, 2019.

24  Matthew Levendusky, "Partisan Media Exposure and Attitudes Toward the Opposition," *Political Communication* 30 (October 2013): 565–81; Jeffrey M. Berry and Sarah Sobieraj, "Anger Is a Business," *Vox*, April 26, 2016; Diana Mutz, *In-Your-Face Politics: The Consequences of Uncivil Media* (Princeton, NJ: Princeton University Press, 2015).

25  Lilliana Mason, *Uncivil Agreement: How Politics Became Our Identity* (Chicago: University of Chicago Press, 2018), 1–16.

26  Vanessa Williamson, Theda Skocpol, and John Coggin, "The Tea Party and the Remaking of Republican Conservatism," *Perspectives on Politics* 9 (March 2011): 26; Theda Skocpol and Vanessa Williamson, *The Tea Party and the Remaking of Republican Conservatism* (Oxford: Oxford University Press, 2012).

27  David Rogers, "Senate Passes $787 Billion Stimulus Bill," *Politico*, February 13, 2009; Skocpol and Williamson, *Tea Party and the Remaking of Republican Conservatism*, 168–71.

28  Mann and Ornstein, *It's Even Worse Than It Looks*, 8–13, 14–25.

29  "Top GOP Priority: Make Obama a One-Term President," *National Journal*, October 23, 2010.

30  Alan I. Abramowitz, *The Great Alignment: Race, Party Transformation, and the Rise of Donald Trump* (New Haven, CT: Yale University Press, 2018), 2, 5.

31  Alan Abramowitz and Steven Webster, "'Negative Partisanship' Explains Everything," *Politico Magazine*, September/October 2017; Elizabeth Bruenig, "In God's Country," *Washington Post*, August 14, 2019; Pew Research Center, "An Examination of the 2016 Electorate, Based on Validated Voters," August 9, 2018, https://www.people-press.org/2018/08/09/an-examination-of-the-2016-electorate-based-on-validated-voters.

32  Michael D. Shear and Maggie Haberman, "Trump Defends Initial Remarks on Charlottesville; Again Blames Both Sides," *New York Times*, August 15, 2017.

33  Julie Hirschfeld Davis and Maggie Haberman, "Trump Pardons Joe Arpaio, Who Became Face of Crackdown on Illegal Immigration," *New York Times*, August 25, 2017; Desmond King and Rogers M. Smith, "White Protectionism in America," in *Perspectives on Politics* (forthcoming).

34  Adam Taylor, "America Has More Female Lawmakers Than Ever," *Washington Post*, January 8, 2019.

35  Kristin Bialik, "For the Fifth Time in a Row, the New Congress Is the Most Racially and Ethnically Diverse Ever," Pew Research Center, February 8, 2019, https://www.pewresearch.org/fact-tank/2019/02/08/for-the-fifth-time-in-a-row-the-new-congress-is-the-most-racially-and-ethnically-diverse-ever; Fredrick C. Harris and Robert C. Lieberman, "Racial Inequality After Racism: How Institutions Hold Back African Americans," *Foreign Affairs* 94 (March/April 2015): 9–20; Kriston McIntosh et al., "Examining the Black-White Wealth Gap," Brookings Institution, February 27, 2020, https://www.brookings.edu/blog/up-front/2020/02/27/examining-the-black-white-wealth-gap/?utm_campaign=Brookings%20Brief&utm_source=hs_email&utm_medium=email&utm_content=84068283; Ana Patricia Muñoz, Marlene Kim, Mariko Chang, Regine O. Jackson, Darrick Hamilton, and William A. Darity Jr., "The Color of Wealth in Boston," Federal Reserve Bank of Boston, March 25, 2015, https://www.bostonfed.org/publications/one-time-pubs/color-of-wealth.aspx.

36  US Census, "A Look at the 1940 Census," https://www.census.gov/newsroom/cspan/1940census/CSPAN_1940slides.pdf, 11; William H. Frey, "The US Will Become 'Minority White' in 2045, Census Projects," Brookings Institution, March 14, 2018, https://www.brookings.edu/blog/the-avenue/2018/03/14/the-us-will-become-minority-white-in-2045-census-projects.

37  Jennifer McCoy and Murat Somer, "Toward a Theory of Pernicious Polarization and How It Harms Democracies: Comparative Evidence and Possible Remedies," *Annals of the American Academy of Political and Social Science* 681 (January 2019): 257.

38  Frances E. Lee, "Populism and the American Party System: Opportunities and Constraints," in *Perspectives on Politics* (forthcoming), https://doi.org/10.1017/S1537592719002664.

39  Tali Mendelberg, *The Race Card: Campaign Strategy, Implicit Messages, and the Norm of Equality* (Princeton, NJ: Princeton University Press, 2001).

40  Benjamin I. Page and Robert Y. Shapiro, *The Rational Public: Fifty Years of Trends in Americans' Policy Preferences* (Chicago: University of Chicago Press, 1992), 68–81; Howard Schuman, Charlotte Steeh, Lawrence Bobo, and Maria Krysan, *Racial Attitudes in America: Trends and Interpretations*, rev. ed. (Cambridge, MA: Harvard University Press, 1997); Fredrick C. Harris and Robert C. Lieberman, "Beyond Discrimination: Racial Inequality in the Age of Obama," in *Beyond Discrimination: Racial Inequality in a Post-Racist Era*, edited by Fredrick C. Harris and Robert C. Lieberman (New York: Russell Sage Foundation, 2013).

41  Donald R. Kinder and David O. Sears, "Prejudice and Politics: Symbolic Racism Versus Racial Threats to the Good Life," *Journal of Personality and Social Psychology* 40, no. 3 (1981): 416; Martin Gilens, *Why Americans Hate Welfare: Race, Media, and the Politics of Antipoverty Policy* (Chicago: University of Chicago Press, 1999); Lawrence Bobo and Ryan A. Smith, "From Jim Crow Racism to Laissez-Faire Racism: The Transformation of Racial Attitudes," in *Beyond Pluralism: The Conception of Groups and Group Identities in America*, edited by Wendy F. Katkin, Ned Landsman, and Andrea Tyree (Urbana: University of Illinois Press, 1998); Abramowitz, *Great Alignment*, 129.

42  Abramowitz, *Great Alignment*, 130–31.

43  Abramowitz, *Great Alignment*, 8–9, 47, 49.

44  Skocpol and Williamson, *Tea Party and the Remaking of Republican Conservatism*, 68–74; Christopher S. Parker and Matthew A. Barreto, *Change They Can't Believe In: The Tea Party and Reactionary Politics in America*, updated ed. (Princeton, NJ: Princeton University Press, 2014), 1; Arlie Russell Hochschild, *Strangers in Their Own Land: Anger and Mourning on the American Right* (New York: New Press, 2016); Fredrick C. Harris and Robert C. Lieberman, "The Return of Racism? Race and Inequality After Charlottesville," *Foreign Affairs*, August 21, 2017.

45  Parker and Barreto, *Change They Can't Believe In*, 2.

46  "Here's Donald Trump's Presidential Announcement Speech," *Time*, June 16, 2015; "Trump Calls for Total and Complete Shutdown of Muslims Entering US," National Public Radio, December 7, 2015.

47  John Sides, Michael Tesler, and Lynn Vavreck, *Identity Crisis: The 2016 Presidential Campaign and the Battle for the Meaning of America* (Princeton, NJ: Princeton University Press, 2018), 86–87.

48  Nicholas A. Valentino, Carly Wayne, and Marzia Oceno, "Mobilizing Sexism: The Interaction of Emotion and Gender Attitudes in the 2016 US Presidential Election," *Public Opinion Quarterly* 82, no. S1 (2018): 801; Sides, Tesler, and Vavreck, *Identity Crisis*, 140.

49  Sides, Tesler, and Vavreck, *Identity Crisis*, 186–88; Valentino, Wayne, and Oceno, "Mobilizing Sexism"; Brian F. Schaffner, Matthew MacWilliams, and Tatishe Nteta, "Understanding White Polarization in the 2016 Vote for President: The Sobering Role of Racism and Sexism," *Political Science Quarterly* 133 (Spring 2018): 9–34.

50  Sides, Tesler, and Vavreck, *Identity Crisis*; Abramowitz, *Great Alignment*; Jacob S. Hacker and Paul Pierson, *Winner-Take-All Politics* (New York: Simon and Schuster, 2010); Ben Steverman, Dave Merrill, and Jeremy C. F. Lin, "A Year After the Middle Class Tax Cut, the Rich Are Winning," *Bloomberg*, December 18, 2018; Paul Pierson, "American Hybrid: Donald Trump and the Strange Merger of Populism and Plutocracy," *British Journal of Sociology* 68 (November 2017): S105–S119; "Tracking Deregulation in the Trump Era," Brookings Institution, https://www.brookings.edu/interactives/tracking-deregulation-in-the-trump-era.

51  Lawrence Mishel, Jared Bernstein, and Heather Boushey, *The State of Working America 2002/2003* (Ithaca, NY: Cornell University Press, 2003), 57; Claudia Goldin, "Egalitarianism and the Returns to Education During the Great Transformation of American Education," *Journal of Political Economy* 107 (December 1999): S65–S92; Claudia Goldin and Robert A. Margo, "The Great Compression: The Wage Structure

in the United States at Mid-Century," *Quarterly Journal of Economics* 107 (February 1992): 1–34.

52 Lawrence Mishel, Jared Bernstein, and Sylvia Allegretto, *The State of Working America 2005* (Ithaca, NY: Cornell University Press, 2005); Deirdre Bloome, "Racial Inequality Trends and the Intergenerational Persistence of Income and Family Structure," *American Sociological Review* 79, no. 6 (2014): 1196–225.

53 Thomas Piketty, Emmanuel Saez, and Gabriel Zucman, "Distributional National Accounts: Methods and Estimates for the United States," *Quarterly Journal of Economics* 133 (May 2018): 557, 578; Mettler, *Government–Citizen Disconnect*, 33–34.

54 Mettler, *Government–Citizen Disconnect*, chap. 2; Suzanne Mettler, *Degrees of Inequality: How the Politics of Higher Education Sabotaged the American Dream* (New York: Basic Books, 2014), 23–28, 118–31.

55 Thomas W. Volscho and Nathan J. Kelly, "The Rise of the Super-Rich: Power Resources, Taxes, Financial Markets, and the Dynamics of the Top 1 Percent, 1949–2008," *American Sociological Review* 77 (October 2012): 679–99; Hacker and Pierson, *Winner-Take-All Politics*; Internal Revenue Service, "Personal Exemptions and Individual Income Tax Rates, 1913–2002," p. 220, https://www.irs.gov/pub/irs-soi/02inpetr.pdf.

56 Allan H. Meltzer and Scott F. Richard, "A Rational Theory of the Size of Government," *Journal of Political Economy* 89 (October 1981): 914–27; Spencer Piston, *Class Attitudes in America: Sympathy for the Poor, Resentment of the Rich, and Political Implications* (Cambridge: Cambridge University Press, 2018); Benjamin I. Page and Lawrence R. Jacobs, *Class War? What Americans Really Think About Economic Inequality* (Chicago: University of Chicago Press, 2009); Larry M. Bartels, *Unequal Democracy: The Political Economy of the New Gilded Age* (Princeton, NJ: Princeton University Press, 2010); Martin Gilens, *Affluence and Influence: Economic Inequality and Political Power in America* (Princeton, NJ: Princeton University Press, 2012); Kristina Miler, *Poor Representation: Congress and the Politics of Poverty in the United States* (Cambridge: Cambridge University Press, 2018).

57 Kay Lehman Schlozman, Sidney Verba, and Henry E. Brady, *The Unheavenly Chorus: Unequal Political Voice and the Broken Promise of American Democracy* (Princeton, NJ: Princeton University Press, 2012), 8, 15, 136.

58 "Cost of Election," Center for Responsive Politics, https://www.opensecrets.org/overview/cost.php; Schlozman, Verba, and Brady, *Unheavenly Chorus*, 125–26.

59 Benjamin I. Page, Jason Seawright, and Matthew J. Lacombe, *Billionaires and Stealth Politics* (Chicago: University of Chicago Press, 2019), 42–43.

60 Theda Skocpol and Alexander Hertel-Fernandez, "The Koch Network and Republican Party Extremism," *Perspectives on Politics* 14 (September 2016): 681–99; Alexander Hertel-Fernandez, *State Capture: How Conservative Activists, Big Businesses, and Wealthy Donors Reshaped the American States—and the Nation* (Oxford: Oxford University Press, 2019).

61 Lee Drutman, *The Business of America Is Lobbying: How Corporations Became Politicized and Politics Became More Corporate* (Oxford: Oxford University Press, 2015), 11, 13–14.

62 John S. Ahlquist, "Labor Unions, Political Representation, and Economic Inequality," *Annual Review of Political Science* 20 (2017): 409–32; "Union Members—2018," Bureau of Labor Statistics, January 18, 2019, https://www.bls.gov/news.release/pdf/union2.pdf; Alexis N. Walker, *Divided Unions: The Wagner Act, Federalism, and Organized Labor* (Philadelphia: University of Pennsylvania Press, 2020); Alexander Hertel-Fernandez, *Politics at Work: How Companies Turn Their Workers into Lobbyists* (Oxford: Oxford University Press, 2018).

63 Sarah Burns, "Trump, Like Obama, Tests the Limits of Presidential War Powers," *Government Executive*, January 10, 2020, https://www.govexec.com/defense/2020/01/trump-obama-tests-limits-presidential-war-powers/162366.

64 Lawrence R. Jacobs, "Trump's Institutional Inheritance: The Legacy of Bipartisan Sup-

port for Presidential Power," memo prepared for conference, "A Republic, if You Can Keep It," Washington, DC, 2018.

65  Nicholas F. Jacobs, Desmond King, and Sidney Milkis, "Building a Conservative State: Partisan Polarization and the Redeployment of Administrative Power," *Perspectives on Politics* 17 (June 2019): 453–69.

66  Kenneth Mayer, *With the Stroke of a Pen: Executive Orders and Presidential Power* (Princeton, NJ: Princeton University Press, 2001); William G. Howell, *Power Without Persuasion: The Politics of Direct Presidential Action* (Princeton, NJ: Princeton University Press, 2003); Robert Mickey, Steven Levitsky, and Lucan Ahmad Way, "Is America Still Safe for Democracy? Why the United States Is in Danger of Backsliding," *Foreign Affairs* 96 (May/June 2017): 20–29; Arthur Schlesinger Jr., *The Imperial Presidency* (Boston: Houghton Mifflin, 1973); Jacobs, "Trump's Institutional Inheritance."

67  John Yoo, "Unitary, Executive, or Both?" *University of Chicago Law Review* 76 (Fall 2009): 1935–2018; John Yoo, *Crisis and Command: The History of Executive Power from George Washington to George W. Bush* (New York: Kaplan, 2009); Steven G. Calabresi and Christopher S. Yoo, *The Unitary Executive: Presidential Power from Washington to Bush* (New Haven, CT: Yale University Press, 2008); James Risen and Eric Lichtblau, "Bush Lets U.S. Spy on Callers Without Courts," *New York Times*, December 16, 2005; James Risen, *State of War: The Secret History of the CIA and the Bush Administration* (New York: Free Press, 2006).

68  Michael Wines, "Deceased G.O.P. Strategist's Hard Drives Reveal New Details on the Census Citizenship Question," *New York Times*, May 30, 2019.

69  Hacker and Pierson, *Winner-Take-All Politics.*

70  Suzanne Mettler, *The Submerged State* (Chicago: University of Chicago Press, 2011).

## Chapter 9: Putting Democracy First

1  Tamara Keith, "Trump, Ukraine, and the Path to the Impeachment Inquiry: A Timeline," National Public Radio, October 12, 2019.

2  "Memorandum of Telephone Conversation," July 25, 2019, declassified by order of the president, September 24, 2019, https://s.wsj.net/public/resources/documents /Unclassifiedukrainetranscript09.2019.pdf?mod=article_inline.

3  "Memorandum of Telephone Conversation."

4  Greg Miller, Ellen Nakashima, and Shane Harris, "Trump's Communications with Foreign Leader Are Part of Whistleblower Complaint That Spurred Standoff Between Spy Chief and Congress, Former Officials Say," *Washington Post*, September 18, 2019; Devlin Barrett, Matt Zapotosky, Josh Dawsey, and Shane Harris, "Whistleblower Claimed That Trump Abused His Office, and That White House Officials Tried to Cover It Up," *Washington Post*, September 26, 2019; Anonymous Letter to Honorable Richard Burr and Honorable Adam Schiff, August 12, 2019, Unclassified, p. 1, https:// games-cdn.washingtonpost.com/notes/prod/default/documents/3b5487de-f987–4cef -b59b-c29bb67687ac/note/ef3465c1–465b–4e68–9b36-08b5946b0df4.pdf#page=1.

5  Domenico Montanaro, "Pelosi Announces Formal Impeachment Inquiry into President Trump," National Public Radio, September 24, 2019.

6  https://twitter.com/realdonaldtrump/status/1179179573541511176; Davey Alba and Nick Corasaniti, "False 'Coup' Claims by Trump Echo as Unifying Theme Against Impeachment," *New York Times*, October 2, 2019; Jelani Cobb, "Why Trump, Facing Impeachment, Warns of Civil War," *New Yorker*, October 5, 2019; Mary B. McCord, "Armed Militias Are Taking Trump's Civil War Seriously," *Lawfare*, October 2, 2019, https://www .lawfareblog.com/armed-militias-are-taking-trumps-civil-war-tweets-seriously.

7  Sheryl Gay Stolberg and Carl Hulse, "Alexander Says Convicting Trump Would 'Pour Gasoline on Cultural Fires,'" *New York Times*, January 31, 2020; Aaron Bycoffe, Ella Koeze, and Nathaniel Rakich, "Do Americans Support Removing Trump from Office?" FiveThirtyEight, January 29, 2020, https://projects.fivethirtyeight.com/impeachment-polls/.

8  See, e.g., Matt Glassman, "The Root of White House Chaos? A Weak President" *New York Times*, March 1, 2018.

9  Patrick Healy and Jonathan Martin, "Donald Trump Won't Say if He'll Accept Result of Election," *New York Times*, October 19, 2016; Eric Bradner, "Fact-Checking Trump's False Claims About Arizona and Florida Elections," CNN, November 12, 2018.

10 Dana Milbank, "Mitch McConnell Is a Russian Asset," *Washington Post*, July 26, 2019; Carl Hulse, "'Moscow Mitch' Tag Enrages McConnell and Squeezes G.O.P. on Election Security," *New York Times*, July 30, 2019.

11 Annie Lowrey, "It's Been Two Years. The President Still Hasn't Released His Tax Returns," *Atlantic*, January 13, 2019; Trump v. Vance (S. D. N.Y., 2019), 8; William K. Rashbaum and Benjamin Weiser, "Trump Taxes: President Ordered to Turn Over Returns to Manhattan D.A.," *New York Times*, October 7, 2019.

12 Clark Packard, "Congress Should Take Back Its Authority over Tariffs," *Foreign Policy*, May 4, 2019.

13 Steve Denning, "How Trump's Cabinet Now Undermines the Rule of Law," *Forbes*, May 19, 2019.

14 Lisa Marie Segarra, "Watch John McCain Strongly Defend Barack Obama," *Time*, August 25, 2018.

15 Michael S. Schmidt, "Mueller Report Reveals Trump's Fixation on Targeting Hillary Clinton," *New York Times*, April 24, 2019; Felicia Sonmez and Elise Viebeck, "Schiff 'Has Not Yet Paid the Price' for Impeachment, Trump Says in What Appears to Be Veiled Threat," *Washington Post*, January 26, 2020.

16 Lilliana Mason, *Uncivil Agreement: How Politics Became Our Identity* (Chicago: University of Chicago Press, 2018); Thomas B. Edsall, "Is Politics a War of Ideas or of Us Against Them?" *New York Times*, November 6, 2019.

17 Dan Mangan, "President Trump Told Lesley Stahl He Bashes Press 'To Demean You and Discredit You So . . . No One Will Believe' Negative Stories About Him," CNBC, May 22, 2018.

18 Desmond S. King and Rogers M. Smith, *Still a House Divided: Race and Politics in Obama's America* (Princeton, NJ: Princeton University Press, 2011); Andra Gillespie, "Race, Remembrance, and Precarity: The Political Determinants of Nostalgia," in *Who Gets What? The New Politics of Insecurity*, edited by Frances Rosenbluth and Margaret Weir (Cambridge: Cambridge University Press, forthcoming); Department of Justice, Hate Crime Statistics 2017, https://www.justice.gov/hatecrimes/hate-crime-statistics; Heidi Beirich, "The Year in Hate: Rage Against Change," Southern Poverty Law Center, February 20, 2019, https://www.splcenter.org/fighting-hate/intelligence-report /2019/year-hate-rage-against-change.

19 Caitlin Dickerson, Jose A. Del Real, and Julie Bosman, "With ICE Raids Looming, Immigrants Worry," *New York Times*, July 13, 2019; "Groups Sue Trump Administration over Fast-Track Deportations," American Civil Liberties Union, August 6, 2019.

20 Robert A. Dahl, *How Democratic Is the American Constitution?* (New Haven, CT: Yale University Press, 2002).

21 Pew Research Center, "Views of American Democratic Values and Principles," April 26, 2018, https://www.people-press.org/2018/04/26/2-views-of-american-democratic -values-and-principles. Experts agree that American democracy does not currently function as well as it should: http://brightlinewatch.org.

22 Jill Lepore, "In Every Dark Hour," *New Yorker*, February 3, 2020.

# Index